THE GAME THAT WAS
The Early Days of Pro Football

OTHER BOOKS BY MYRON COPE
Off My Chest (with Jim Brown)
Broken Cigars

THE
Game
THAT WAS

The Early Days of Pro Football

by MYRON COPE

The World Publishing Company
NEW YORK AND CLEVELAND

Published by The World Publishing Company
2231 West 110th Street, Cleveland, Ohio 44102
Published simultaneously in Canada by
Nelson, Foster & Scott Ltd.

First Printing—1970

Library of Congress Catalog Card Number: 79-124281

Printed in the United States of America

WORLD PUBLISHING
TIMES MIRROR

To Dad, and to the memory of
my beloved mother

CONTENTS

PREFACE   3
1. ED HEALEY   13
   "An absolutely vicious football player"
2. INDIAN JOE GUYON   35
   "You can't sneak up on an Indian."
3. RED GRANGE   43
   The first plutocrat
4. JOHNNY BLOOD   59
   A high resistance to culture
5. OLE HAUGSRUD   71
   The franchise that sold for a dollar
6. DUTCH CLARK   83
   When the bank ran out of money
7. CLARKE HINKLE   95
   Joe College
8. CLIFF BATTLES   113
   Life with George Marshall
9. ART ROONEY   121
   "What I'm telling you is that we've tried."
10. DON HUTSON   141
    The five-dollar bidding war
11. TUFFY LEEMANS   151
    "My name is Alphonse . . . but it never took."

12. SAMMY BAUGH   159
    "If they could cripple you, fine."
13. ALEX WOJCIECHOWICZ   173
    The thirty-letter man
14. BULLDOG TURNER   187
    The raconteur of Cowhouse Creek
15. BULLET BILL DUDLEY   219
    The time the Steelers might have won
16. STEVE VAN BUREN   229
    "Money meant nothing to me.
    I was stupid, that's why."
17. MARION MOTLEY and BILL WILLIS   237
    The color line is broken
18. BOBBY LAYNE   257
    "I sleep fast!"
19. GEORGE HALAS   275
    Father of the game
    EPILOGUE   287
    INDEX   289

Illustrations following pages 118 and 182

THE GAME THAT WAS
The Early Days of Pro Football

PREFACE

One day soon, every pro-football field in America will be covered by synthetic grass, and in time the stadiums of a good many cities will be enclosed by domes. Playing conditions will be ideal, unless one chooses to believe that football is a game that was not meant to be played like chess, with every board alike and the room temperature adjusted to comfort. For some of us, professional football will have lost a part of its flavor. It will remain a strong man's game, of course, but the mud-caked uniform—somehow a badge of great struggle —and the steamlike breath on a quarterback's lips will be gone. In the days building up to the big game, nobody will speculate on the possibility of poor weather, that old ally of underdogs, nor will a checkered blanket or a thermos of hot coffee be part of the festive preparations a fan makes on the morning of a game—at least not where the great steel bubbles rise.

Unless the players themselves come to be bred by selective genetics (their progenitors perhaps being under personal-service contract to clubowners), football soon will have reached the ultimate in modernization. This book, then, is an attempt to recall pro football as it existed in a less sophisticated time. It is a book for the young who are curious and for their seniors who can find time for nostalgia.

It is only right that I plead guilty, immediately, to having camped upon ground broken by another. In 1966 Lawrence S. Ritter, a New York University economist of considerable distinction in his field, published *The Glory of Their Times,* a work as foreign to finance as the Standard & Poor's Index would have been to Babe Ruth's locker gear. Professor Ritter had succumbed to a lifelong weakness for baseball and gone off on a journey to find the great players who in the early decades of the century had made baseball our national sport. Tracking down the Rube Marquards and the Sam Crawfords, he switched on a tape recorder and persuaded them to reminisce. From those interviews came *The Glory,* an affectionate remembrance of baseball as it was played in another day in another America. It was only a matter of time, then, that someone would ask, why not a professional-football counterpart to *The Glory?*

The question occurred to the editors of *Sports Illustrated.* Pro football, thanks largely to television riches, had become an enormously profitable and meticulously managed industry. But what had it been before the invention of the picture tube? How did a pro-football player make ends meet in a time when there were no offers to endorse shaving cream, when men rode drafty day coaches into the north to play Green Bay on frozen fields that no one dreamed could be thawed by underground electrical coils? The editors of *SI* were ambitious to serialize excerpts from a book that not only would explain the life of the pretelevision pro but would tell something of America as she existed before the great electronic take-over. They suggested I take a year away from my magazine writing to visit the old greats at their firesides, their offices, their farms, and that I turn on a recorder and see if

I could carry them back to a time that surely deserves to be remembered. How could any football buff resist the assignment? Senior Editor Ray Cave needn't have bought me those three martinis before lunch.

In determining which men I would seek out, we established only two firm ground rules. The first was that the earliest of my ballplayers would not predate 1920, the year when football evolved into its first professional league—the American Professional Football Association, soon to become the National Football League. My cutoff point would be the early 1950s, when television money began to come into the game in a meaningful way. And because we could not resist the lure of a Bobby Layne interview, why not stretch the rule to include one player who arrived before television bonanzas but prospered long into the age of TV?

Our second ground rule was that every ballplayer in this book would be one of exceptional talent. The problem, however, was that three decades of professional football turn up more brilliance than one volume can accommodate. The field had to be thinned. An expedient method would have been simply to have visited only those ballplayers who have been voted into the Pro Football Hall of Fame, but somehow such a solution seemed too pat, to say nothing of being too limiting.

Our first step, then, was to bring into play *Sports Illustrated's* vast network of correspondents—"stringers," they are called in the trade. *SI* has one in every major American city. To each of them a wire went out instructing them to track down names and addresses of every exceptional old-timer known to reside in their territory. It was the sort of assignment, no doubt, that causes stringers to mutter darkly and go out for a stiff drink, for how does one define exceptional? We could not define it ourselves. The result, naturally, was that some stringers limited their catch only to those of the gaudiest performance statistics, while others wired in lists that included everyone down to the old pro who once gave their Uncle Harry an autograph at the Pottsville train station.

That was all right. I had names and addresses to work with. Now I had to develop criteria for making final selections. Hall of Fame membership, of course, was one consideration. Unscientific as it may seem, the ring of a man's name was another factor to be weighed alongside excellence. If this book was to be an experience in nostalgia, a field for the sentimental to wander, surely there was no harm in my yielding to the lure of names whose euphonics cause them to linger with us over the years. Johnny Blood, Cliff Battles, Indian Joe Guyon, Bulldog Turner, Tuffy Leemans (who wanted desperately to be called Al), and Bullet Bill Dudley. One wonders what has become of the American gift for nicknames. Should another author undertake a book such as this fifty years from now, I suspect his pulse will not be quickened by the ring of such names as Johnny Unitas, Jim Brown, or Gale Sayers. Unhappily, there exist today many ballplayers who would want to strike down the first sportswriter who tried to christen them Whirlwind or Killer in the sports pages. I am saddened that the limitations of time and space were reached before I was able to travel down to Mississippi to see Bruiser Kinard.

Certainly no account of pro football's early triumphs and struggles would be complete if it did not revisit Bill Willis and Marion Motley, the pioneers of black participation in modern pro ball. Histories of the game have largely overlooked the fact that long before baseball wiped out its color line in 1947, pro football routinely welcomed the black man, and that, alas, he then vanished from the game. In the 1930s pro football became exclusively white. Judging from available evidence, no purge had taken place. Indeed, Chicago Bears owner George Halas was startled when I suggested to him that there may have been one. There had been no ban on black ballplayers, he said—"in no way, shape, or form."

Why, then, had the blacks vanished? "I don't know!" Halas exclaimed. "Probably it was due to the fact that no great black players were in the colleges then. That could be the reason. But I've never given this a thought until you mentioned it. At no time has it ever been brought up. Isn't that strange?"

Perhaps the best guess is that the blacks disappeared because pro football in the 1930s was evolving into a game played solely by men who had proven themselves in college ball, but the colleges, while showing occasional interest in black trackmen, had little interest in black football recruits. Still, there no doubt existed clubowners who found pure-white football to their liking, for as black players increasingly trickled into college ball in the late '30s, the pros expressed no interest in their futures. In short, pro football probably had drifted into an unwritten ban on blacks. It was not until the days immediately following World War II that Coach Paul Brown of the Cleveland Browns shrugged off taboos and brought the great talents of Willis and Motley to the public eye. The two men are here in these pages to tell their story.

The unforgettable Bronko Nagurski, sad to say, is not here. Alone among the old pros I telephoned for permission to visit, the bruising ballcarrier who as much as anyone helped make the Chicago Bears the "Monsters of the Midway" declined to see me. From his home in International Falls, Minnesota, on the Ontario border, he told me, "I don't like to rehash. I don't have time to reminisce." The finality in his voice served notice, just as the sight of his thundering form once did to tacklers, that there was little to be gained by attempting to alter his resolve.

Probably it is unforgivable that New York Giant Mel Hein, reckoned by many to have been the greatest of all centers, is not between these covers. Blame it on my weakness for quaint names. By the time I had visited Bulldog Turner and Wojie Wojciechowicz, both of them Hall of Fame centers and rich with spellbinding memories of the past, I felt that in the interest of balance it would not do to include yet another center. Again in the interest of balance, I regretfully omitted many superb performers with the Chicago Bears and Green Bay Packers, the two clubs that dominated the early years of pro football. Otherwise, this would have been a book about the Bears and Packers. But Turner and Red Grange and Ed Healey and George Halas of the Bears are here, as are Johnny Blood and Clarke Hinkle and Don Hutson of the Packers. So, too, are men who pioneered pro football in the great cities of the east.

There was this difference between my pro-football players and the baseball players of *The Glory of Their Times*: Whereas the baseball stars were household names, men who enjoyed recognition if not wealth, the football players while in their prime suffered the double indignity of low pay and obscurity. In the 1920s and '30s great sections of the nation remained ignorant even of the fact that pro football existed. "You'd get back into the hinterlands," Red Grange told me, "and tell them that pro football was a good game, that the pros blocked hard and tackled hard, and they'd laugh at you." College football owned the headlines, relegating the pros to one-paragraph fillers. Baseball was America's premier game. The truth was that many of the football pros—Sammy Baugh, for example—had pointed themselves in the beginning toward a baseball career but for one reason or another strayed from the path. In football, frequently going without medical attention and sometimes without a weekly paycheck, they built a professional sport whose following would become the envy of baseball. They consider it patronizing to be told that they "contributed" much to pro football. "Heaven's sake!" explodes Clarke Hinkle. "We *established* the game." Often they lived in rooming houses or hotel rooms. They frequently played sixty minutes of a game, convinced that to be removed, even because of injury, amounted to personal disgrace. Time and again I heard the old-timers choose identical words to sum up their motive. "Well, you see, we wanted to play."

The reader will find them to be more proud than complaining of the conditions they played under, and equipped with a fine sense of comedy that enables them to savor the most preposterous circumstances in which they found themselves. Our meetings were thoroughly informal, as Mrs. Julie Haller, who transcribed the resulting tapes, will attest. "I thought it was great fun having four of you on the Bulldog Turner tapes," she pointed out to me. "I mean, there were the two of you in the evening session, with the ice clinking in the background, and then the other two men, the sober ones, in the next morning's session."

Although Mrs. Haller served me faithfully, frantically typing away to keep pace with a mounting pile of tapes, her presence in this project in one instance created a problem. In Detroit, Dutch Clark checked himself when about to utter a mildly off-color expression. He glanced apprehensively at my recorder, sensing that his words might reach the ears of a delicate secretary. "Don't worry about the machine," I told him, hoping to put him at ease with a white lie. "My typist swears like a sailor herself." Several weeks later Mrs. Haller, a demure mother of four, delivered the transcript of the Dutch Clark interview, and as I read it I was brought up short on page 32 by a parenthetical aside headed "Comment from Typist." It read: "Goddammit, Myron, why would you say such a thing about me?"

Although the chapters that follow are transcribed interviews, I have eliminated the questions that I put to the old pros and edited their answers in such fashion as to meld them into a contiguous flow of reminiscence. In other words, where necessary I have rearranged the sequence of the conversation so as to present the material in an orderly way, much as a newspaper columnist does when he reviews his notes following an interview. Again where necessary, I have inserted a word, a phrase, or a sentence for the sake of transition, lest the reader be jolted by abrupt shifts in the conversation. And because the meaning of words spoken informally can be distorted when transferred verbatim to paper, I have reconstructed sentences where it was essential to do so. Otherwise, these chapters are the unvarnished memories of the men who related them.

Professor Ritter, in *The Glory*, marveled at the detail that his baseball players were able to bring to recollection of events long gone, but he was reassured by psychologists "that it is not at all unusual as one gets older for the more distant past to be remembered more clearly than what happened three weeks ago, especially if the distant past was particularly memorable." Such were the powers of recall that I found among the old football stars. Let the reader be assured that, wherever possible, a conscientious effort was made to check and double-check the most minute details of their reminiscences, and that in the end discrepancies between memory and existing evidence amounted to no more than a few overripe oranges in a carload of perfect specimens.

I have no doubt that somewhere in this country, at least one elderly fan who keeps football archives in his attic will find in these pages an occasional fact to challenge. But in researching professional football's past, one can only grope as best he can among the many blind alleys that exist. Roger Treat, editor of *The Official Encyclopedia of Football*, was of valuable assistance to me, but he warned me during the early going that the fathers of pro football, unlike those of big-league baseball, kept scant records. Pro football was too busy trying to survive. Besides, the cost of file cabinets might have spelled the difference between survival and death.

At any rate, this book is not a history in the classic sense. It is merely a story. It is a story of a game that was, and of an America that we shall never see again.

Myron Cope

1

ED HEALEY

"An absolutely vicious football player"

We had never met, but as I came through the gate and entered the South Bend air-terminal building I guessed from his size that the big man in the straw hat was Ed Healey. When Chicago Bears owner George Halas, in 1922, purchased Healey's contract from the Rock Island Independents for one hundred dollars, he became—or so it is generally believed—the first pro-football player to be sold. Now, in steel-framed glasses and a dark suit, his appearance was that of a successful man, a retired-banker type. We drove in his cream-colored Continental to the Indiana Club, where in the card room we were served lunch by his favorite waiter, Albert.

Then we proceeded north across the line into Michigan and swung off the road into Riverbrook Farm. It was not a large farm—in fact, in its most productive years it required only a handful of help—and when Ed Healey decided that his retirement, so to speak, should be one of activity, he let the help go in order to disencumber himself and reduced the farming operation to what he could handle himself. The venerable farmhouse, according to documents found by the Healeys when they restored it, was built by an exiled French general during the Civil War period. It is white-painted brick with green shutters—an intimate home in the French manor style.

We talked in the knotty-pine study, whose walls were liberally appointed with remembrances of the past. Healey sat by an open window that looked out on a backyard running down through sycamores and walnuts and locusts to the St. Joseph River. A fine June breeze came up from the river, and like the movement of the breeze itself, vivid memories of an America long gone flowed across Ed Healey's mind's eye.

He had played the tackle position. Standing six feet, one and one half inches, and weighing 220 pounds, he earned a reputation in the 1920s for toughness—a reputation that carried him into the Hall of Fame. "He was as good a tackle as I've ever seen," the great halfback Red Grange told me at another stop in my travels. "Oh, how Healey loved to come downfield under a punt! He was an absolutely vicious football player."

———

With reference to my fashioning a successful career in professional football, all that came about, as I witness it now, by reason of my growing up on a farm and putting on acts such as this: The hogs would get loose and Dad would say, "Now, Ed, we've got to get those hogs back in the pen before we start work today." He would turn me loose and I would come up with a flying tackle and snare that hog, and Father would say, "Eddie, you're a good boy. You're a good boy, Eddie." That's the way he encouraged me. That man never so much as put a hand on me, but I had respect in capital letters for him. He was unquestionably one of stick-to-itiveness, or in other words, stay with the ship until she went down. My greatest recollection of Father was that by example he taught me never to be afraid to work and to give of myself to the utmost. That led to punishing myself, particularly where it came to athletics. At the time, it might have seemed a little burdensome to do the many chores that Father requested of me, but it paid dividends later in life. As a matter of fact, here I am at seventy-five, for Christ's sake, and I'm going all the time.

Father would say to me, "Eddie, someday you'll be meeting many different friends from all walks of life. Be kind to them, regardless of their creed or color. They're all children of God on earth." And again, he would say, "Eddie, my boy —if you haven't got a good word to say about a man, just withhold comment. Think it over." That was a creature of the soul talking.

On the other side was the dear mother, who gave forth of herself to the extent of nine children, all girls except myself, who was second from the last. Lovewise, I gave it in bushels to the mother. I distinctly recall that any number of times, when one of the sisters said something unkindly about a neighboring child, possibly about something that had happened in school, Mother would say, "Well, now, remember that 'even the snowflake lets a shadow fall/ as to the ground it softly falls to rest./ So may the sweetest, purest, kindest soul of all/ seem sometimes wrong to those who know them best.'" It was a kindly, heavenly atmosphere.

There was all this femininity in the home, but it was a femininity of refinement. A wonderful influence. All the sisters had their various attributes, don't you know. Yet by reason of all this femininity it seemed advisable that I become able to take care of myself under any condition that might arise, so I took up boxing. Not professionally, not for any mercenary return, you understand. But I sought to make myself well-informed in connection with the art of self-defense, and my mother and sisters were not aware of it until I had the marks on my face that necessitated an honest answer. Mother said to me, "There's many a man that's serving

his whole life behind the bars for the very thing you're doing." So then you had to stop and think that surely you didn't
want to be behind the bars. But by the same token, you had
to be able to cope with any situation that might arise in life.

Our farm was located just outside of Springfield, Massa-
chusetts, in a place called Indian Orchard. We had about two
hundred acres, and then we moved to a farm even closer to
Springfield. It was only about thirty acres, but there was still
plenty of work to be done. At Classical High in Springfield,
I was big enough that the coach asked me to come out for
football, so I addressed Dad one day and said, "Dad, I've
been asked to go out for football. How about it?" Father said
that it would be with his approval but that I should remember
there were too many duties on the farm for me to be running
out for all the other sports. So I started to play football, and
it came sort of natural for me. Fear was most remote in my
makeup. I mean, I *loved* bodily contact. I just thrived on it.
I ate it up. If you have the stuff, then you should be ignited
by reason of being plugged by somebody. I played tackle from
the beginning and thrived on the explosiveness that playing
in the line presented you. It was most self-sacrificing, as you
know, because on offense you were always helping out the
man in the backfield with the ball. That back isn't going
anyplace unless someone busts them for him. And in the
event that a fellow lineman was having trouble, you were in
there assisting him in a dynamite way, never hesitating to
give your best to assist your fellow man.

In time I attended Dartmouth College, and it's rather an
interesting story as to how that came to pass. You see, in
1914 I was director of a playground in Springfield, and was
coaching a little bunch of what you might call midgets in
playground baseball. My team, midgetwise, had beaten all
the other midget teams in the various playgrounds. So we

went out to Forest Park to play for the championship. Frank Cavenaugh, the Iron Major, who as coach of Dartmouth was the Knute Rockne of that era, drove down to Forest Park in an automobile, which at that time was novel. He sent a chap to get me off to one side. Cav looked at me and said, "Healey, I hear quite a bit about you. And most of it is good." He said, "You've turned out to be quite a football player, and you kind of like it." "Well," I said, "I guess your last statement is correct. I do like it." And Cav said, "I'd like very much to have you come up to Dartmouth."

So I came home that evening and spoke to Dad. Now I should explain that Dad not only had the farm but also had a number of teams that conveyed traprock used for building roads. He had teamsters working for him that had come from Ireland. They were all tough Turks—I always called them Turks—and they were a grand group of men. But they loved the spirits. When they'd get to town, they might imbibe a little too freely, and then, when they got back to the farm, someone would have to complete their work for them. It usually befell me to unhitch their teams and take off the harnesses and knock the snow out of the horses' feet. So I said to Father, "Dad, really I'm getting kind of tired of this business that you're in, being exposed to these booze hounds that run into these saloons." And he said, "Well, Eddie, I've never had an education and I want you to have one. I'm glad you're going to Dartmouth. It's up there where you won't be troubled with a lot of women, and you'll like that kind of going that they have there. You'll like the hunting and trapping and fishing."

I loved Dartmouth. I was studying premedicine. But in my junior year we entered World War I, so I enlisted. I enlisted as a horseman, having been informed that this was the only service that would take me overseas immediately. I joined an outfit of 150 horsemen from Camp Lewis, Washington, who predominantly were men that had ridden the range, don't you know, and we saw quite a bit of service, particularly in the Argonne Forest. Now, then, since you want to know why I, a Dartmouth man, later would choose to play professional football, let me answer that in this way. It was shortly after the Armistice, on a trip that we made on horseback from Marseilles, France, proceeding through Luxembourg and along the Moselle to Koblenz. This particular situation developed in the course of our journey.

It was a very hazy, foggy late-November morning over a kind of rolling country where you would drop off a hilltop, coming out of a cloud, and descend into the valley below the fog. That is just what we did. And much to my amazement, there in a meadow adjacent to the Moselle River I beheld in a formation the shape of a gridiron all the caissons, all the artillery field pieces of two companies of the 42d Division. Seated thereon was the personnel of those companies in their OD uniforms. Now engaged within that enclosure was none other than personnel that loved football.

They were having the very first fun they had had, no doubt, since the Armistice was signed. Now I ask you if that wasn't an affection and devotion to football, to be out there playing not in football uniforms but in their ODs, being witnessed by the pals of their company. Well, that was the way that football was looked upon in that era. And I daresay the very same thing that prompted them to be engaged in a football game immediately after getting through with a war, prompted me in due course to continue on with football into the professional ranks. One loved the game.

I went back to Dartmouth for my final year, but I did so with a firm determination to go into the business world rather than into medicine. In Europe, you see, the army had instructed me to report to the University of Montpellier, where I was supposed to study, medicalwise. But I could not understand the French professors. French always seemed to be an obstacle to me. As a matter of fact, I had taken one year of it in high school and I can recall this darling teacher saying to me that she would pass me but that I should never take any further French. So what with the language difficulty and other interests, I lost my desire to enter medicine.

After Dartmouth, I went west immediately. In the fall of 1920 I landed in Omaha, Nebraska. My primary object was to get west into the open spaces, into the kind of country that I thought I might enjoy. Omaha was about as far from home as I dared go, because if I were to be notified that my mother had only a short time left on earth, and if I were 'way out in Colorado, say, I would not be able to get home before they buried her. We did not have much airplane travel at that time, so I gauged it and made Omaha the limit of my distance. I obtained employment loading beef into railroad cars.

It was a comedown for a college man, yes, but let me say this to you—there wasn't very much to be had. There was a recession on, there surely was. Of course, if you wanted to be just another man that punched the clock, you could have gone to work for the New York Bell Telephone, say, and put your card in the socket and punched it when you went out, or something like that.

Anyhow, we loaded cars from about four in the morning until two in the afternoon, and then I would go out to Creighton University and assist the football coach as line coach. One day I ran into Ed (Buck) Shaw, who had been the captain of the University of Nebraska football team. He said to me, "You tell me you're from Dartmouth?" I said, "Yes, I am," and then he referred to a copy of the Spalding Guide that he was carrying. It had my picture in it. So he said, "I see they organized a pro league over at Canton, Ohio." I said, "Well, where is the nearest team?" and he told me it was at Rock Island, Illinois, which was four hundred miles across Iowa, the state of tall corn. So on a Friday night I hopped the train and went over there. I announced to the Rock Island club that I was a Dartmouth football player, and they referred to the Spalding Guide and said, "Well, we're looking for men like you."

(At this point in Ed Healey's reminiscences, he handed me a recent copy of *The Roar*, a Dartmouth alumni publication to which he had made a contribution that read as follows:

Recently my dear wife Luke interrupted the silence of our livingroom by casually calling my attention to the fact that football was violent. I took time out from a feature article in the January issue of *Outdoor Life* that I was reading with affectionate interest titled "The Grouse and I," by Cecil Heacox, a Dartmouth graduate of later vintage than ours, and inquired what prompted her to state football was violent.

Luke's reply was that on the front page of her *T.V. Guide* it read, "When Football Was Violent" by Don Doll. I hesitated before replying, and then said, "I remember him. He played for U.S.C. and the Rams when they used six officials to blow the whistle, just fifteen years ago."

"Now, Luke," I said, "I shall tell you a story that involved your husband when they employed three officials with either handicapped vision or heartache for the home team." In early September of the year 1920 . . . I took the sleeper coach jump on Friday night across the state of tall corn, silver dollars and round haircuts. Saturday morning on arrival in Rock Island I ran down the owner, Mr. Walter Flanigan, and discovered that I was welcome, so I practiced with the team on Saturday p.m. for Sunday's engagement, before 5,000 fans in Douglas Park —against the Chicago Tigers, a team composed of giants with such prominent names as Milt Ghee, Shorty DesJardiens, Gil Falcon, etc. Chicago also had playing in the line that day some prominent wrestlers—for instance, Marty Cutler at 250 pounds, none other than your husband's opponent. Mrs. Healey, are you trembling?

Marty was most expert with all the holds in the game of wrestling. He not only applied an armlock on my right ankle but was also clever enough to use his cleats for disfiguring my face to the tune of seven stitches.

The next morning, after the game and back to Omaha, I headed for Dr. Dermody's office for repairs to the ankle and face. The $100 I received (as salary for the game) just about took care of the doctor's bill. . . . Yes, Luke, *T.V. Guide* is correct in calling football a violent game.

Although Healey had taken a physical beating at the hands of Cutler, apparently he impressed Rock Island management, for at the finish of the game he was pleasantly surprised when handed the one hundred dollars, high pay at the time. "My play that day," he told me, "was not so bad as to evidence that I did not know what the game was all about." And as a Dartmouth man, from the famed Ivy League, he increased the prestige of the Rock Island club.)

You must bear in mind that my whole theme in playing professional football was that I was enjoying a life that I was designed for. In other words, doing something you like to do and consequently becoming more successful at it. I always enjoyed the great spirit of football and the fun that came therefrom. I was a young man doing a lot of moving around. I didn't stay with that beef job more than three or four weeks. I was on the move, and of course I commuted weekly to Rock Island via the sleeper. I took any kind of work. Why, I would even unload a carload of coal, which I did in Plains, Kansas, when a bum—or a knight of the grip that rode the rails— wouldn't do it.

In other words, I went to Old Man Collingwood, the banker out there in Plains, and asked him for a job when I was blowing through that grasshopper country. He said, "A job! Well, if you want to unload that carload of coal out there, you can." It was about the first of July, and you could feel the heat waves coming across there. I had on a pair of white flannels that I had brought out from Dartmouth—I was lucky to *have* a pair of pants!—and I started unloading that coal in the morning. I came in that night black. Old Man Collingwood gave me a five-dollar bill or something like that. All the bums riding through on the rails, they needed to eat, too, but they wouldn't unload that coal.

In *my* book, however, it was a very wholesome era to have lived in. If I'm any judge, people found themselves far more satisfied in mind than they are today. They could plan their lives with more security. They enjoyed the little things in life —raising their little families and educating them to the extent of their income and at the same time recognizing lack of capability in their children. In rare instances was anyone of questionable intelligence ever sent away to college, such as youngsters are today. And today, everything has gone so big that the small man has been completely submerged—like the chain stores versus the little man that has his own individual store. I'm fearful of what the future holds as the result of that.

You're asking me about such things, so we will discuss them some. Now Mrs. Healey and I regularly get up about six-thirty, quarter of seven. My dear wife gets breakfast and immediately I turn on the television set, awaiting the breakfast, which is served right here on this panel that slides out of my desk. And as I sit here and watch the television program unfold with Hugh Downs, I am first given the news. Not only is the news unpleasant to listen to, but likewise those whom they later interview. In predominance, the people whom they interview are such that you can tell shortly that they are people extremely conscious of their success in the movies or of their ability to sing a song. In other words, I get up—honestly, I get out of here as fast as I can, before they show them a second time. I want to get outside to the dogs that are happy to see you, that lick your hand and make you feel like you're welcome. You see what I mean? I want to get someplace where it's peaceful, because when you start hearing all this stuff about Vietnam and Biafra and Egypt and Jerusalem—well, everything is un*kindly.* Un*wholesome.* We're living in an era of hate, and for what? God put us on this earth to love our fellow man, not to hate him.

You know, I wrote to John Dickey, the president of Dartmouth, whom I know personally. There's a feeling of affection between us, so I happened to think of John, knowing of all these disturbances we've been having on campuses. I told John that I recall from boyhood that when Mother would bake a cake she would gather all the flour that was necessary, and she would gather the eggs and break them. She'd gather the various spices and other things that went into this particular 'coction. And she'd start stirring with a great big spoon. It was the damnedest-looking mess you ever saw. But there was a mastermind behind that spoon! And I told John Dickey that in this era we're living in, if with God's help we only can come up with some person who can handle the spoon in this situation that we're confronted with, this can be a beautiful country to live in. But where is that person going to come from? How is he going to be heard?

All right, let's return to the days at Rock Island. You know, no pro team at that time could afford a coach. The clubs may have paid a quarterback an extra twenty-five bucks to do the coaching. They might have extended their purse strings to that extent. For example, at Rock Island we had a quarterback named Rube Ursella as coach, and then in 1921 Frank Coughlin right out of Notre Dame was our coach. We progressed fairly well underneath his coaching, but his ability as a tackle was lacking. I had been set on the bench to substitute for him, but after the third game I was in there playing and he didn't command too much respect after I took his job away from him. So they made Jimmy Conzelman the coach. He was a very intelligent quarterback, and we had a moderately successful season.

In '22 the Rock Island Independents sold me to the Chicago Bears following a game that I remember as clearly as if it were just played today. Just listen carefully. Gee, we had a great team! We had lost just once. And on the Sunday prior to Thanksgiving we played the Bears at Wrigley Field.

Now understand, in Chicago the officialdom was such that on occasion it made it a little difficult for the outsider to win. On this day the game was really a tight one. In fact, it was going along 0-0, and they don't come much tighter than that. George Halas, who along with Dutch Sternaman owned the Bears and played for them, was at right end, the opponent for myself, who was the left tackle. Halas had a habit of grabbing ahold of my jersey, see? My sleeve. That would throw me a little off balance. It would twist me just enough so that my head wasn't going where I was going.

So I said to Halas on a couple of occasions, "You know, George, I've often heard that you were getting old awfully young." I didn't enjoy being the victim with reference to his holding, so I forewarned him of what I intended to do about it. Likewise it was necessary for me to forewarn the head linesman, whose name was Roy. His last name I don't seem to recall, but anyhow, I said, "Now, Roy, I understand to start with that you're on the payroll of the Bears. I know that your eyesight must be failing you, because this man Halas is holding me on occasion and it is completely destroying all the things that I'm designed to do in that line." I said, "Roy, I'll

tell you what I'm gonna do. In the event that Halas holds me
again, I am going to commit mayhem. As a matter of fact, I
am going to attempt to take his block right off those shoulders
of his."

Now bear in mind, please, that we had a squad of about
fifteen or sixteen men. Neither Duke Slater, our right tackle,
nor I had a substitute on the bench. So I said, "Roy, you can't
put me out of the game, because we don't have another
tackle. And I can't really afford to be put out of this ballgame
because of your failure to call Halas's holding. I have notified
him, and I am about to commit mayhem."

Well, the condition of the field was muddy and slippery—
a very unsafe field. Halas pulled his little trick once more, and
I come across with a right, because his head was going to my
right. Fortunately for him, he slipped somehow—or maybe I
slipped—and my fist went whizzing right past that head of
his, right into the terra firma, which was soft and mucky. My
fist was buried. When I pulled it out, it was with an effort like
a suction pump. But I'm telling you, I felt very, very happy
that I had not connected. I'm just telling you that, had I
connected, I might have dismantled Halas. So I was happy
that I hadn't, because this was on a Sunday and on the following Tuesday, I believe it was, I was told to report to the Bears.
George Halas had bought me for a hundred dollars.

The Bears had beaten us in that game, 3-0, with a field goal
on the part of Dutch Sternaman, so that had ended our schedule. Had we defeated the Bears, you see, we would have
acquired sufficient prestige to justify booking more games in
the expectation that they would attract patronage. Unfortunately, the victory had eluded us. Green Bay, however, was
planning several more games, and my own intention was to
go up to Green Bay and play the rest of the season for the
Packers. But Mr. Flanigan called me in and told me to report

to Halas and Sternaman, that they wanted to talk to me. So I said, "Well, yeh, I might do that." I was the first profession-al-football player to have his contract sold, but at the time I knew nothing about that.* I mean, I was totally not cognizant of the fact that I was actually the Bears' property.

But I went to Chicago and talked with Halas and Sterna-man in their "private" office, which was the lobby of the Planters Hotel. They offered to pay me seventy-five dollars a game. I said, "I wouldn't sit on your bench for seventy-five dollars a game." So after a discussion of remuneration which lasted two hours, they agreed, and rightfully so, to pay me a hundred bucks a game. Two days later I played sixty minutes on Thanksgiving Day against the Chicago Cardinals and learned a hell of a lot about Chicago and the atmosphere that existed there.

In that game Halas raced downfield on a punt to tackle Paddy Driscoll, the Cardinal star, but Halas wasn't holding on to him very well. Driscoll was one of my dear friends— I had a lot of friends on the Cardinal team—but I was going in to give him an affectionate enclosure, don't you know. I was going to make him secure. And then, holy cow! Out from the Cardinal bench poured a group of men with rods on! They were going out there to protect their idol, Paddy Driscoll.

As you may recall, the vogue at that time was that all the gansters in the world were functioning in Chicago. You had Regan's Colts from back in the yards. You had the O'Donnell crowd. You had the Al Capone crowd. You had the Schemer Drucci crowd. So here came that bunch of South Side root-ers, flowing out from the bench with rods on.

Immediately I stopped in my tracks. I stood there in

*The NFL's questionable archives state that in 1920, the first year of organized pro ball, Buffalo purchased Bob Nash, a lineman, from Buffalo. But most pro-football histories have described Ed Healey as the first player to be sold.

amazement. All I could think of was that a couple of days before, I'd signed up for a hundred bucks, and now I'm out here liable to be killed. I said, "Jesus, Mary, and Joseph! For a hundred bucks?" Luckily, George Halas hung on and completed the tackle of Paddy Driscoll.

Well, I performed for the Bears from 1922 through 1927, and did you know that one year we played eight games in eleven days? As I recall, we won six of the eight, but it was a schedule fit for neither man nor beast. It came about as a result of the club signing none other than the Redhead—the great Red Grange.

I had first witnessed the Redhead in what was only the fourth game that he ever played for Illinois University. Northwestern was the opponent, and the game happened to be played at Wrigley Field. The Bears always practiced at about eleven o'clock on Saturday mornings, so on this particular occasion—along in the fall of 1923—we concluded our practice and returned to our dressing room, which I might say was palatial. I mean, we had training quarters and shower baths and lockers in sufficient numbers, and you were proud to hang your clothes there, knowing that they would not be encumbered in any way by anything that crawls, nor would your pockets be pilfered. Well, we got dressed after showering and made way for the Illinois group. The park being sold out, we were advised to go to the Illinois bench if we cared to see the game.

All right, here's a clean-cut kid from Wheaton, Illinois, just out of the freshman class, you know. But the first thing you know, he intercepts a pass. Well, gee, he goes off to the left and a guy's coming toward him, but he feints and sidesteps and goes to the right. Another guy takes a cut at him. Jesus! He stiff-arms the guy and marches up the center and cuts toward the west sideline, and away he goes, ninety yards for a touchdown. Three touchdowns did he score that day, exhibiting all the ability that an old back would. So it ends up the coach decides to pull in this prize package and give him a rest on the bench. I'm telling you, I had never witnessed any such performance in my lifetime.

Now this brings us back to the cause of our playing eight ballgames in eleven days. On a Saturday prior to Thanksgiving, 1925, Red performed in his last game for his alma mater. He played against Ohio State at Columbus, then took the sleeper to Chicago and the next day joined the club. And then, with none other than the great Red Grange as the main attraction, we set out on a trip and exploded the eastern coast, playing by day and hopping to the next city by overnight sleeper. Of course, we did not always play up to our capability because the human body can stand just so much. But the Redhead broke away in Philadelphia on a Saturday. He broke away in New York on Sunday. I could tell you where he broke away in any of those games. Still, if I were choosing between Red Grange and Jim Thorpe, I would take Thorpe.

I had seen Thorpe perform for the Carlisle Indians against the Springfield YMCA College in 1912, and I played against him in pro ball. Grange was not punishing, but Thorpe was. Mr. Thorpe was well-gifted by nature with terrific joints and could hurt you both offensively and defensively. When he was in shape, he could go sixty minutes at top clip. He was the best in my era, without question.

At any rate, with Red Grange, a gentleman and a scholar, we exploded not only the eastern coast but likewise the western coast and the south with the introduction of professional football, and about the middle of February we got back to Chicago. Now I must tell you a story that involved none other than Mr. C. C. Pyle, Red Grange, and Company.

C. C. Pyle, of course, was the Redhead's business manager, and during the lengthy trip he apparently had been impressed with the performance that I had exhibited, both on the field and off. George Halas, you see, had turned over to me the keeping of the men in tow. Like the others, I, too, enjoyed the frivolity of our travels, but you must have somebody who evidences leadership, who takes charge. So I was that man, and apparently C. C. Pyle was impressed. He addressed a letter to me, inviting me to the Morrison Hotel in Chicago.

He had a room engaged for me there, and when I arrived I found that likewise in residence at the hotel were such personalities as Suzanne Lenglen, the great tennis player; Joie Ray, the great runner; Red Grange, the great performer on the field. And not to leave out another member of the female sex, C. C. Pyle, who had been married and divorced three or four times, had in another room someone that did not answer to the name of Mrs. Pyle.

The prime purpose of my being there, I found out, was that C. C. Pyle had a proposition for me. He was forming a football team to be known as the New York Yanks that would open in the fall of 1926 with Grange as the attraction. And he propositioned me to not only coach the club but select and manage the playing personnel. I listened very attentively.

He offered me ten thousand dollars to change the scene of my activity. Ten thousand dollars! That was more than I was making altogether from Mr. Halas and from another employer, Mr. George A. France of the France Stone Company, which by now employed me in the quarry business in the state of Indiana. And mind you, I had gotten $150 a game for thirty ballgames that season, which figures out to $4,500, doesn't it? Furthermore, pro football by this time was a week-long proposition, although Halas would give me a few days off from practice to attend to my other job when necessary.

I was the only player he would exempt from practice. He could rest assured I would keep myself physically capable.

So having listened to evidence of a magnanimous parting of money on the part of Mr. Pyle, I said, "Charley"—that was his name, Charley—I said, "Charley, I'll give you an answer on that today."

"Oh, you don't have to answer me today," he said. And I said, "Well, this *is* shocking. I've never really been up against anything where I had to make a decision with reference to leaving people I'm established with." So I immediately made my departure and went across the street to the Conway Building. Halas and Sternaman had graduated from the lobby of the Planters to an office.

I told them the true story and nothing else but. Mind you, both had become dear friends of mine. I said, "There's the situation, boys. There it is, right in a package. Now what am I to do?"

Naturally they could not justify any such money as Pyle had offered me, because the attendance didn't justify an expenditure of ten thousand dollars for one individual. Even the great Paddy Driscoll might have commanded only five thousand dollars or something like that. So after much deliberation, George S. Halas and Edward C. Sternaman came up with a figure which, as far as I was concerned, was satisfactory not to leave them. So I walked back across the street and told Pyle that he had better look for someone else. And one of the things that prompted me to make such a quick decision was this—that I figured that any man that could be married and divorced three times and come up with a broad in another room, I didn't have any business working for him. If I had gone with him to New York, he might have taken care of my situation, and then again, he might not have.

I had no reason to regret my decision. In that connection, my thoughts are of poor Ralph Scott. He was our right tackle. Walter Camp had chosen him All-American when he played for Wisconsin, so you have to give him credit for being a pretty good tackle. He came from Montana and was a World War I veteran, shot up a bit. On our travels through the west, we had come out of Seattle and were en route back to Chicago on the train, passing through Montana. I do not know that Ralph Scott was an Indian, but at one of the depots a crowd of Indians on horseback and half the state of Montana came out to meet us. Ralph Scott got off the train, and he had a great big smile on his puss. It was a tremendous display of loyalty to him on the part of those Indians and those people of Montana, and so later I said to him, "Scotty, you could be elected governor of Montana." I said, "Scotty, go back home. Let those Indians and those wonderful people of Montana have the benefit of your tremendous personality. I doubt you'll ever miss football."

Well, Ralph Scott was the damn fool that took that job Pyle was offering. Scotty didn't have any more business being in New York than I did. I mean, New York is a fast town. The last I heard, the poor guy shot himself. I don't know whether he killed himself or somebody killed him, but he never came back from New York.

I myself had very many happy and satisfying moments playing this great game of football, but the most thrilling moment of all happened in January of 1926, while we were on that western trip. We were advertised out there as the Chicago Red Grange All-Stars. And so we were playing an exhibition against a team advertised, I believe, as George Wilson's Los Angeles All-Stars. We had a full house. Everybody was anxious to see the Redhead, but there was a personality on the opposing team who on the West Coast was an equally famous back. A boy by the name of George (Wildcat) Wilson, who had played for Washington.

Now I recall that on the very first play from scrimmage, George Wilson received the ball at his right-halfback position. The flow of traffic all moved to the Los Angeles team's left, or to the opposite side from where I was playing. I noticed that the other side of our line was being knocked down or held, so the bodies were lying all over, and in order to get up momentum with reference to my catching up with Wilson, it necessitated my hurdling several downtrodden bodies that were men of my team.

So the hurdling action took some time. But once on the loose, I pursued George Wilson with determination and will-power. And at about the ten-yard line, let's say, I eventually caught the culprit. I caught him from the rear. Of course, I tell you all this because our opponents never scored. And I don't hesitate to tell you—I might just as well be honest about this—I was terrifically fast and wonderfully conditioned. So I did catch the culprit from the rear, although his heel came up through my outstretched hands and there was a removal of a tooth.

I got married on November 17, 1927, and played only a couple or three games of pro football after that. I had had wonderful enjoyments on the gridiron, but marriage revised my life. That, plus the fact that the France Stone Company had taken on additional quarries, which gave me a responsibility for same. Eventually, I became general manager of operations and sales in the states of Illinois and Indiana. However, it is this farm, where you and I are engaged in conversation, that has been the fulfillment of a dream, one that I planned during the days of the 1930s, when Roosevelt informed us to plow under cotton and corn and kill off the hogs.

Well, that was *wrong*. I mean, there were too many people in our own country that needed those hogs and needed that cotton. Throughout the world, people are underfed. We don't need to kill those things or stow them away. So I said, "That's all wrong. You got to get back on a farm, Ed."

I was, at the time, in New York for a luncheon engagement with Mr. John McGinley, vice-president of Travelers Insurance, and a Mr. Towner of the Towner Rating Bureau. Meeting these gentlemen for the first time, I felt that I should do a bit of listening. So here were these two wonderful big men with Scotch tweeds on during the cold weather, and I heard Mr. Towner say to Mr. McGinley, "You know, John, I was telling my dear wife, Nancy, the other evening, after hearing this Roosevelt say we should plow under the cotton and kill off the hogs—I was telling dear Nancy that here we are enjoying the evening of life. You know, we've raised a beautiful family. We lived in Park Avenue. We've had doormen and we've had chauffeurs. We've had everything that's wonderful during life. We now have these wonderful grandchildren growing up, and I told Nancy that if the good Lord should call me prior to her, that I could close my eyes happily and go to the dear Lord knowing that my family could go back on that farm we have outside of Brattleboro, Vermont."

Well, knowing that area—Brattleboro—and the ruggedness of the granite that lies beneath the surface, all I could think of was Cal Coolidge and how he and his father had struggled and strived to grow a little bit here and a little bit there. That's tough country to farm. But I had taken Mr. Towner's point, and I just decided, "Well, I'll get a farm, but it will be where it's a lot more fertile." I came right back here and put the matter into the hands of a real-estate agent. That's what I did, and this is what I came up with. With Mr. France's consent, I continued with my position in the quarry business until ten years ago, but resided here, a gentleman farmer, so to speak.

Ofttimes, when I'm sitting here at my desk by the window, I'll be watching wild ducks and wild geese on the river. Actually and honestly, during the hunting season last fall, here comes a great big buck down the river, probably having been disturbed elsewhere by hunters. Of course, I don't shoot him, and he kindly gets out of the river on the far side, so that I can witness him crawl out. A fascinating sight. While I still retain three great male Labradors, I don't do much hunting myself, and mostly, I just like to see the deer and the geese and the birds around. I got back to the land, and it's been delightful. Let me say to you—and I don't mind telling you —that it's been a real privilege on my part, and a happy few hours, to have you not only as a guest for lunch but as one visiting with me in my home and meeting my dear wife.

2

INDIAN JOE GUYON

"You can't sneak up on an Indian."

The late Ralph McGill, the distinguished Atlanta newspaper publisher and author, once wrote, "There is really no argument about the identity of the greatest football player who ever performed in Dixie. There is a grand argument about second place, but for first place there is Joe Guyon, the Chippewa brave." Bill Fincher, a onetime line coach at Georgia Tech, where Indian Joe devoted a phase of his football travels, observed that "tackling Guyon was like grabbing an airplane propeller." The 1916 Cumberland College team would not have disagreed. Trapped on the same field with Guyon and his Georgia Tech teammates, Cumberland lost by a score of 222-0.

Indian Joe began playing football, first as a tackle, for the Carlisle Indian School at Carlisle, Pennsylvania, there succeeding the storied Jim Thorpe as Carlisle's backfield threat. In pro football he played for no fewer than six clubs, fashioning a career that in 1966 won him induction into the Pro Football Hall of Fame. Widowed in middle age, he worked as a press-box attendant at Louisville's old minor-league baseball park, Parkway Field, where one day he was introduced to a southern widow lady attending her first game. "That all the players they put on the field?" she inquired of him. He replied, "If they had any more, they'd be climbing up each other's backs." Listen, mister," said the widow lady, "don't get smart with me!"

They were married soon after, and I found them living in a small frame house in a workingmen's section of Louisville. Mrs. Guyon, a plump, cordial woman, explained that not long ago Indian Joe had suffered head injuries in an auto accident. In order to assist his memory of times gone by, she sat nearby in a kitchen adjacent to the living room where Joe Guyon and I talked.

━━━━━━

I'll wager you can't guess my age. Take a guess. Try a double number. That's right, seventy-seven, but I'm the same damn weight as when I played ball. One-eighty-five. Indians are simply terrific, physically. The Indians who came off the reservations to play ball were agile and strong and quick. Wrestling is where they got their tricks. Even now, I can protect myself. You just run at me, and boy, I'll floor you. I mean *anybody*, see? I'll floor them before they can say scat. They'll wonder what the hell hit 'em. Because I was drilled on the reservation.

How long we been living in this house, sweetheart? Four years? See, years ago I played baseball here. I skyrocketed the Louisville Colonels of the American Association to two pennants in a row. I'm a terrific baseball player. I played the outfield, and I led them to two pennants in a row. I led 'em in base hits, runs scored, stolen bases, sacrifice hits, and *everything*. That was '25 and '26, wasn't it, darling?

I didn't go up to the big leagues because I got hurt. Kid let me run into a fence at Indianapolis when I was going like— oh, God, hitting around .400 my third year. Gee whiz. Yeh, a kid from the University of Kentucky did it. I call him a kid because he just come out of school. He thought he knew all about baseball. I played right field and he played center, so I told him, "Now this is professional baseball. We play together. I'll take care of you, and you take care of me. I'll be over there to help you, and you help me." But he let me run into a fence on a fly ball. I was always a high stepper, you know, and goddarn it, I got stuck way up there on that old board fence. I had on new spikes, and I just embedded them into that wood and I got hung up there. Absolutely.

Two boys come from the bench, gonna pull me off. Why, they couldn't move me! So two more come running out, and, oh, they pulled me out but they tore my knee, goddamn. That was just about the end of all my athletics, baseball and pro football. I had been going like crazy. And *hit* a ball? Baseball is really my love.

I came off a Chippewa reservation at White Earth, Minnesota. Up there I loved to hunt and trap. I had to make my own bow and arrows, and I remember I got five partridges out of one tree. That's right. Five out of one tree. The funny thing about a partridge, you start and hit that lower one and he goes down, and then you hit the next one and the next one. Ain't that something? Just make your bow hit that lower partridge, and it won't make no mess. Down it goes. The noise won't bother the others. But if they see that top one coming down, well, he's the boss, that guy up there. And when he gets off, everybody goes. You didn't know that, see?

My mother's folks—her mother and father—they were medicine men. Expert on herbs. Later I was playing baseball for the Atlanta Crackers, and my son and daughter had diarrhea so damn bad that the best doctors in town couldn't stop those kids. So I wrote up to my mother and she sent me medicine wrapped in a little deerskin pouch. It was from herbs and the bark of the red willow. She said to give them a little pinch of that medicine, and it stopped them just like that. So that's what made my children go to the professions that they went to. They were much impressed that their ancestors could cure them when nobody else could. My son now is a doctor. How about that? My daughter's a public-health nurse. Can you imagine that!

In 1912, when I was about nineteen, I enrolled at the Carlisle Indian School, and that's where I first met Jim Thorpe. That was the year Jim went over to Stockholm and won the pentathlon and the decathlon in the Olympics. He was a Sac and Fox from Oklahoma, and I guess he was five or six years older than me, about twenty-four or twenty-five, and of course, he already was an All-American football star at Carlisle. I got to wrestling the boys there at the school, and Jim wanted to see who in the hell that damn Chippewa was that had come off the reservation and was flipping all these guys. So we wrestled. I couldn't throw him because he was quick and fast himself. We wrestled to a standoff and we became buddies right away. I was the best man at his wedding, and my first marriage was to a cousin of Jim's in Oklahoma.

The funny thing, Carlisle wasn't nothing but an eighth-grade school, but they called us a college.* Of course, some of us were pretty old by the time we got there, because those reservation schools weren't always real good, but anyhow, those Carlisle teams used to beat Harvard, Pittsburgh, Army, Pennsylvania, and a lot of those big univeristies. They didn't

---

*Actually, the Carlisle Indian Industrial Training School was a vocational-training institution, operated by the federal government. Whether its academic program could have been equated accurately with high-school grade levels, be they eighth grade or higher, is open to question. In the summer of 1918, the government closed the school and converted it into a hospital for World War I wounded.

want to have to say, "Well, a damn grammar school beat us," so they just called us a college.

Gosh, that Jim Thorpe was a ballplayer. When he tackled you, goddang, he'd almost kill you. Give him the ball and he delighted in running through a whole team. He'd say, "What's the matter? Can't you handle ol' Jim?" He always kidded them.

Jim hated the training table, because it never had enough on it to eat. He loved steaks. Pop Warner, our coach at Carlisle, would ration off steaks to us, and Jim would buy them off the other players. He could do that. Oklahoma Indians had money.

Arithmetic used to give Jim hell, but he had to pass, you know, to be eligible for football, and that's what kept his grades up. Jim loved football, although he hated practice. Sometimes he'd hang his head and go off like an Indian and pout a lot. Then Warner would come up to him and say, "All right, what the hell's going on here?" Jim wouldn't say nothing. Then Warner would say, "Goddamned Indian! You don't want to learn. You just want to pout." Warner would jab him.

As it turned out, Jim was the one that hired me for my first job in pro football. I had put in two years at Carlisle and made second-team All-American, but then I had to go to prep school in order to get enough credits to go to college, see? So I went to Keewatin Academy, located at Prairie du Chien, Wisconsin. We beat hell out of the high schools. We'd just slap them down. Then Georgia Tech grabbed me and I made All-American again. Then in 1919, a group of people who sponsored a pro-football team in Canton, Ohio, hired Jim to coach it and play in the backfield. So he called me over there. I guess I was twenty-six or twenty-seven by then, I don't know.

I played halfback on offense, and on defense I played side-back, which I suppose is what they later started calling "defensive halfback." I had more damn tricks, and brother, I could hit you. Elbows, knees, or whatchamacallit—boy, I could use 'em. Yes, and it's true that I used to laugh like the dickens when I saw other players get injured. Self-protection is the first thing they should have learned. You take care of yourself, you know. I think it's a sin if you don't. It's a rough game, so you've got to *equip* yourself and know what to do. I saw my friend Jim Thorpe get double-teamed once, and I had to go over and pick him up. I laughed at *him*.

Jim paid me a good salary, maybe a hundred dollars a game, and I carried the team. I did the punting, the passing, all that derned stuff. I was the key man. Jim and I, we'd alternate in the backfield.

In those times, you only had one day of practice for a game. There had to be one day of practice to get your plays. You had to get your end runs, your off-tackles, your plunges, your fakes, your crisscrosses—all those things. But with the experience we had, all that stuff fell right in, you know. Patterns were pretty much alike everywhere.

Gamblers tried to buy us off. They would approach us at the hotel, where we stayed on the weekend. 'Course, you couldn't tell who was a gambler, but I mean they'd start talking football. Then they'd say, "Joe, I want to talk to you. What about this game today?" Then they'd go into their proposition. "Well, how about fifty dollars?" They didn't fool with me because they found out soon enough that I wouldn't talk to them. I said, "I'm not interested," and walked away. But there were guys who took their money, I guess. I guess some did. We had one guy. Oh, he was a high traveler. A halfback. We saw his contacts at the hotel. Then we saw his play. He was detailed to cover a man, and when he didn't,

why, we said it was an accident. But the second time, it was
too obvious. I said, "What the hell is going on?" I went over
to the bench and said, "He didn't cover his man, Jim. This
guy is not covering his man." Jim braced him right there. He
fired him. The game was what we were after. We ain't going
to sell the darned game for no goddarned nothing.

The games that were real scraps were the ones in Chicago.
George Halas ran that team, and he was a scrapper. There'd
be a fight every time we met those son of a biscuits. Halas
knew that I was the key man. He knew that getting me out
of there would make a difference. I was playing defense one
time and I saw him coming after me from a long ways off. I
was always alert. But I pretended I didn't see him. When he
got close, I wheeled around and kicked him, goddamn. I
brought my knee right up into him. Broke three of his ribs.
And as they carried him off, I said to him, "What the hell,
Halas. Don't you know you can't sneak up on an Indian?"

You've asked me, is it true that Jim Thorpe drank too
much? Well, he participated pretty much after he got back
from the Olympic games and everybody wanted to entertain
him. But I can't tell you a lot about Jim's drinking because
we didn't enjoy the same things. I never touched the stuff.
Nightclubs didn't appeal to me. But I'll say this—if it was a
big game coming up, Jim knew he had to take care of himself.
Pop Warner put the theory of conditioning into him, and he
knew the importance of it. But if it wasn't a big game coming
up, then, yes, he'd go out and fill up.

Jim took some tough blows in his lifetime. Like the time
they took away his Olympic medals because they found he
had played some professional baseball. Oh, gosh, he took that
hard. He said, "Well, they can have the damn things but they
can't take back the honor." And then he lost his boy, just a
youngster, and that really knocked him down.

I would have to say that Red Grange was a better runner than Jim Thorpe, but Jim was the better all-around player. Do everything. But Grange was a better runner because he was equally fast and more elusive, although he never got by me. I always tied him up. My middle name is Napoleon, and I guess it suits. I've always been aggressive.

Take like when I went to the New York Giants in '27. I must have been about thirty-five then. But I spearheaded the Giants to their first world championship. Spearheaded them, yeh. Did everything. I kicked kickoffs clear through the uprights. I could still outrun those pro ballplayers. That was my last year of pro football, because that baseball injury ruined everything, but gosh-darn, I enjoyed New York. Just getting an opportunity to see that town! My roommate was Pete Calac, a great fullback who had been at Carlisle with me and could carry four men on his back. Pete didn't drink and, of course, neither did I. We'd take a ferry and go sight-seeing. I ran up to the top of the Statue of Liberty twice, just to see what kind of condition I was in. Yes, sir, my big moment in football was going to New York. Goddamn, I give that old city hell.

3

RED GRANGE

The first plutocrat

Seated at the side of his pool, Red Grange looked the part of a retired sportsman. He wore sunglasses, a light-yellow shirt, tattersall slacks, and blue-cloth shoes. The sunlight, filtering through the skylight-type roof over the pool, revealed a tint of the old red hair among the gray. With his wife he had settled at Indian Lake Estates, a peaceful Central Florida development populated by well-to-do senior citizens. Beyond the far side of the swimming pool, in a quiet lagoon, Grange's powerboat lay tied to his private pier, where once each day the fish gathered to receive breadcrumbs from Mrs. Grange's hand.

Harold Grange was, of course, the Wheaton Iceman, so known because as a youth he worked on an ice truck in his home town of Wheaton, Illinois. At the University of Illinois, he at once became the nation's premier football star, a half-back who disappeared from the grasp of tacklers like a vapor. The Galloping Ghost, Grantland Rice named him.

Alone among all the players of the pro-football decades that preceded television, Red Grange earned from football the six-figure income that stars of the 1960s were to realize. Tax-free dollars flowed into his hands and went from there into real estate. His ace in the hole was a unique operator named C. C. (Cash & Carry) Pyle, probably the first player's agent known to football. With Pyle calling the shots, Red

Grange played for the Chicago Bears, then jumped to the New York Yankees in an outlaw league Pyle created, and continued through a second season with the Yankees after they won admission to the NFL. Then he returned to the Bears. In the Roaring Twenties, the Golden Age of Sport, Grange was the beloved plutocrat of pro football.

Charley Pyle was about forty-four years old when I met him. He was the most dapper man I have ever seen. He went to the barbershop every day of his life. He had a little moustache that he'd have trimmed, and he would have a manicure and he'd have his hair trimmed up a little, and every day he would get a rubdown. He was the greatest clotheshorse you ever saw. All his clothes were tailor-made. His suits cost a hundred or two hundred dollars, which was a lot of money in the 1920s. He wore a derby and spats and carried a cane, and believe me, he was a handsome guy. The greatest ladies' man that ever lived. The girls loved him.

Money was of no consequence to Charley. I would say that at the time I met him, he had made pretty near a million dollars and lost it. He had sold pipe organs to theaters at one time, and at this particular time he owned three movie theaters—two in Champagne, Illinois, and one in Kokomo, Indiana. One night during my senior year at Illinois, I went down to the Virginia Theater in Champagne, and one of the ushers located me and told me, "Mr. Pyle wants to see you in his office." Well, the first words Charley Pyle said to me were "Red, how would you like to make a hundred thousand dollars?" I couldn't figure what he was talking about. But he said, "I have a plan. I will go out and set up about ten or twelve football games throughout the United States. I think I can talk George Halas and Dutch Sternaman of the Chicago Bears into making their team available, and as soon as the college season ends, we will make this tour, and I'll guarantee you that you'll make at least a hundred thousand out of it."

Of course, I was flabbergasted. But Charley made good his word. He lined it up for me to play with the Bears and then went out on the road and set up the whole program. We started after Thanksgiving Day and played the first game of the tour at Coral Gables, outside of Miami, at a time when Florida was swinging. In 1925 everybody there was selling real estate and building things. Three days before the game, we looked around and there was no place to play a football game, so we said, "Where are we going to play?" The people there told us, "Out here in this field." Well, there wasn't anything there except a field. But two days before the game, they put two hundred carpenters to work and built a wooden stadium that seated twenty-five thousand. They sold tickets for fancy prices up to twenty dollars apiece, and the day after the game, they tore down the stadium. You'd never know a ballgame had taken place there. They were going to build houses on that field.

Dollarwise, I couldn't really tell you how much money I made with Charley Pyle, but, yes, I got my hundred thousand dollars out of that tour. Then we made two pictures out in Hollywood. One of them was called *One Minute to Play*, and it called for a lot of football sequences. We wanted to get a lot of crowd shots, but to get crowd shots you had to hire extras and pay them about fifteen dollars a day. We needed thousands of them. We wanted to show a big crowd on a crisp fall day in the northeast.

Now Charley was never one to pay out money indiscriminately, you know, so he hit on a plan. He brought in Wildcat Wilson, the All-American from Washington, and furnished him with a football team made up of a lot of local fellows from USC and California and places like those. And Charley furnished me with a team of about the same caliber. We advertised in the newspapers that Wildcat Wilson's team was going to play Red Grange's team in the Rose Bowl, and that everybody who wore an overcoat and a felt hat would be allowed in free. Likewise, women wearing coats.

This was July, mind you. The temperature in the shade must have been a hundred and at the stadium it must have been 110. But we had about twelve thousand people setting up there all bundled up in their overcoats and hats, and we got all the crowd shots we needed. It never cost us a dime, except that we had to hire maybe fifteen players on each side and pay them something like twenty-five or fifty bucks apiece.

Well, it's like Tom Gallery told me about a year ago. Tom was then head of NBC sports and had been a great pal of Charley's, and he said to me, "If Charley was around today, wouldn't he have a field day with all this big money rolling around?" We endorsed sporting equipment and meat loaf and football dolls and soft drinks and had a Red Grange candy bar. You name it, we had it. And where the average fellow would ask for five thousand dollars, Charley would ask twenty-five thousand. Mostly, he got cash. Cash or a check. He didn't fool around very much.

The guy was a genius. He went over to Europe and brought back Suzanne Lenglen and was the first man to put on an indoor tennis tour in this country. In 1927 he put on a footrace from Los Angeles to New York. He had three hundred entries, and fifty-five of them finished, and he paid a twenty-five-thousand-dollar first prize to Andy Payne, that little farmer boy from down in Oklahoma. Charley sold half a million programs on that race—at fifty cents apiece, I believe. Wherever the runners stopped for the night, the town had to pay Charley a certain amount for the publicity. The sportswriters got to kidding the race and calling it the Bunion Derby, but it was, I think, the greatest athletic feat that has ever been put on in this country. Those fellows ran every day! Not five days a week, but seven days a week. And they ran twenty-five to seventy-five miles a day. It was a tremendous thing!

I was out in Los Angeles with Charley about two or three weeks before that footrace started, and he said, "I haven't got a car out here. I ought to have an automobile." So I said, "Yeh, how are you going to go along the road with these runners if you don't have a car?" Well, the average fellow would then have gone out and bought a car. But not Pyle. He went up to Oakland to a bus company and had a bus custom-made for twenty-five thousand dollars. I've never seen anything like it. It slept eight or nine. He had a shower bath and a galley and berths and a radio. It was the most palatial thing you ever saw, and that was the way he traveled from Los Angeles to New York.

Let me tell you about another idea Charley had. You hear all this talk about the Houston Astrodome these days, but I'm talking about 1926. Charley had a set of blueprints drawn up for a domed stadium. He paid five thousand dollars to get the rundown on all the engineering details and have the blueprints made. And on those plans he had a stadium that would seat seventy thousand people. It had a roof that you could open and close. It had a helicopter landing place on top. All the aisles were escalators. They would turn them on after the game, and all you would do was step out of your seat and be whizzed right out. Charley had a glass company develop a formula for special glass—magnifying glass. You would have a crank at your seat, so that you could roll up this piece of glass or roll it down, whatever you wanted, and it would be like watching the game through binoculars. The farther back you were, the higher the glass would magnify. Charley had so many innovations! The whole place would be electrically run. He could turn it into an ice rink, or practically anything else. He said, "Anyone who gets three or four of these stadiums will control sports in America."

But he never built one. He finally said, "It's impossible. It's impossible because it would cost three million dollars." Today it would cost $150 million.

Charley made a million three or four times and lost it. As I said, the money itself meant nothing to him. But he did like to hear his name mentioned. He would go to the six-day bike races and sponsor three-hundred-dollar sprints just to hear his name come over the loudspeaker. He rode the Twentieth Century Limited between Chicago and New York quite a bit, and whenever one of the waiters would say, "Mr. Pyle, how are you?" he would leave a ten-dollar tip. If the waiter didn't know his name, Charley wouldn't tip him a nickel. He loved that acclaim.

He was a fellow you would *like*. The greatest mixer, a great storyteller. He loved to set around and have a drink with anyone. A lovable guy. I never met anyone who did not like Charley Pyle. A number of the big sportswriters, he was the closest friend they had. Westbrook Pegler, the political columnist who at the time was a prominent sportswriter, was a very good friend of mine and Charley Pyle's. In his column he could cut you up into little pieces, you know, but his alibi was "If I didn't like you, I wouldn't write about you." I never read anything favorable that he wrote about anyone, but personally I liked Westbrook. Nobody took a punch at him, because for one thing, he was a big guy who could take pretty good care of himself. And he was a nice guy, but his way of writing was just that he would tear everything apart.

In 1926, the year that Charley set up a new league, the American Football League, he had an office in the Hotel Astor. Westbrook would be down there every morning. This was during Prohibition, you know, and each morning when Westbrook left, he would take a couple of bottles of Pyle's Scotch with him, and then he would turn around and write a column and call Pyle everything he could lay his tongue to that could go on paper. Charley sometimes would complain, but Westbrook would say, "Well, just as long as I keep your name singular, don't holler."

Not counting that first football tour that I made with the Bears, I played two years under contract to Charley Pyle, and then I left him. He was very busy, going great guns in a lot of things, and I figured I could handle my affairs myself. I had fulfilled my contract with him, and he'd fulfilled his obligations to me, and we remained great friends. Some years later, in his latter years, he had a stroke and I thought it was the end for him. He was very, very badly crippled. He couldn't talk and his whole right side was useless. But I'll tell you what a dogmatic fellow Charley was.

It was two years before I saw him again, and this time he was just as active and spry as I was. It seemed impossible. I said, "What happened?" And he said, "Well, they told me I'd never walk again or use my arm or be able to talk. So I hired a young fellow to drive my car, and I went up into northern Wisconsin. I rented a cottage 'way out in the country and stayed up there for ten months. I had some pulleys lined up in a tree, and every day I sat out under that tree and had some kids that I'd hired tie a rope to my bad arm and pull that rope. I did that for months, and then I did it with my legs for months, and finally I got back the use of all my limbs." Now I ask you, how many people would have done that?

Charley passed away about fifteen years ago. He was a good fellow. He was a great guy to have on your side. He was a good-time guy. And talk about swinging, nobody could swing like Pyle could! They don't make 'em that way any-more.

Actually, football was not my favorite game. I liked football, but I did not like it as well as basketball and track. I loved to practice baseball all day long, but I detested football prac-tice. It was just hard work. When I was at Illinois Bob Zuppke was the coach, and if he could find one mud puddle on the field, he'd throw the ball there and that's where you'd have to roll on it. We'd practice out there from 3:30 until it got dark, and then they'd turn the lights on and we would prac-tice some more. We would scrimmage by the hour.

Coach Zuppke, who of course has always been one of my top guys, never could pronounce my name. He'd give it that German pronunciation—Grainche. You couldn't loaf on him, because he had eyes in the back of his head. I never heard him swear in my life, but he had three words that were the ultra of ultras. He would say, "You *lemon*, you!" And if you heard those words, it usually followed that an hour after everyone had gone in, you'd still be out there running around those goalposts. Coach Zuppke would get you in shape or kill you, one of the two.

He used to contend that any back who carried the ball thirteen times and did not score shouldn't be playing football. You see, the guy who makes the touchdowns is very unim-portant. It's a heck of a lot easier carrying that ball than blocking, believe me. Blocking is the toughest job in the world. It's always amusing to me when I read about how great some individual is. Nobody's great in football. You're only as great as the other ten guys make you. I would carry the ball, oh, from thirty to forty times a game, but I was just the representative is all, and if I didn't score at least two or three times, why, I would be a pretty lousy halfback. Yet when O. J. Simpson carried the ball thirty or forty times a game for USC, they made a big thing of it. Of course, I think he's a top football player, because he's got the moves. Those straight runners are a dime a dozen.

I haven't seen a new football play since I was in high school. You have just so many holes in a line and you have eleven men playing, and there's only so many ways you can go through those holes, and those ways have been used for forty, fifty years. There isn't that much science in football. Television announcers just make you think there is. Well, I don't care how complicated they make the game seem, it's really based on two principles and those are blocking and tackling. The Green Bay Packers under Vince Lombardi were a great team, because they blocked. When I view football I can't watch the ballcarrier. I pick out a lineman and never take my eyes off him. Two-thirds of the time, he just runs over and falls down someplace, you know. You don't see the great blocking that we used to have. But I pick out a lineman and watch the blocking anyhow, because that's what makes a football team. I'm not interested in watching the others score touchdowns. I don't care about touchdowns.

I don't think there's any way you can develop a new play or a new offense. How many offenses are there? Years ago, we had them all. When they brought out the I formation, somebody asked me if I'd ever seen it before. Well, yes, we used it in the eighth grade. We called it the tandem formation. And as far as today's pro offenses are concerned, it's just a conglomeration of spreads. We called them spreads, but now they call those guys out there a split end or something like that. Phraseology has changed, that's all. When I was a kid we used spreads that they haven't come back to yet. They will someday, and they'll say, "Look at this new brand of football!"

They talk about the great passers today. But remember that the football has been changed in size three times since the early 1930s, and each time it has been made narrower and the axis pulled in. Anybody can throw today's football. You go back to Benny Friedman playing with the New York Giants in the late 1920s and early '30s. He threw that old balloon. Now who's to tell what Benny Friedman might do with this modern football? He'd probably be the greatest passer that ever lived.

What made professional football big was only one thing, television. When I played in the late 1920s and '30s, outside of your franchise towns the people hardly knew anything about pro ball. You'd get back into the hinterlands and tell them that pro football was a good game, that the pros blocked hard and tackled hard, and they'd laugh at you. A U.S. senator took me to the White House and introduced me to Calvin Coolidge and said, "Mr. President, I want you to meet Red Grange. He's with the Chicago Bears." I remember Calvin Coolidge's reply very plainly. He said, "Well, Mr. Grange, I'm glad to meet you. I have always liked animal acts."

The college coaches of my day condemned pro football, you know. When I joined the Bears in 1925, I would have been much more popular had I joined the Capone mob. My own coach, Bob Zuppke, got so down on me that for a while he wouldn't speak to me. I said to him, "You're making *your* living out of football. What's the difference if you make a living coaching it or playing it?" Of course, the college coaches wanted to keep the football business within the colleges. I liked playing college ball better than pro ball, because in college you had all those people rooting for you—you had the student body behind you. And I always felt, just as George Halas has said many times, that I would get out of pro football if it ever harmed college ball, but I don't think it ever has.

Personally, I did not believe that pro football had a future. Charley Pyle believed it did. So did Don Maxwell, the sports editor of the Chicago *Tribune* in the 1920s. The *Tribune* probably was the first to start building up the game. That newspaper believed in it. In the big cities, New York and Chicago, you had a hard core of pro fans, maybe fifteen or twenty thousand, but out in the country, nothing. Still, the 1920s were, as they called them, the Golden Age of Sports. Each sport had a number of outstanding individuals, really big stars, and they were publicized to death. You had Bill Tilden in tennis, Earl Sande in horseracing, Charley Paddock in track, Dempsey in boxing, and of course Babe Ruth in baseball. I'll always remember meeting the Babe. He had been one of my heroes. It was in Boston in the winter, 1926 or '27, and he came up to my hotel room. He just wanted to say hello. He said, "Kid, don't pay any attention to what they write about you or to what they say about you, and don't pick up too many checks." Of course, that's just what the Babe was always doing—picking up too many checks.

Everybody just seemed to let their hair down a little after the First World War, and when the '20s came along the people were ready for some entertainment. It was a great generation. Everybody seemed to be enjoying themselves. People wore felt hats with big three-inch brims. Your clothes were big and baggy. You wore overcoats that pretty near touched your shoes, and neckties that were wide, same as they're coming back into style today. Most of the kids who came into pro football were from small towns and had never had a dime in their life. They'd get into the big cities and buy a new suit of clothes and a nice pair of shoes and an automobile on time, and although a lot of them would have to hold down a part-time job in a garage or someplace, a lot of them were real swingers. You read about Joe Namath today! Well, shucks, drinking and sex were not just recently invented, you know. We had a lot of guys that were better swingers than Namath will ever be. They found places in New York that he hasn't located yet.

That sort of thing has been going on for a long, long time, but in my day they kept it out of the papers. Prohibition made no difference. There was more drinking in Prohibition than there is today.

Talk about swingers, what about Johnny Blood? One year, I played a couple of post-season exhibition games for Green Bay and roomed with Blood. What a guy! I remember a couple of girls wanted Johnny to sign a program, and he said, "I'll do better than that. I'll sign it in blood." He cut his wrist with a knife and signed that program in blood, and he had to have about four stitches taken in his wrist.

He was a lovable guy, a very learned guy, and one whale of a football player. A long-legged guy who could kill you every way. Run, punt, pass, catch passes, a great football player. He used to drive Curly Lambeau crazy. We were staying in Los Angeles, and Johnny and I had a hotel room next to Coach Lambeau. Curly was in the corner room. Johnny knew that Curly had a case of whiskey in his room, so when Curly went out, Johnny climbed out on the ledge, which was on the ninth floor and must have been about a foot wide, and he walked along that ledge for about twenty feet and got through Curley's window and took a couple of bottles and came back. I don't think Curly ever did learn who stole his whiskey.

Now I don't mean pro ballplayers were a bunch of drunks, because they were not. They played tough football. We used to practice at nine o'clock in the morning and get through about noon, and then about three times a week we'd have a meeting at night. The afternoons generally were your own. I've seen more doggone fights among football players, because they didn't have anything else to do. I've even seen 'em fight the owners. I remember that when the Bears were playing in San Francisco, Dutch Sternaman, who owned half of the club, got up in the dressing room and said that he was not going to start George Trafton, our center. George stood up and knocked Dutch right through the dressing-room window onto the lawn. It was an insult in those days to tell a ballplayer he was not going to start, or to take him out of the game. The only way you came out was to be dragged out with an injury that prevented you from walking.

Sure, your ballplayers had a lot of fights, but they held no grudges. I've seen some vicious fights off the field, but the next day you'd see the two guys with their arms around each other. However, the year after George Trafton knocked Dutch Sternaman through the window, the two of them and a couple of other players were walking from Wrigley Field to the elevated railroad when they started talking about that punch Trafton threw at Sternaman in San Francisco. So George and Dutch decided to fight it out again. Trafton had on a big overcoat, and Sternaman said, "Go ahead and take off your overcoat and we'll finish this thing." Well, just as Trafton got his overcoat down over his arms, where it would prevent him from swinging, Sternaman started in on him. Dutch gave him a very good whaling.

My second full year in pro ball, I hurt my knee playing for the New York Yankees against the Chicago Bears at Wrigley Field, and from then on, I was just a so-so football player. I walked on crutches for eight months. The doctors would tell you that if they operated, they couldn't guarantee anything, and you might have a stiff leg or not even be able to walk again. I went to doctors from coast to coast. One of them put my leg in a barrel of ice. Another fellow put it in a cast. Oh, I had everything done to that knee. And all of those doctors told me to stay off it.

So that's what I did. It puffed up. I had water on it. But finally, I got out to Los Angeles, still getting around on crutches, and went to a Dr. Spencer. He said, "Do you play golf?" I said, "Well, I hack around a little." And he said, "I want you to go out and play golf." I told him I couldn't even walk, that I was on *crutches*, but he said, "I don't care if you're on four pairs of crutches. Go out and start playing golf. If you don't use that knee, you'll never walk again."

So I went out and hobbled around the golf course, and inside of a few months I was walking fairly good again. I came back and played seven more years and made all-league two of those years, but I was strictly a straight runner from then on. The woods are full of straight runners.

Personally, I don't think today's football players are any better than the old-timers at all. You hear that they're bigger and faster. We had fellows that could run just as fast. And they wore equipment that held all that perspiration and weighed three times as much as today's equipment. On the average, today's players are bigger, I'll grant you that. We had a few fellows who weighed 250, 255, but that was a big man in those days. Size, however, has nothing to do with making a football player. I don't mean that a 125-pounder can go out and play against a 300-pounder, but after a man weighs 250, I don't think size has an awful lot to do with it. I see many big guys that weigh 260 that aren't much good at football.

I would just as soon have a three-hundred-pound man tackle me as a one-hundred-pound man, providing I could see him. The way you get hurt is being tackled by someone you can't see. You're not prepared for it. But I don't think you get hurt because the tackler is especially big. I've seen so many big guys who you point your finger at them and they're hurt. And I've seen a lot of little guys like Keith Molesworth, who played with the Bears for a while. Moley weighed about, oh, 150 pounds soaking wet. You could drop a building on him and not hurt him. It's not the size of the man that counts at all. I'll agree that the modern players are better when they can block and tackle better than the old-timers.

I think the pro game has deteriorated tremendously in the last four or five years. I just don't believe you can stock twenty-six football clubs with forty players each—that's 1,040 football players—as well as you can stock twelve or fourteen teams. I don't think there are that many good football players in the United States. But of course, the average viewer, what does he care? Even a high-school game is good as long as it's even and it looks right.

To me, the big change in football is in the defensive alignments. Years ago, you'd have maybe two or three set defenses and a couple of variations off of them. Today a pro team will have eight, nine, or ten defenses and half a dozen variations off of them. You never know what they're going to do. I remember Coach Zuppke at Illinois saying, "The best defense in the world is to have no defense. Just everybody do something different on every play so they can't figure you out." And maybe that might be the idea today. They do practically that today.

Football nowadays is on a much different scale, of course. It's big-money business. You're dealing with millions of dollars. It's important, and there isn't anything very funny in it. I think that in the old days we had more laughs and more unusual experiences to remember, because when a fellow's making seventy-five or a hundred dollars a game he can have a few laughs. The fate of the nation did not depend on whether you won or lost. But we liked to win. Everybody likes to win. In fact, the only football players in my time were fellows who really loved to play football. They were not in it for the money. There wasn't much money there. They would have played football for nothing.

4

JOHNNY BLOOD

A high resistance to culture

Known as the Vagabond Halfback, Johnny Blood was a lanky, fatalistic itinerant whose Irish twinkle and adventuresome outlook not only brought him proposals of marriage but a sense of certainty that life was his apple. Although from time to time his misadventures nonplussed his coaches, they usually understood that Blood's transgressions sprang from a blithe spirit. St. Louis police, sirens screaming, chased him down and arrested him for stealing a taxicab, but he had not meant to keep it. Minutes earlier, he had had a chorus girl on his arm and no transportation. "The cab was standing there with the motor running, but I couldn't find the driver," he explained. "So I borrowed it." Long on gallantry, Blood hesitated no more than a few moments before forking up his last seventy-five dollars to bail out the chorus girl, and then settled down to a night's rest behind bars.

He ranked among the swiftest men in pro football and possessed an uncanny knack for scoring a touchdown when one was most needed. He would snatch a touchdown pass while covered by as many as three defenders. His fifteen-year NFL career, 1925–39, included seven stops: Milwaukee, Duluth, and next, John O'Hara's Pottsville, Pa., where the local firehouse, which served beer twenty-four hours a day, enabled Blood and his teammates to beat Prohibition; Green Bay was the fourth stop, then Pittsburgh as a player-coach.

59

His real name was John Victor McNally, his beginnings, classic Midwest. In New Richmond, Wisconsin, the rather elegant white frame house where he grew up still stands on a tree-shaded corner lot, suggesting a time when the smells a boy knew were those of fresh bread and muffins baking, and when the sounds of an evening were those of voices around the parlor upright. The McNallys were people of means. Yet at a time when a large segment of the public looked upon pro football as a tramp's occupation, their son made it his calling. He did not marry till the age of forty-five, and later, after a divorce, remarried at sixty-two. With his second wife, he now leads a quiet, contemplative life in St. Paul, Minnesota, having sown a good deal more wild oats than most of us have had the pleasure or stamina to sow.

———————

I couldn't say, particularly, that I was the black sheep in my family, though some people were inclined to view some of my episodes with less than applause. Well, by way of explanation, there *is* a difference between pro football now and pro football then. I'm referring to, say, the early 1930s, during the Depression. In 1931 I was all-pro right halfback. I had scored thirteen touchdowns, which at that time was a league record, and I was in the all-pro backfield along with Red Grange, Ernie Nevers, and Dutch Clark. I had played for Green Bay three years and we had won three championships. But when it came time to go back to Green Bay for the '32 season, I had no money to get across the state from my home in New Richmond. I had only a dollar or two in my pocket.

So I decided to ride free on the train. They called it the Soo Line, but its real name was the Minneapolis, St. Paul & Sault Sainte Marie Railroad, and in order to get to Green Bay you would have to change trains at Amherst Junction to the Green Bay & Western. I got on the Soo Line and rode the blinds down to a place called Stevens Point, where there was a stop. I got off and inquired about connections at Amherst Junction and was told that the Green Bay & Western would get into Amherst Junction a couple of minutes before the Soo Line but if you wired ahead they would hold the train. They did this for passengers. So I wired ahead and then got back on the blinds again and rode to Amherst Junction. There I got off the Soo and ran down a cut and grabbed on to the blinds of the Green Bay & Western. After the trainmen waited around for a few minutes for the passenger who had wired ahead, they gave up and started the train.

Well, about ten miles from Green Bay, the door of a freight car opened and one of the crew looked out and saw me and said, "John, what are you doing out there?" Everybody on the Green Bay & Western knew the Packer football players. The guy said, "Come on in and wash up." So I got me a bowl of water, and while I was washing up, he looked at me and said, "Say, where did you get on?" I said, "Amherst Junction." And he started laughing. He said, "Oh, so you're the guy who wired ahead! Well, you're the first hobo I ever heard of holding a train for." And this, in essence, shows you the difference between pro football in 1932 and pro football today.

By the way, when I told Ollie Kuechle, a Milwaukee sportswriter, how I got to camp, he said, "We're going to call you the Hobo Halfback." I didn't say anything. That was his business if he wanted to call me the Hobo Halfback. But Curly Lambeau, our coach, didn't like it. He thought we were on the big time and going to win another championship. He didn't like the term. So Ollie said, "Well, okay. We'll call him the Vagabond Halfback." For years after, I was known as the

Vagabond Halfback, and maybe all this is a partial answer to your question as to whether my relatives regarded me as the black sheep.

I'm a schizophrenic personality. I was born under the sign of Sagittarius, which is half stud and half philosopher. The stud, of course, is the body of a horse, and I was always full of *run*. Running all the time when I was a kid. In the sign of Sagittarius the body of the horse joins with the chest of a man, who is aiming a bow and arrow. This is a man who's looking for a target and is going to hit it, which I take represents the philosopher in him. So with that combination of philosopher and stud, I always felt I was going two ways. My life illustrates it. Let me put it this way. I had an aunt, a big, husky doll, and one day she asked me, "John, what are you really interested in?"

"Well," I said, "I guess I'm really interested in the theory of morals and the theory of money."

She started to laugh. I said, "What are you laughing at, Aunt?" And she said, "Well, isn't that funny! You'll never have any of either!"

I come from a group of Irish people. The names of my eight great-grandparents were McNally, Barrett, Reilly, McCormick, Murphy, McGraw, McGannon, and McGough. Our outfit came over and settled in Wisconsin because it was just opening up around 1850, and from that group, some of them succeeded quite well and some did not. They all stayed out of jail and all got decent funerals, and some of them did quite well, that's correct. My father was a McNally and my mother was a Murphy. Father became the general manager of a successful flour mill, and my mother's two brothers became publishers of the Minneapolis *Tribune*. But I claim my poor relatives as well as my rich ones.

I got out of high school at fourteen and a half, really. It

wasn't that I was precocious but that I was *pushed* along by my mother, who had been a schoolteacher. I had no signs of athletic ability, because I was too small. Even later, when I matured, I matured late. My parents had tried to make me master the violin and be a debater and recite poems. They wanted to made a cultured individual out of me, but I had a high resistance. In the seventh or eighth grade I once put on a very poor public performance with the violin, playing "Turkey in the Straw," which was a very humiliating experience for me. I haven't gotten over it yet.

Well, as I say, I was a runner. I used to run away from home. I'd catch freights. The fact is, I can remember my father giving me several memorable drummings with a shillelagh, which I recall with no malice at all. I was still in knee pants when I graduated from high school and a little young to go to college, so I studied bookkeeping and typewriting, and the following year, 1919, my parents sent me to River Falls State Normal, about twenty miles away. They went to California and left me with a checkbook, which turned out to be a mistake. Because of that, I eventually decided to join the navy to avoid a confrontation with my parents.

The navy, however, turned me down because my eyesight wasn't up to standards, although I subsequently made a living in football with my eyesight, and in World War II, when they weren't quite so choosy, the Army took me and I served as a cryptographer in China. Anyhow, I left River Falls State Normal and went to work in a packing plant at New Richmond and then went up to Dakota to put in the crops. I slept in a wagon. I can remember that on the longest day of the year, June 21, 1919, after I got up and finished getting the bugs off me, I fed the horses before the sun came up and then spent the entire day, till sundown, alone on a section of half-broken land, which I was cultivating—"disking," they called it. So I figured out that this was too tough a way to make a living. That was my terminal experience on the farm.

From there I went to St. John's University in Minnesota, which was where Eugene McCarthy later went to school. At the time, there were about six hundred students in the university, but that's what they called it—a university. It was a Benedictine institution, but I was an antitheological misfit. However, I played my first football game there, in the intramural league. I played for a team called the Cat's Pajamas. That was an expression current at the time—it meant something like "a superior guy." Anyway, I was an immediate success with the Cat's Pajamas. By that time I was sixteen and a half. I was tall but frightfully skinny, but the summer up in Dakota had toughened me up. We won the intramural league, and later I started competing for the college team.

After three years there, I had a little confidence in myself and felt ready for a bigger sphere. I went down to Notre Dame and went out for the freshman squad. The Four Horsemen were playing for Notre Dame that season, and as it turned out, the only contribution I made to Notre Dame football was that I wrote Harry Stuhldreher's poetry assignments. You see, they wanted to make a tackle out of me. I was six feet tall, but I weighed only 160 pounds and felt that my function was to avoid contact rather than to make it. So I did not stay long on the football squad, and the following St. Patrick's Day I took a little trip and had an unexplained absence from school. When the officials began investigating my absence, they discovered that in addition to my dormitory room, I kept another room in town. They took exception to the nature of my existence and suspended me. So I got a motorcycle and took a big trip. About thirty years later, when I decided to resume my education, I went back to Notre Dame to inquire about my credits, if any. They showed me my record. Inscribed upon it was no mention of any accomplishments but only the words, "Gone, never to return."

After the motorcycle trip, I went to work on a Minneapolis newspaper as a stereotyper, but it didn't take me long to see that a stereotyper's work was not for me. Meanwhile, I heard that there was a way of making a little money in the fall playing football. There were four teams in a semi-pro league in Minneapolis, and one of these teams was called the East 26th Street Liberties. They had a small practice field alongside the railroad track with one light, which was in the center of the field. That was the lighting by which they practiced. Well, I and another stereotyper decided to try out. As we went out to the field, riding my motorcycle, we went by a theater where the marquee advertised a picture titled *Blood and Sand*. Being that both of us still felt we might have some college eligibility left, and knowing that semi-pro football would ruin our amateur standing, I realized we had to have fake names if we played semi-pro ball. So when the East 26th Street Liberties asked us what our names were, it popped into my head right there. I said, "My name is Blood and this guy's name is Sand."

We won the league championship that fall, and then were paid for the entire season. We got ten dollars for our effort. We spent it that night.

The following year, 1925, I got an offer to play for a team in Ironwood, Michigan, for seventy-five dollars a game. I played three games there, then jumped the team for an offer from the Milwaukee Badgers of the National Football League. I remember we played in Steubenville, Ohio—that was really quite a fun city—and it was there that I became convinced that I might have a future in pro ball. Steubenville had a guy named Sol Butler, who had been a broad jumper in the Olympics. I caught a pass and ran away from Sol

Butler, and that was the first time I really thought I was a ballplayer. Nobody believed in the future of pro ball at that point, but I believed I was a pro ballplayer.

You see, I had been drifting along in the sense that I was looking for my life-style, as they say nowadays. I wanted a life in which I could do something I enjoyed and still have leisure to do other things that I enjoyed. Football was an escape, certainly, but an escape into something that I enjoyed. In the off-season I would ship out to the Orient as an ordinary seaman and enjoy the beauty of the Pacific islands. Or I would winter on Catalina Island off the coast of Los Angeles. Understand, I was not afraid of work. I had sufficient energy that work did not bother me at all. I was a hard worker. To me, freedom did not mean being able to do only the nondifficult but, rather, to do what I chose to do. One winter in Catalina, I worked three shifts. I worked in the brickyard all day, making bricks. I worked the next eight hours in a gambling hall as a bouncer. And the next eight hours, I "honeymooned" with a redhead.

The football season was a great time of year. During the seasons I played for Green Bay, the ballplayers stayed at the Astor Hotel. They'd sit around the hotel and gossip, or they'd go to libraries—well, maybe one out of a hundred pro ballplayers would go to a library. We played golf, we went hunting, we drank—the ordinary activities of young men when they're at leisure. We had no difficulty passing the day. The fall weather in Green Bay was beautiful, and just to do *nothing* was marvelous. Just watching the autumn turn golden was a pleasure.

The ordinary ballplayer made seventy-five to a hundred dollars a week, but it was tax-free and it was a dollar worth twice as much as the dollar is worth today. There weren't too many people getting that kind of money at our age. And right across the street from the hotel was the YWCA, where you could get a good dinner for seventy-five cents. That's where we usually ate. The boys from the South watched their money, because things were tough down South and they were trained that way. But as for myself, I can say that in spite of my interest in monetary theory, I always remembered that "they who harvested the golden grain, and they who flung it to the winds like rain, alike to the same aureate earth are borne." It takes a guy who's really loose with money to think about it freely.

Curly Lambeau used to say that I trained harder than anybody on the club. That is, I spent more energy on the training field than the average guy, and I believe that to be true or I would not repeat it. But in 1933 Lambeau fired me. We were in New York that year to play the Giants, and we were having a medium season, with about three or four games to go. It was a Friday night, about eight o'clock, and I got a call at the hotel from some millionaire's wife—the wife of some millionaire from the Fox River Valley around Green Bay. She wanted me to meet her at the Stork Club.

I said, "Oh, no. I couldn't do that. The game's only day after tomorrow." So I got ready to go to bed, and here two goddamned nurses rapped on the door. So my roommate and I ordered up a few drinks. Well, we got pretty loaded. Next morning, I went out to practice in not the best of condition. Alcohol, you see, hangs on to me. I don't sober up real fast. It's a family characteristic—I have plenty of recuperative power, but alcohol doesn't fall out of me. It hangs on to me.

So I went out to practice and got ready to punt, and the first ball I kicked, I fell flat on my ass. Lambeau sent me back to the hotel. He came up afterward and said, "I've got to let you go." I didn't argue with him. I never argued. Well, the team played New York without me and lost the game, but the fact was that I was fired. I went over to Paterson, New Jersey, and played a couple games with a Paterson semi-pro team, and finally the Packers were playing Chicago in their last game of the season, and Lambeau got in touch with me to come back. He got to thinking about next year, I suppose, and that I'd be a free agent if I was still fired. About June the next year, 1934, he sold me to Pittsburgh.

Art Rooney, the Pittsburgh owner, had taken a fancy to me. He liked Irishmen. But after I got to Pittsburgh he no doubt was a little disappointed in me. He pressed me to go to confession, to make a better Roman Catholic of me. Let's just say that I came under the heading, but spell it with an *i*, an *n*, and an apostrophe. I *was* a roamin' Catholic.

Anyway, after a season in Pittsburgh I decided the next summer that I wanted to get back with Green Bay. I knew that the Packers were training up in northern Wisconsin and that they had scheduled an exibition game with the Chippewa Falls Marines and two more with the La Crosse Loggers. So I got on with both of those semi-pro teams and played three games against Green Bay and did all right. I talked to Art Rooney and told him I had a chance to go back with the Packers, and he said okay, go ahead. But it was from that point on that I started having real trouble with Lambeau.

He began to push me around. This was because I had gotten quite a reputation around Green Bay. Lambeau was football in that town. He became jealous of me. He would sit me on the bench. The game would be practically lost and the fans would be hollering, "Put him in! Put Blood in!" So then, when we were just about dead, he'd say to me, "Get in!" I'd have to come up with a big play, and that's how I got the reputation of being a clutch player. Lambeau wouldn't play me unless he had to play me!

After two years of that, I went back to Pittsburgh as a player and head coach, and later, in the early 1950s, I was head coach at St. John's for three years. We won about 75 percent of our games. I'm neither awfully proud of my coaching record nor am I ashamed of it. But I would not say that my temperament was designed for coaching. A coach can't be concerned with the poor ballplayer. If the player can't make it, he's got to be out right away. It's a very tough aspect of coaching, and in this aspect I was weak. Also, some guys get fat on coaching—they get healthy and strong—but other guys get ulcers. At St. John's, I got ulcers. All those guys in black suits who had been there all their lives, they'd say, "We know all about this coaching. We have the best boys. We know our boys are the best boys. *Why* are they the best boys? They're at St. John's, *that's* why they're the best boys." So I got ulcers, which is not necessarily inconsistent with my temperament. A lot of clowns have ulcers.

I gave up coaching in 1953 and since then have spent the years meditating. I inherited enough money to take it a little easier. I wrote a book called *Spend Yourself Rich*, which deals with my theory that riches consist of consuming products. Actually, I wrote the book a long time ago, in 1940, and then got it out to rework it twenty years later. The first time, I had written it in a madhouse. Yes, in a madhouse. See, I had some friends who once said, "John, you've been on a big song and dance. Maybe you'd better slow down." At Winnebago there was a hospital run by the State of Wisconsin, so I went there and stayed ninety days and dashed off this tome. Twenty years later I went back to the manuscript to see if there was anything wrong with it, and I decided there wasn't anything wrong with it. The book is now out of print. Well, actually, it was never published. But hell, it didn't do me any harm to get it off my chest. I'd been carrying a typewriter in the back of my car for years, not knowing why.

5

OLE HAUGSRUD

The franchise that sold for a dollar

As I was saying good-bye to Johnny Blood in St. Paul, he suddenly offered a suggestion. "There's a gentleman up in Duluth you ought to see. His name is Ole Haugsrud." I had never heard of Haugsrud, but I became curious to meet him when Blood explained that in 1926 Haugsrud had bought an NFL franchise for the almost incredible sum of one dollar.

Early the next morning, Blood picked me up at my motel, then drove to a residential neighborhood where we were joined by a white-haired giant named Dan Williams, who along with Blood had played for the Duluth Eskimos, the team Ole Haugsrud bought for a dollar. During the 150 miles or so north to Duluth, the two men briefed me on that unusual transaction, which, as it turned out, may have saved the National Football League from death in its infancy.

Originally the Duluth club was a fine semi-pro outfit called the Kelly-Duluths, having been named for the Kelly-Duluth Hardware Store. The Kelly-Duluths' opposition came largely from teams in nearby towns in the iron-ore range. But in 1923, in order to obtain a professional schedule, Dan Williams and three others—the trainer and two other players—put up $250 apiece and bought a National Football League franchise for $1,000. Even then, the renamed Duluth Eskimos were able to arrange no more than seven, and as few as five, league games a season. Due bills piled up. Finally the four owners offered to make a gift of the franchise to Ole Haugsrud, by avocation the club's secretary-treasurer. To make the transaction legal, Haugsrud handed them a dollar, which the four men immediately squandered drinking nickel beer. The dollar that paid for those twenty beers would be one Dan Williams and his colleagues would never forget.

The year was 1926, and the struggling NFL was fighting for its life. C. C. Pyle, the flamboyant business agent, had the great Red Grange under contract and with Grange as his box-office attraction was formulating his new eight-team league, to be known as the American Football League. Pyle spread the word that he also had signed the celebrated All-American back, Ernie Nevers, a handsome blond of English-Irish-French extraction who, though just emerging from Stanford, had captured the nation's fancy. Nevers bore the imprimatur of Pop Warner, who before moving on to Stanford had coached the nonpareil Jim Thorpe at Carlisle and now rated Nevers superior to Thorpe himself. The NFL knew Nevers to be the only big name with whom the league could salvage its slim prestige, but NFL clubowners took Pyle at his word and made no effort to sign Nevers.

Alone, Ole Haugsrud, a mild-looking little Swede, was skeptical. He had been a high-school classmate of Ernie Nevers in Superior, Wisconsin. When he paid a dollar for the Duluth franchise, he had it in the back of his mind to travel to St. Louis (where Nevers was pitching baseball for the St. Louis Browns) to see for himself if Pyle actually had Nevers under contract.

Ernie was very glad to see me, and I was glad to see him. I met with him and his wife at their apartment, and Ernie showed me a letter he had from C. C. Pyle. Ernie told me, "Ole, if you can meet the terms Pyle is offering in this letter, it's okay with me. I'll play for Duluth." And really, that's all there was to it. I would have to pay Ernie fifteen thousand dollars, plus a percentage of the larger gates. I had the money to do it. I believe I was only twenty-two or twenty-three years old, but I had various holdings—buildings and things like that. I had inherited a little money.

Of course, I couldn't be certain that the league would give me the kind of schedule I needed to pay Ernie that kind of money, so what I did was sign him to a document that gave me an option on his services. I didn't pay him five cents to sign. Oh, maybe I gave him a dollar to make it legal, but really, a handshake was all Ernie wanted. A handshake with an old friend was good enough for Ernie.

The next thing, I came home and got our ballplayers together. There were about ten or eleven of them in town. I called a meeting in the office of Doc Kelly, a dentist across the bay in Superior. Doc played halfback for us—he played behind Johnny Blood—and was known as the Superior Tooth Carpenter. We met up at Doc's office in the evening, and I told the boys how much I would have to pay Ernie Nevers. I said, "Here's what it is. Now, how much do you guys want?" I left it up to them. They were probably the only team that ever drew up their own contracts. But it was very, very easy for me to do this, because they wanted to play.

I said, "I'll step out of the room while you make up your minds." But I no more got out the door when they called me back. Actually, I think they'd had it all worked out. Dan Williams, I think it was, said, "Well, how does this sound? Fifty dollars lose, sixty dollars tie, and seventy-five win?" I said, "That's okay. Now if you don't mind, I'll take this as an option and go down to the league meeting in Chicago and see what I can do about a schedule."

The league meeting was at the Morrison Hotel, and it was getting on close to August, I believe. See, they didn't hold meetings 'way ahead of the season, because a lot of teams didn't know if they could operate for another season and had to get some funds behind them before they'd go to a meeting. Anyway, in Chicago the first fellows I got ahold of were Tim Mara of the New York Giants and George Halas of the Chicago Bears. I had called Tim Mara prior to that, and he was really the one that knew the entire contract I had with Ernie Nevers. He was like a father to me from the beginning. He said, "I'll tell you, kid. We got to do something here to make this a *league*." He said, "Now we'll go through with the regular meeting, and when it gets halfways through and you got two, three ballgames, I will give you the high sign." There were twenty-two clubs in the league, you see, and none of the others knew we had Nevers on option.

This was kind of a historic point for the National League, because here everybody was, sitting with the threat that Pyle had hanging over them, and the league really didn't know if it was going to operate again. So Mara said to me, "Wait till I highball you, and then you go up to the league president with your option on Nevers." Well, I did as he told me to. I showed the option to Joe Carr, who was being paid five hundred dollars to be president. He read that little document and then looked up and said, "Gentlemen! I got a surprise for you."

He read the option paper, and some of them out front got up and yelled like a bunch of kids. Joe Carr said to me, "You saved the league!" Everyone figured that Pyle not only had

Grange and Wildcat Wilson and the Four Horsemen of Notre Dame, but Ernie Nevers, too. So all those people at the meeting cheered, and there was almost a celebration right there. But Tim Mara said, "Gentlemen, we got to make a league out of this, so we'll start all over by first rehiring the president and paying him a salary that means something." Mr. Mara made a motion, and we voted Joe Carr a salary of $2,500.

Then Mara said, "Now let's start over and have a new draft." By that, he meant a new draft of games. The way they would do it was you would name a date, and Mara would ask another clubowner, "Would you like to play him on that date?" And the clubowner would say yes or no, and you got whatever games you could. Well, we started putting down that 1926 schedule, and I had nineteen league games as fast as I could write them down. And before I got back to Duluth I had ten exhibition games, which made a total of twenty-nine. And all because I had Nevers. Some of them wanted two games with us.

Now here's something I skipped. Mr. Mara had got up and said, "What we've got to do is to fill the ballparks in the big cities. So we've got to make road teams out of the Duluth Eskimos and the Kansas City Cowboys." He figured Duluth would draw the big-city crowds with Ernie, and the Kansas City Cowboys were good at drawing crowds because they had a gimmick. When they arrived in a town, they'd borrow a lot of horses and ride horseback down the main street. They rode horseback down Broadway and drew thirty-nine thousand people in New York.

So we had only two home games—one in Duluth and one over in Superior, where the ball park had railroad tracks on both sides. The railroad men would leave boxcars lined up all along there. We drew three or four thousand at the box office in Superior, but there were just as many standing on the boxcars, watching free.

I believe it was September 6 that we hit the road, and we didn't get back till February 5. We traveled by train and occasionally by bus, and one time we took a boat from New York to Providence. During one stretch we played five games in eight days, with a squad of seventeen men. Most of the time we were down to thirteen players—just two men on the bench. But our boys played with broken noses and broken fingers and all sorts of injuries. In Sacramento, where we stopped on a postseason exhibition swing, our quarterback, Cobb Rooney, went to the hospital with his eyeball laying out on his cheek, but the next day he turns up at my hotel room in San Francisco with his head all wrapped up and his nurse along with him. He says to me, "I want to introduce you to my future wife."

When we played the Giants a league game in New York, we had fourteen players. Mr. Mara looked at us and said, "I don't know what you'd call this, a football team?" And Grantland Rice, the big sportswriter, said, "Well, that's the Iron Men from the North." And that's the way we were dubbed from there on.

We won nineteen ballgames, lost seven, and tied three, and in some places we got good crowds, very good crowds, although not like the ones they draw today. The boys had that contract for fifty-lose, sixty-tie, and seventy-five-win, but at the end of the season they all got paid off on the seventy-five basis, and the club netted a profit of four thousand dollars. But there were times when we were six, seven thousand in the hole.

See, when we got paid off for a game, I would send the check back to a Duluth bank, and as we traveled, I would write checks on our account in Duluth. But in Providence early one morning, I got a telegram at the hotel from the banker in Duluth. It read: OLE, YOU BETTER GET THOSE ES-KIMOS HOME WHILE YOU STILL GOT ENOUGH BLUBBER MEAT TO FEED THEM. It turned out that our checking account was about dry. What happened was that we had been paid four thousand dollars in New Britain, Connecticut, but when the Duluth bank put the check through, it bounced. And we had gotten three thousand dollars in Hartford, and that check also had got kicked in the tail. So I called all the boys together at breakfast and read them that telegram telling us to come home.

I'll always remember that Cobb Rooney got up and said, "Ole, tell that banker to stick that telegram up his you-know-where. You just pay us fifteen bucks a week to eat on, and pay our room rent and our transportation." All of the other boys said, "Amen!" They said, "You can pay us our salary when you catch up."

So we kept going. But actually, there was something I could do about those rubber checks. Every club had to put up five thousand dollars with the league to cover this kind of situation, and the rule was that when a club was putting out bum checks, why, the first ones who got in there with their claim got the money. And that year, we happened to be first. So we got our money back, and in two weeks all the boys were paid off.

In St. Louis one time, we were playing an exhibition against the St. Louis Gunners, and the manager of the Gun-ners came up to me on the sideline and handed me a check for better than three thousand dollars, which was our guaran-tee. He walked away before I realized that he hadn't paid me an additional seventy dollars that he owed us to cover an expense item. I hollered to him, but he knew what was on and started running. I chased him right across the football field and up the steps of the grandstand and across an open causeway. Then he ran into the ladies' room. There was a colored fellow standing outside the ladies' room, and he said to me, "You can't go in there!" I said "I'm going in!" And I did. I cornered the fellow in a toilet, and he gave me the seventy bucks.

All along, Ernie Nevers was everything we expected him to be. Against the Pottsville Maroons he completed seventeen consecutive passes.

(Johnny Blood, an attentive audience to Haugsrud's account, at this point interjected the advice that Nevers not only played fullback but helped Coach Dewey Scanlon plan strategy as well. Being the box-office attraction upon whom the club's success was dependent, Nevers installed the Pop Warner Stanford offense in which the fullback received the snap from center on every play. Nevers called the plays, handled the ball every time, and thus was the hub of the offense, all of which amounted to good business. As it happened, however, both the National League and C. C. Pyle's American League were hindered by bad weather much of the season. Soon after, the two leagues made peace. The National League granted Pyle's New York Yankees a franchise, which had been his goal all along but had been opposed by New York Giants owner Tim Mara. Back to Ole Haugsrud's story.)

In the entire twenty-nine games we played in 1926, Ernie Nevers sat out a total of just twenty-nine minutes. And here's something that will tell you the type of fellow he was. The league had me put a clause into his contract saying that he had to be in each game a certain number of minutes. I think it was twenty-five minutes. But when Ernie read that clause he said, "Ole, you can shove this up yours, and up Joe Carr's,

too!" It provoked him that the league thought he was the
kind of guy who would want to be out of the game. I said to
him, "Ernie, it'd just be a lot of trouble for me to go back to
the league and get this clause out, so what's the difference?"
We left it in, but Ernie took it as an insult to his integrity.

In those days you didn't have the money to hire bands and
marching units and things like that to entertain the crowd. So
what we would do, sometimes before the game and sometimes at the half, was put on kicking exhibitions. We'd put
Nevers and Blood and Russ Method and Walt Gilbert out
there kicking, and I'd always stand about halfway to the
goalposts and relay the ball back. I liked to drop-kick myself
—in fact, I kicked with either foot—so once in a while I'd
catch the ball from the fellows behind the goalposts and make
a kick. You know—from the twenty-yard line, just for the fun
of it. I'd be wearing the moleskins for this job, and I used to
carry the water bucket, too. I would often say to Ernie Nevers, "When we run up a big lead, why don't you put me in
to kick?" But Ernie would say, "You'll get hurt, Swede."

Well, that day in St. Louis, the day I had to chase the guy
for our money, the score was 52-0. And geez, Ernie calls me
into the game and throws me a headgear. We had just scored
a touchdown, and I'm to kick the extra point. But unbeknown
to me, our center, Bill Stein, passed the word to the opposition. "This is the boss kicking," he said. "We'll let you get
him." So that's what happened, and I was at the bottom of
a pile, and when I got out of there, why, I realized that the
gates had been opened on me and these guys had just flooded
in. Our boys were standing there laughing. Well, I was pretty
mad. And so after I chased the St. Louis guy for our money,
I went back to the hotel and I was still mad. I got the biggest
godderned towel I could find and put my arm in it. I put on
that towel like a sling. And you know? I couldn't write a

check for a couple of weeks. The boys never put me in another ballgame after that.

One problem we ran into all the time was getting publicity. You'd see items in the newspapers *after* a game, but we had a hard time getting anything into the newspapers *before* a game. The news media as a whole were afraid to publicize professional ball, because college ball was big and the colleges frowned on us. In fact, they had a rule that if you played professional ball, you could never get a college coaching job. I remember a time a little later, around 1930, I took a trip east with the Chicago Cardinals, and we were on the same train as the University of Chicago football team. They were going east to play Princeton. The two teams were in adjoining coaches. But Amos Alonzo Stagg, the Chicago coach, locked the doors between the two coaches. He thought the pros would contaminate his players. He had a rule that if, after a boy was graduated from Chicago, he played pro ball, his varsity letter would be recalled. I recall going out on the platform during a stop in Ohio. Stagg got out on the platform, too, and I said, "How do you do, Mr. Stagg?" If I said it once, I said it ten times, but he never gave me an answer.

Well, as I told you before, we made a profit of a few thousand in 1926, but the next year we came out only about a thousand ahead. We couldn't get the games we needed. One reason was the league cut down from twenty-two clubs to twelve, and another reason was that we were asking a four-thousand-dollar guarantee and the weaker clubs would rather schedule a team that asked, say, $1,500 less. After that '27 season, Nevers took a year off from pro ball to go back to Stanford to coach the backfield for Pop Warner, and I put the club in mothballs. I had a year's leave to sell the franchise. I sold it for two thousand to a buyer from New Jersey who put the franchise in Orange. In 1932 it was transferred to

Boston, and in 1937 George Marshall took it to Washington. The franchise I paid a dollar for is now worth, I suppose, fifteen million, if not more.

But I didn't do so bad by selling. You see, we negotiated the deal at a league meeting in Cleveland, and the fellows from the other clubs were anxious to see the deal settled and get away, because they didn't always have money enough to stay three, four days in a high-priced hotel. I wanted three thousand but the fellow from Orange wanted to give me two thousand. The others said to me, "Come on, Swede. We got to get going home." So I said, "All right, but with one stipulation. The next time a franchise is granted in the state of Minnesota, I will have the first opportunity to bid for it." In order to get out of there, they gave me a letter to that effect, and over the years I kept letting the National Football League know about it. In 1961, when the Minnesota Vikings were created, I got ten percent of the stock. The franchise cost $600,000, and for my share I paid sixty thousand dollars. Since then, we've had offers of between twelve and fifteen million for the franchise. So I guess you would have to say that as a result of originally buying a franchise for a dollar, and later investing sixty thousand, I now own stock that is worth about a million and a half.

6

DUTCH CLARK

When the bank ran out of money

According to the custom of the 1930s, Earl (Dutch) Clark
was called a quarterback because he called his team's plays.
Actually, he played left halfback (also known as tailback) in
the single wing and three times led the National Football
League in scoring. "Somewhere," recalls Clarke Hinkle, the
old Green Bay fullback, "we got the word that Dutch Clark
was blind in one eye." Clark really wasn't—he was only
partially blind. "We thought that if the story was true, we
could have a picnic throwing to his blind side when he was
back there on defense. So, of course, we tried it. He intercepted two passes and ran both of them back for touchdowns."

In a sense Dutch Clark symbolized an important stage in
the growth of professional football, for he began his career
with the Portsmouth (Ohio) Spartans, next to Green Bay the
last of the NFL's small-town clubs, and with them moved to
Detroit in 1934 when they became the Detroit Lions. Ohio
had been the hub of the league during its infancy. Toledo,
Columbus, Marion, Canton, Akron, Dayton, Cleveland—
each of these towns at one time or another in the 1920s
sported an NFL franchise. But as the league grew bolder,
testing its product in more and more big cities, the small-
town franchises gradually disappeared.

Like pro football itself, Dutch Clark was a small-town boy

who went to the city and stayed. He received me in a borrowed office at the University of Detroit field house, a place he often visits for old time's sake. A tall, husky man of impassive nature, he was for a time the university's director of athletics, a job that, because of its proximity to the young, obliged him to forgo his penchant for playing the horses. In the early 1950s, when his wife died and his son reached his senior year of college, Dutch found himself free of responsibilities, so he resigned from the university, became a sales representative for a Detroit tool company, and returned to the pleasures of the parimutuel windows.

"I do what I want to now," he said. "Of course, I got a boss at the tool company, and once in a while he jumps me. But they're pretty nice about it over there."

═══════════

You know, I think it's a bad thing nowadays that they start these kids in Little League football when they're ten years old, and people are screaming at 'em, hollering at 'em, and they get no fun out of it. They get into junior high school and people are at 'em, so before they get into high school, it's already a matter of life and death with these kids. If they're ever going to have any fun, they got to have it when they're young, you know. But people are digging at them. At least I got into college, about the third year of college, before I got to worrying about whether I was going to die if we didn't win.

I enjoyed football till it got to the point where they tried to make me feel it was life and death. When I was younger I could laugh at the coaches—when they weren't looking, of course. But as you mature you get to thinking, "Well, maybe this *is* kind of serious." Good old alma mater, you know. So you worry, and it quits being fun. I always liked to play football, even professional ball, but it was never as much fun as it was in the beginning.

I came from Colorado, and although I'm called Dutch Clark, I'm not a Dutchman. Fact is, Clark is an Irish name. And my father was a Welshman. But I had two brothers and one of them didn't talk very plain when he was young, so an uncle named him Dutch. Then they started calling my other brother Big Dutch, and they called me Little Dutch. My brothers never got to high school, neither one of them, because in those times there were problems, like eating and things like that. My father had a small farm, and then later he worked for the railroad in a town called La Junta. But he got let out, so he traveled around, anyplace he could find work, and sent home money. Then we moved to Pueblo, about 1920, and I quit school and started working for the railroad when I was fourteen.

I was a callboy. I would sit in the master mechanic's office when they made up the trains, then I would go get the brakemen and engineers from their little rooming houses along the street. You didn't have phones then. You had to roust them out, maybe at 3:30 in the morning. So that's what I did for a few years. But in the meantime I saw kids coming home from school and playing touch football in the park. I thought I could play that game as well as they could, so I went over and got in those games, and then I finally decided to go back to school. I went out for the school team and started out as a center, 137 pounds, and all the while I worked another year on the railroad and then as a desk clerk at the YMCA, from six till midnight.

The high-school coach turned me into a back, and quite a few colleges became interested in me. I chose Northwestern, but I was a little country kid and I didn't like it there much. The people were wonderful to me, but they kept talking to me, yakking at me. They wouldn't leave me alone. I was homesick, though I would have gotten over that if they would have left me alone. I was there about two weeks, I guess, when one night a businessman back home, a fellow who wanted me to play for Colorado College, told me to wire him if I didn't like Northwestern. A little later, that's what I did, right in the middle of the night. I wired for money and went back home to Colorado College.

In my junior year I made All-American quarterback, which caused quite an argument. Alan Gould of the Associated Press put me on his All-American team, and he took a beating because of that. He picked me over Howard Harpster, a great ballplayer at Carnegie Tech. A lot of people criticized Alan Gould for that, but in later years, whenever I had a big game, Gould took great pleasure in sticking the knife into the people who had criticized him.

Having played for a small school, I wondered if I really could play well. I was curious to see if I could play pro ball. And hell, the Depression was on when I came out of school, and nobody had any money. So in 1931 I signed up with Portsmouth for $140 a game. That was good money. A lot of players made ninety-five or a hundred dollars, and even then you didn't get all your pay.

They said the first game was a practice game, so we would get only thirty-five dollars. But the first game happened to be against Brooklyn, a league game, actually the league opener, yet they gave us only forty-five dollars. It was in the contract —"first game." What could you do?

Portsmouth was a town that was crazy about football. There were maybe thirty-five, forty thousand people in the town. The Selby shoe factory was there, but the people weren't working, So at practice, when we were going to scrimmage, we would have maybe five thousand people out watching us. If we didn't scrimmage, they'd scream and holler. Then we'd get up to the day of the game, and we wouldn't have two thousand people there. They were nice people in Portsmouth, but they didn't have the money.

The ball club was more or less a civic setup, although there were certain businessmen who would put up money to keep it going and owned stock. Our coach was Potsy Clark, a tough little guy. We played the old single wing, and I can remember that after we got beat one time, 7-6, the ballplayers went around complaining about the kind of offense we played. They would complain on the streets and, of course, it got back to Potsy. Then the people started criticizing him, and, boy, did he let loose then! He called us together and said, "This offense is good enough for Haughton of Harvard, and it's good enough for you!" He took us out and worked us like dogs, for days. Potsy believed in practice. We traveled to road games by bus, so if we were going from Portsmouth to New York, say, we'd carry our football shoes, and when we came to a level field out there in the country, Potsy would stop the bus and we would get out and run signals.

In Portsmouth the ballplayers slept in rooming houses scattered around town. You'd pay maybe $1.50 or $2.00 a week for a room, and you could get the biggest meal in town for six bits, probably. So actually you could keep a little money in your pocket. The club had its office upstairs above a loan office. You'd go there to get your pay, but there was a rule in those days that the club held back 25 percent of your pay. It was supposed to help the boys. At the end of the season they would give you the 25 percent, and that way, you would have some money when you went home. But you know, when we'd get to the end of the season, the club wouldn't have any money either, so how could you get the 25 percent?

As I said, you would go to the office and pick up your check, but then you had to go to the bank to get it cashed, and if you weren't one of the early ones, you sometimes wouldn't get your check cashed. The bank would be out of money. When they ran out of money, they just ran out of money.

My first year, we were right up near the top of the standings near the end of the season. We had a game tentatively arranged with Green Bay for the championship. If we beat them, we would be the champions. The game was to be played at Portsmouth, and it figured to get the club out of the red, because people would be coming from everywhere to see it. I had a job coaching basketball back at Colorado College and had to get back there, but I said I would come back to Portsmouth for the Green Bay game. Before I left for the west, I asked for my money. See, I had a couple of checks that hadn't been cashed, and I had the 25 percent coming.

It was on a Sunday, and we had just played the Chicago Bears and there hadn't been many people at the game, but I told the general manager, a man named Griffiths, "Griff, if I don't get my money, I ain't coming back." He said, "All right, can I give you a check?" And I said, "I don't want any checks. I want that money."

So Griff took me up there to the office. He owed me about eight hundred dollars all together. He counted out that money from the gate receipts, and it was mostly in dollar bills. In fact, I had six hundred dollars in one-dollar bills—six different rolls. I rode a bus to Cincinnati and then a train to Colorado, with those rolls of dollar bills stuffed in every pocket. After I got to Colorado, they canceled the champion-

ship game. Why, I don't know. I haven't the slightest idea. I
guess Green Bay decided not to play it. Green Bay finished
on top that year, because they had lost two games and we had
lost three.

My second year at Portsmouth, I got a raise, but the club
kept running behind on paychecks. I would get provoked and
say, "Well, I'm going home." In fact, I didn't care whether
I stayed or not. The ballplayers would have meetings over at
the Elks Club, and they would say, "Shall we quit, or shall
we play?" Everyone hung around the Elks Club, because they
had slot machines and cards there, and things like that. Of
course, Potsy would hear about those meetings, and he'd
come in and scream. He would say, "If you quit now, you'll
be quitting things the rest of your life!" A couple of times, the
club was going to pay me but not pay the other guys. I said,
"No, I don't get paid if the others don't." Frankly, I'd just as
soon have gone home. But somebody always came through
with the dough.

We played the Bears in Chicago that year for the championship, but I missed that game. I had to go home for the
basketball season, and I couldn't get back, that's all. In
Chicago they had snow up to their waists, so they hauled
some dirt into Chicago Stadium and played the game indoors.
I understand the field wasn't even a hundred yards long. That
was the championship.

I made all-league the first six years I played—in fact, every
year except my last in pro ball. I wasn't terrifically fast, but
I seemed to make lots of yardage. I could drop-kick field goals
up to forty, forty-five yards. But the longer I played, the less
accurate I became, because the ball was getting trimmer all
the time. In the beginning we played with a big ball that was
easier to kick. Some of your kickers were terrific. I was not
as long as a lot of them, because I held the ball very close to

the ground to try to get accuracy out of it. And in my last year I place-kicked instead of drop-kicking, because the ball had gotten so narrow. But, then, nobody kicked many field goals in those days anyway. In 1932 I led the league in field goals. I think I had three.

I'm kind of blind, I guess. When I was playing pro ball, I had 20/100 in the right eye and 20/200 in the left. But it didn't bother me at all. I had bad eyes from the time I was in grade school, but in those days you didn't go buy a pair of glasses. You didn't have enough money to eat on. So I didn't get glasses till I was in college. But anyway, maybe the eye trouble helped me. Maybe I dodged quicker. But I do know it never bothered me at that time, and I don't see how it would bother me particularly if I were playing football today. On defense, playing safety, I'd stand back where I could see the whole field and I knew where they were coming from. I was a real good defensive back.

I passed well, too, but we didn't pass much. Come to think of it, though, passing was the one thing where my left eye, the worst one, would give me a little trouble. See, in the single wing you'd run to the right, faking the run, and then drop back and throw quick. My best vision was always to the right. But there were times when we'd have a man open to the left, where I couldn't see him.

After my second year at Portsmouth, I quit pro ball for a year, because it was so difficult to get my money. I said, "What the heck," and quit. I went to work as athletic director and coach of football, basketball, and baseball at the Colorado School of Mines. I got three thousand dollars for doing everything. But the following year the Portsmouth franchise was sold and moved to Detroit by George Richards, who owned radio stations. Potsy Clark talked to me, and I saw that the club was going to be a different type of operation, so I quit my job and went back. I guess I had pro ball in my blood by then. And I felt that by going back, I would get a better opportunity in coaching.

In Detroit, we didn't pack 'em in at first, even though we went seven straight games without being scored on. We played out here at the university stadium, which holds about fifteen thousand. The next year we played the New York Giants here for the 1935 championship and won it and got $174 a man for winning. But in 1937 we moved to Briggs Stadium, and for a spell there the Lions used to get crowds of forty thousand, till the team went bad.

After I came out of retirement and went with the franchise to Detroit, I got homesick again—my wife was in Colorado —but I stayed because I knew that I would become the coach when Potsy Clark left. Richards more or less told me so. Potsy used to quit every so often, and at other times Richards would fire him. Then they'd get back together again. Whenever Potsy would quit or be fired, Richards would offer me the job, but I'd say, "Well, I don't know. I've got to wait to see what happens to Potsy."

Potsy had confidence in me, I guess. If Potsy had nine running plays and nine passing plays for us, he figured that was enough. But half the time I was playing, I would put in new plays. See, early in the season Potsy would place me in charge of the young guys, the rookies, and I would work out new plays with them, and later, in the games, I would use them. Potsy would be seeing them for the first time. But he'd go along with that. He was very fine about anything like that.

Finally, the thing between Potsy and Richards got to the point where Richards fired him and Potsy quit and never did come back. So in 1937 I became a player-coach. But I had a lot of trouble with Richards. He was an eccentric, you know. For example, he liked to bet on the Lions and he would get some of the players to go in with him. Today the ballplayers aren't allowed to bet on their own team, but Richards figured they'd play twice as hard to win twenty-five bucks, or maybe fifty bucks. So he got them going along with him.

He was a sick man and he was staying home, but every day he'd have his chauffeur run down to my hotel with a handful of notes, telling me how to coach the club. He'd write, "God-damn it, Dutch. Why don't you send that Klewicki out there like Green Bay sends out Hutson and throw to him like they throw to Hutson?" Well, Klewicki was five-eleven and about 218, see? Hutson could go fifty yards while this boy was going fourteen. Oh, I was having horrible trouble with Richards.

The men who ran his radio stations for him said to me, "Well, just forget it now. We'll get him out to California. We'll get him away." So they got him to California, but hell, he'd get on the long-distance phone. There was a kid named Harry Wismer, who was Richards' boy. Richards had put him in as an announcer at one of his stations, and Wismer would watch practice all the time and call Richards every night to give him a report. Then Richards would call me and say, "What the hell are you doing *that* for?"

Just before a game against the Bears in Chicago, Wismer was standing inside the dressing-room door and he had a little box—a kind of loudspeaker, I guess—and he turned that son of a bitch on, and there was Richards on the other end, giving us a pep talk. Well, when you played the Bears you didn't have to get ready, because you were fighting for your life when you went out there. But there was Richards cussing and telling us through that box to get in there and kick the hell out of the Bears, and that he wished he could be there with us, and all that. In one way, it was a good thing, because all the players laughed so hard that they went out the door loose. And that day, we beat the Bears.

The last years of Richards' life, he hated Harry Wismer. Harry had been his boy and his best friend, but Harry cut his throat. What Harry did to him, I don't know. It had something to do with a lawsuit, I think. Something that cost Richards some of his radio stations, I believe, but I don't really know. Anyhow, at the end Richards hated the man.

For me it was rather an odd existence. I coached the Lions for two years, then got out. In '38 we had to beat the Philadelphia Eagles in order to tie Green Bay for the western division title. But the Eagles got ahead of us on a couple of flea-flicker passes and beat us, 21-7. Richards was furious. I figured he was going to fire me if I didn't quit. So I told Bill Alfs, who was the vice president of the club, that the Cleveland Rams wanted me to come over there and coach. Bill said, "If I were you I'd take it, because this guy's liable to fire you any day."

So I went over to Cleveland, but I had to quit my playing career. Richards wouldn't let me play for Cleveland. He said, "If Clark wants to play, let the Rams give us Johnny Drake." Drake was our star back at Cleveland. Well, I was at the tail end of my playing days anyhow—I had hurt an ankle the year before in training and hadn't played much, and I didn't care about playing anymore. So I hung 'em up, and that was that.

7

CLARKE HINKLE

Joe College

Old-timers say he may well have been the toughest man who has played professional football—tougher, if not stronger, than Nagurski. "Clarke Hinkle was near the end of the line when I first played against him," says Bulldog Turner, the illustrious Chicago Bears linebacker, "but he was still the hardest runner I ever tried to tackle. He didn't bend over. He run just about straight up. And when you hit him it would just pop every joint all the way down to your toes."

Fullback, linebacker, sometimes passer, place-kicker, and punter, Hinkle performed with a sense of dedication that made him glassy-eyed. Opponents searching to explain his competitive pitch circulated a groundless rumor that he keyed himself up with drugs. He usually played at only 207 pounds, yet left big men shattered.

I found him living alone in an eight-room house in Toronto, Ohio, one of those dreary industrial towns that pockmark the banks of the Ohio. The old frame house on North Fourth Street stood on the corner, two blocks from the riverbank. As we talked in the living room, the house trembled from time to time as a trailer truck rumbled down North Fourth Street or a Pennsylvania Railroad Freight clattered along the tracks that virtually ran through the Hinkle backyard.

Trim and sharp-featured at sixty-two, his hair attractively

white around the edges, he had welcomed me cheerily, attired in a youthful ensemble consisting of a maroon turtleneck with gold piping around the neck, eggshell Levi's, matching maroon socks, and loafers. He settled into a rocker in front of a black stone mantel on which rested a plaster-of-paris replica of a bust that sits in the Pro Football Hall of Fame. A likeness of the young ballplaying Hinkle had been intended, but the art bore no resemblance to the man, now or earlier. "I think they made a mistake and copied from a picture of somebody else," he reflected without rancor.

He said that he gets along by selling industrial supplies, mostly lubricants, and at the time he supplemented his income by doing a sports show for the television station down the river in Steubenville. In the dining room, on the opposite side of the center hallway, some twenty hats lay strewn about the dining-room table. Later, as Hinkle passed through the room to get us coffee, he paused and explained that they were but a fraction of his hat supply—he has at least fifty. On the table were checked hats, porkpie hats, Alpine chapeaus, fur hats, everyday felt hats—all manner of hats except homburgs and silks. "These are new hats, not collector's items," Hinkle said. "I wear 'em all. I'm a sucker for hats."

This house has been in the family for about a hundred years, I guess. My grandfather built it. I live in the whole house— I live in all of it, actually. I still have a coal furnace, and I stoke about four or five ton of coal a year in here. I keep the place in shape. It's my home. My roots are here.

I've been married twice. I married a Park Avenue gal back in 1936. Came from a very fine family—very wealthy family. She was raised by maids. When we first got married, she couldn't boil water without scorching it. Still, a very lovely girl. But when I came back from service after the war, I got off the beam a little bit. I didn't get adjusted right away. I was out of football, by then, you know, and it caused a little bit of a problem to me because I'd been in the limelight so long. I went a little haywire, and so my wife divorced me.

Then I got married to a girl from near here. We took a honcymoon for a week and had cocktails at the Top o' the Mark and luncheon at the St. Francis and all that sort of thing. But the marriage only lasted about thirty-three days. Now I go with a very nice girl, real nice, and we get along real well. She comes around and cleans up the house for me. Of course, I get out the dirt that I can see, you know, and I do my own washing and ironing, and altogether, I get along real good. I came back here in '48 and been here ever since.

When I went out to Green Bay in '32 I was an easterner, one of the few easterners that were out there in what you might call the Northwest. I was a real dude. The day I got off the train I had on brown-suede shoes and maybe a velour hat and a black suit with a gray shirt and a purple tie. See, I'd played at Bucknell University, and that's the way they dressed back east. I always went for clothes.

Well, it was about two o'clock in the afternoon when I arrived at the hotel. The players were sitting around in the lobby, being as a lot of them lived at the hotel. Nobody said a thing. They just looked at me. I went back to the desk to register, and all the while they analyzed me. I'm sure they thought, "Here's another one of those fancy dans." I looked like a dandy. Oh, hell, yeah. Till I got on the football field.

I'd had pretty good years at Bucknell, and in '31 I'd been invited to play in the East-West Shrine game at San Francisco. I was voted the most outstanding ballplayer in that game. Now there was no professional-football draft in those days, so after the game Curly Lambeau, who ran the Green

Bay Packers, came up to my room at the Palace Hotel to talk me into signing a contract with the Packers. Actually, Lambeau was one of the few pro-football people who made a practice of going to the East-West game, although that's where you found a lot of your good pro material. You see, there were only two postseason games in the country at that time—the Rose Bowl and the East-West game—and naturally, with all the players that were available, why, you had to be pretty good to make that East-West game. So Lambeau scouted it. He was the founder of the Green Bay club, and a driving coach. He was dedicated. And he was doing some traveling, whereas George Halas and some of those others weren't. Halas was picking up his ballplayers around Chicago, while Lambeau was out beating the bushes. He was one of those rare coaches like Paul Brown or Vince Lombardi —he could see things in a ballplayer that other coaches couldn't.

The New York Giants were the only other team interested in me. They'd approached me after a game we played against Fordham in New York. But the Packers had been champions for the last three years—1929, '30, and '31—and then, too, what really decided me was a game I'd seen the Packers play in '31. They had a lineman by the name of Cal Hubbard, and, boy, he looked like a mountain. He was six-five and about 265, and real tough. I saw him and I thought, "By God, I believe I'd rather be on his side than play against him." So I signed up with the Packers for $125 a game.

Because of the way I dressed, the Green Bay players called me Joe College. But right away we had a couple of scrimmages, and they found out that I could take it and that I did have some ability. In fact, I had to beat out two pretty damned good veteran fullbacks, Bo Molenda and Hurdis McCrary, and I did. My rookie year we played twenty-two games, fourteen of them league games and eight exhibitions, and we were still playing in February, almost in March, and the reason we were was Johnny Blood. Now there's a guy! Let me tell you about him.

He was a rangy halfback, about six-two and 190, and he had great speed. When he was about thirty-five and Don Hutson was about twenty-four, he raced Hutson a hundred yards. Hutson could outrun the wind, but he beat Johnny in that race by only a step. Johnny was the kind of a guy who would read Shakespeare, Chaucer, and all those kind of people, although when he was drinking he would read filthy dime novels.

Johnny's life was probably even more glamorous off the field than on. After a game he'd buy up whorehouses. He purchased them and closed them up. Yes, he'd close them up so he could stay there with those girls all by himself. I doubt if he had relations with any of them, but that's just the way he was. He liked an unusual conversation. He just liked to do things like that. So during my rookie season he was corresponding with some people in Honolulu, and one day he came to us and said, "Do you want to play a few postseason exhibition games in Honolulu? All you got to do is say yes, and I'll arrange it."

Nobody took him seriously. Lambeau said, "Okay, John. I'll let you handle it. You make all the arrangements."

Well, darned if Johnny didn't get us all lined up for Honolulu. We went over on a boat—it took us five and a half days—and played three games against Hawaiian teams. We stayed there twenty-two days, then came back and played Ernie Nevers' All-Stars in San Francisco and then played them again the following week in Los Angeles. But before that, on the boat coming back from the islands one night, we couldn't find Johnny Blood. We were having a good time on the boat, when suddenly we couldn't find Blood. So Milt Gantenbein, who was my roommate at the time—Milt and I walked out on the main deck and went back toward the stern. The sea was a little rough, and that ship was pitching. But we walked back there toward the stern, and then we turned white. We froze.

Johnny Blood was outside the safety railing, on the extreme stern end of that ship. He was hanging on to the flagpole. There he was, in the middle of that pitch-black night, with the ship pitching, and he was swinging around that flagpole. He didn't even know he was in any danger.

He'd been drinking that Okole Hao, that native drink. Made from pineapple juice or tea roots or something. Hell of a drink, I'll tell you. Anyway, we eased out there and got him out of there, but if h'd have dropped off that stern, nobody would have ever found him. And that's just one of the things he did.

Oh, we had some real football players up there at Green Bay. Arnie Herber, I would say, was the most accurate long passer that ever lived. He had very stubby hands, so he never gripped the ball. He just laid it on his hand and let 'er go. He was more accurate at fifty yards than he was at ten. We had linemen like Hubbard and Buckets Goldenberg, who was as serious a competitor as I ever saw, though I don't think he ever made more than $110 a game. Later on, we had Don Hutson, who had that gliding, deceptive speed and would get under those long passes that Herber threw. That gave us a perfect combination. And still later, we had Cece Isbell, a terrific passer and a better strategist than Herber.

You know, a lot of people today think Green Bay was never a great football town till after Vince Lombardi got there and organized things and built all those winners in the 1960s. It kind of annoys me. They talk like we were a bunch of guys that got together on weekends. Listen, Lambeau was a great administrator. He won six world championships, and in his early days he was just as tough and mean as anybody else. You think Lombardi's tough? Lambeau was tougher.

We were kings in Green Bay. We traveled in the best of society. Whenever they had the charity balls that people attended in evening gowns and all that, we were invited. There was a lot of money up there—a lot of money made in lumber and in the paper industry. The best society would invite you to their homes for dinner. And women! When the Packers came back to Green Bay to begin training for another season, the gals would say, "The Depression's over!" And they would go by our hotel in Packards and all kind of big cars, just wanting to be with the Green Bay Packers. I'm telling you, it spoiled you, because you had the pick of the most beautiful gals in town, and that town had real good-looking gals of French and Belgian descent and some who were Indian. Beautiful gals.

Of course, you *knew* everybody in town, so when you lost a ballgame you didn't want to face anybody. You'd keep pretty much to the alleys. In those days—and I presume it's the same there today—if a fan saw you out drinking during the middle of the week, he would call Lambeau and say, "I saw Hinkle having a glass of beer tonight." And Lambeau would fine you twenty-five dollars on the strength of what that fan said. The fans told the truth, too. They were interested enough that if a guy was drinking on Wednesday or Thursday, why, they felt it was their duty to report it.

We always traveled first-class. That was one of Lambeau's principles. We traveled in nothing but the best Pullmans. We even carried our own dining car connected to the two Pullmans we had for the squad. We stayed in the best hotels and ate the finest food. Most of the other teams went to cheaper hotels, but Lambeau felt we should project an image to the public. After Hubbard and some of the rougher players were gone, Lambeau even got a little tough on dress. We were one of the first to wear team jackets—blazers. And we were one of the first teams to fly. In 1941 Lambeau decided we'd fly to New York. I said, "I'll see you there. I'm going by train. I'm afraid of planes." Lambeau said, "You are suspended without pay if you don't fly." So I flew. But we got grounded in Cleveland and had to go the rest of the way by train.

Lambeau used to give us our pay on the train coming home from the games, yet a lot of times guys would get off the train in Green Bay without a cent. They'd play bridge or shoot craps on the train, and between Chicago and Green Bay, say, they'd lose their whole pay. That sort of thing was prevalent throughout the league. It was affecting the ballplayers' mental attitude and their spirit. So Lambeau put a stop to it. What the other ball clubs did about it I don't know, but if Lambeau found anybody gambling, he fined them.

Lambeau allowed us to smoke but he kind of frowned on us smoking in public, because he thought it created a bad image. However, I smoked like a fiend. I smoked more during the football season than any other time. See, we figured in those days that during the season you're running a lot every day and you're blowing that residual air out of your lungs—you're exhaling that bad air out of your lungs. So we didn't feel that cigarettes affected us much.

Actually, I think we were very strict in our training habits. Lambeau gave us a written diet to follow. No fried foods of any kind. Chocolate drinks were out because in those days we felt they built fat around the lungs. Coca-Cola was out, yet they all drink it today. We were told that it took forty-eight hours to digest a bottle of Coke, and that the sugar wasn't good for your wind.

After a ballgame, the lid would either be off or it would not be off. If it was off, that meant, "You can go out if you stay out of the gutters. Don't get in jail." Lambeau didn't say anything about Mondays, but if you'd gotten pretty well boiled on Sunday night, you were expected to taper off the next day—a couple of beers or something. As for Tuesday, well, you'd better be out there ready to play our Tuesday touch-football game, and if you were caught taking one beer the rest of the week, you were fined. Listen, it makes me angry when they picture us as carousers. You just couldn't drink beer all week and play that sixty-minute football that we played. That was demanding football. Where would we have played Joe Namath in our day? Where the hell would we put him on defense? What would you do with a guy like Bob Hayes that in our day had to block for you once in a while? Well, anyway, you had to be in shape to play both ways. I don't think the other teams were as strict as we were in Green Bay, but in my time I never knew any player to become an alcoholic or anything like that. And I'll tell you, there have been some pro ballplayers today turning into alcoholics. Hell, they have to dry them out. And we never took pep pills. A lot of guys today choke up, and a pep pill gives them that fire.

But getting back to Lambeau, he was a great psychologist. I always felt I ought to give a 300-percent effort and I always tried to, but all week Lambeau would make snide little remarks to me. He'd have me boiling by the time Sunday came around. He'd say I wasn't putting out. After the Tuesday meeting at the hotel, he'd come by and say, "Well, you weren't yourself Sunday." And this would be after I'd had a pretty good day.

I'd say to myself, "Son of a gun, what does this guy want?" I'd go storming out of there. I'd say to myself, "I'll show that guy." But I must tell you this—he worked it the other way, too. He wouldn't exactly pat me on the back, but sometimes he'd tell me, "Well, it all depends on you, Clarke. If you're on today, we can beat this club." And that would work, too. I'd go out of there with fire in my eyes.

In 1934 we had one of the worst teams we ever had. We won seven ballgames but lost six. The Chicago Cardinals made us look real bad in a game at Milwaukee, and after the game Lambeau fined all of us half our week's salary. He said, "You're all fined, even the ones who tried." At that time, boy!—that was like cutting a guy's arm off. I was making about $175 a game. So there went $87.50 out of my pocket. However, Lambeau then said, "If you go out and beat the Detroit Lions next week, I'll give you the money back." The Lions were leading the league at the time. Nobody figured we had any business on the same field with them.

Still, we went over to Detroit and beat 'em, 3-0. I kicked a forty-seven-yard field goal, and we knocked them out of first place. Actually, the field goal was about sixty yards, because I always kicked at least twelve yards back from the line of scrimmage. I kicked from 'way back there because I always took three steps to get power. Everything I did, I had to do with force. That's just the way I was built.

I'd rather run into tacklers than use a little finesse, you know, so I lost a lot of yards that way. But I felt I wanted to be tougher than the next guy. If they were going to tackle me, they were going to pay for it. But let me tell you something. I don't have a bad shoulder, a bad knee, a bad ankle, or a bad anything. It's amazing, isn't it? The Lord took real good care of me. I got my leg broken in high school once, and that was the only serious injury I ever had.

In 1941, my tenth and last year of professional football, we played the Bears in Chicago. This was the Bears' wonder team that had beaten Washington for the chamionship the year before, 73-0. They had a fullback, Bill Osmanski, who liked to file his cleats real sharp, although he was a good, clean ballplayer. Well, those games between the Bears and Packers were always bloodbaths, and in this one I was backing up the line when Osmanski came through on those sharpened cleats and tore open my leg so bad that the shinbone was all exposed. So about three plays later I called time-out. I went over to the sideline. But as soon as I got there, Lambeau really chewed me out for calling a time-out so early. We were still in the first half, maybe the first quarter. He said, "We'll need those time-outs!" And I said to Lambeau, "I want to tell you something. Listen, my shinbone's showing. I come over here to get a bandage on it, because, you know, it kind of makes me sick to look at my shinbone."

Well, I played the rest of that half. In the second half I got a little rest, but not much. For the second-half kickoff Lambeau put in Eddie Jankowski, a fullback we had from the University of Wisconsin. Jankowski took the kickoff and got coldcocked. So Lambeau took him out, and I played the whole second half and I kicked the field goal that beat 'em, 16-14, and I haven't got that wound dressed yet. We were so elated that we had beaten that Bear team that in the dressing room I was completely ignored. Finally, one of the trainers put a little bandage over my leg, and I got dressed. You couldn't get a cab outside Wrigley Field that day, so I walked fifteen blocks to the hotel. And they talk about tough football today. Huh!

We had no pain-killers in those days. Nothing. You lived with pain. I don't think there was ever a ballgame that most of us didn't live with pain. But you were so wrought-up playing the game that you didn't think about it. Outside of getting a little rest now and then, the one and only time I ever left a game was when Bronko Nagurski put seven stitches in my face. They took me down to the emergency room of the hospital and put the stitches in, and they brought me back in a taxicab and I went back into the ballgame. It happened in the first quarter. I got back just before the half ended and started the second half. Didn't do bad, either. I believe we played the Bears to a 0-0 tie.

I think I began to get my reputation as a tough player as a result of a famous collision that Nagurski and I had. I'd been in the league about two or three years. As you probably know, Nagurski and I both played fullback and linebacker, and actually, I'd already raised a few eyebrows because opponents who tackled me felt like I weighed about 240, and because when I played against Nagurski I held my own. The time he put seven stitches on my chin, I'd made a mistake on defense. I waited for him to come to me. Then, as I sat there, I said, "Clarke, you better learn how to play this game or they'll kill you." From then on, I tried to get to Bronk before he got to me. So we had this big collision in Green Bay.

I was back to punt on third down. In those days it was common to punt on third down. But sometimes I would fake a punt and run with the ball or throw to Hutson. It was an option play, really. Well, this time I ran with the ball to my right. I got through a hole. I started upfield, and out of the corner of my eye I could see Nagurski coming over to really nail me to the cross. He was edging me to the sideline. Bronk outweighed me by about twenty or so pounds, and what he would do instead of tackling you was run right through you. But I had the advantage because as the man carrying the ball I knew what I was going to do.

So just before I got to the sideline I cut abruptly, right back into him. I thought, "I might as well get it now as any other time." I caught him wide open and met him head-on.

The collision knocked me back ten yards, actually, and I sat there for a few seconds to see if I was all right. I was shook up pretty good. Then I looked over at Bronk. His nose was over on the side of his face. It was bleeding and broken in two places, I think. His hip was cracked, they say. Whether it was or not, I don't know. But he was out cold. They took him off the field, and that's the first time he'd ever been jolted. After that, people began to want to see Hinkle.

It was two weeks later, as I recall, and Nagurski was back in action—and we were playing the Bears again. They had George Musso playing middle guard on defense. Musso weighed about 265, but on this particular play two of our linemen, Buckets Goldenberg and George Svendsen, pinned him there and gave me a big hole. Musso couldn't do anything but watch. But just as I got through that hole, Nagurski came from somewhere.

Boy, he hit me so hard he knocked me right back through that hole and all the way back through my own backfield. But I didn't go down, see? My legs were still churning. So I came back through that same hole, where they still had Musso pinned, and I went fifty-six yards for a touchdown. After the game somebody asked Musso what he thought of that play, and he said, "It's the only time in my career that a back passed me three times on the same play."

I had no fear of Bronko Nagurski, and I'm sure he never had any fear of me. Today we're the finest of friends, yet there are a lot of people who say, "How come you two guys didn't get into a fight?" Well, Bronko and I, neither one of us ever played a dirty game in our life. Wouldn't think of it. So what happened on the field was forgotten about as soon as the game was over.

Some of those jolts you took out there would mess you up a little. I used to get some vertebrae shook up, you know. But if I got up on the training table to get a rubdown, Lambeau would come along and panic. He'd say, "What are you doing on the table, Hinkle?" I think he was afraid that I wasn't going to play the next Sunday. I think he was afraid because I did so many different things for him on the field. So I couldn't get on the training table for a rubdown. And on my wedding day he played me fifty-eight minutes, although we were beating the Boston Redskins by 15 points. I finally got him to take me out by forming a circle with my thumb and index finger and motioning like I was putting on the wedding ring.

I don't think Lambeau had a friend in the world, as far as football players were concerned. Yet all of them respected him, as I think players respect Vince Lombardi. In 1937 we were in California after the season to make a movie for M-G-M, and some of us were given screen tests. The next season, when I reported, I said to Lambeau, "I never did hear anything about that screen test. Did you hear anything from those movie people?" And Lambeau said, "Oh, yeh. They wrote me that you passed, all right. But I told them you weren't interested. I didn't think you would be interested." That's how he was. He wasn't going to take any chance of losing a ballplayer. In later years, when it came to getting job references or things like that, George Halas did more for me than Lambeau ever did. I would never go to Lambeau for a reference or suggest to someone that they speak to him about me, because you never knew what he was liable to say. However, Curly did say in an interview that I was the greatest he ever had. He always mentioned me as his best, so I appreciate that.

In the ten years I spent with the Packers, I got an increase every year, until I'd gone from $125 per game to $10,000 for my last season, when they paid by the season. I was a holdout twice. The first time, I said to Lambeau, "Trade me." He said, "I can't. Nobody wants you." Which I knew was a lie, because I was in my prime then. But I knew I didn't have a chance to get traded, and I needed the money, so I signed. But my last year of football, in '41, I got tough. I held out two weeks on him while the team was already in practice. Fortunately the sportswriters got on my side and the people began writing letters to the paper, saying that I should have more money. So finally, I got what I wanted, ten thousand, which wasn't bad money in those years. But let me tell you what Lambeau did.

He said, "All right, we'll pay it. Be at practice this afternoon." And that afternoon he scrimmaged me for two solid hours.

Luckily, I'd been riding a racing bike in the off-season to keep my legs in shape, but even so, after an hour and a half of solid scrimmage I said to Lambeau, "How about a rest?" He said, "If you'd have signed on time, you wouldn't be suffering like that." He kept me going for two hours and damn near killed me. I went home that day and stayed in bed all day and all night, and I could barely get out of bed the next morning, my muscles were so sore. But I never let Lambeau know that. I went through agony in calisthenics the second day and finally worked out the soreness. But he nearly killed me. He was getting even because I'd gotten the best of him.

The think I'm most proud of is that in my last year of football, just before World War II started, I was able to make all-pro. Counting high school, college, and pro, that was my eighteenth year of football, but I beat out Norm Standlee of the Bears for all-pro. I was still working on my punting and drop-kicking and place-kicking, and I led the league that year in field goals. So I like to say that even in my eighteenth year I was still trying to perfect myself. People say to me now,

"Could you make today's football?" I say, "Very definitely I could. What category would you want me to make it in?" I mean, maybe I'm bragging a little, but I had a ten-year punting average of 43.4 yards, and that's probably better than almost any punter in the National Football League today. Yet it was never even talked about in my time. One game against the Detroit Lions, I had nine punts for a fifty-three-yard average, and it wasn't hardly mentioned.

I feel that I could have played offensive football in today's game. And if I wouldn't have been big enough for linebacker I could have played cornerback or safety, because, you know, only once in my career did a man get behind me. Also, if nothing else, I could have been a field-goal kicker.

It annoys me very much when I hear anyone say that we "contributed" a lot to pro football. Heaven's sake! We *established* the game. From 1936 on, pro football was developing each year and getting more popular. From '36 on, we played regularly to capacity crowds of twenty-five thousand in City Stadium. We played to sellouts in Wrigley Field. We played to fifty thousand in Briggs Stadium, Detroit, and to forty or fifty thousand in New York. We established the game. But we're not included in the pension plan, and I don't think there'll ever be a time that we will be. We established the type of game the players and owners are making their money on today, but they couldn't care less about us.

Well, the big mistake I made was that during my first few years of football I lived on the football money I made, where I should have been getting into some type of business or profession. During the war they took me into the Coast Guard and I ended up with my own command. I finished up with my own ship and came out a lieutenant commander. I still had Green Bay in my blood, so I went back there and got into the insurance business, but I couldn't bulldog people. I couldn't hound them and pressure them till I got the policy. So in 1948 I came back home.

I don't have any money, but I'm able to pay my bills. My health is good, and I sleep good at nights. So what else is there?

8

CLIFF BATTLES

Life with George Marshall

In the 1930s, pro football had no network of scouts to comb small, out-of-the-way colleges for unknown players who had the talent to make it big. Pro ballplayers largely were men who came from major colleges, armed with press clippings. Yet there was an occasional sleeper from the boondocks, and I can recall that as a boy I would hear my father deride the big-school All-Americans by saying, "Look at Cliff Battles! Cliff Battles came out of the woods and tore the pro league apart."

Cliff Battles came out of Kenmore, Ohio, a suburb of Akron, to play halfback for West Virginia Wesleyan at Buckhannon, West Virginia. In reality, he was not hidden in obscurity, for Wesleyan was a popular, though scrappy, schedule breather for such major powers as Army, Navy, New York University, and others. Word of Battles' performances spread. He blasted through the line with power, and ran swiftly and deceptively in open field. When he joined the Boston Braves of the NFL in 1932, he was not without references.

I called upon him at his spacious executive office in General Electric quarters, downtown Washington. A big, bald, ruddy man, he is Manager of Civic Relations for G.E., working with civic organizations and defense people to keep up the corporation's image. Well adjusted to the changing times, he wore a mod blue shirt and yellow tie beneath his gray business suit, and spoke of the past with little emotion and certainly with no sign of either longing for it or wanting to bury it.

———

At an early age I studied violin and bass viola, but just as I was about to be launched in the church orchestra, why, I discovered sports, and that was about the end of it as far as music was concerned. My father, who was a laborer with Goodrich and Firestone and then in the saltworks, took a dim view of athletics. He was the one who had put me and my sister—she's an accomplished musician—he put us into music. But in my junior year of high school, I began to play football, and my mother covered for me. She signed the permission papers. My old man probably would have refused to.

He had no idea I was playing football. He never read the sports pages. Of course, word got around, but when my father would hear something about my playing ball, we would pretend that people were talking about my cousin Roy, who also played on the team. At school I had a nickname—"Gip" Battles. What little publicity I received, we pretended that Gip Battles was Roy. My senior year, we figured that maybe I would receive more prominence than I had, so we decided to make a clean breast of it. Tearfully, I got my father's consent to play.

At West Virginia Wesleyan I majored in English but was prepping for law. In those days the football varsity played freshmen, and I made the team as an end in my freshman year, but in a game against Morris Harvey, or some small school like that, the coach was resting the VIPs for a big game with Navy, so he put me into the backfield. For a freshman, I did pretty well, so they moved me into the backfield and that's where I stayed. I began to attract some attention with long runs, and in my senior year, George Marshall, who owned the new Boston Braves in the National Football League and originally was a West Virginian, sent a man down to Wesleyan to sign me. The story is that he told the fellow, "If you don't sign him, keep going south and don't come back."

I signed for about $175 a game, as I recall, or something like $2,500 a season. It was 1932 and there was pretty much of a Depression, so I could not afford to go to law school. Everybody was having a hell of a time getting a job, so pro ball seemed exciting. If somebody handed you almost a couple of hundred dollars a week for doing something you enjoyed, why, it seemed like a pretty good thing.

My first coach in Boston was Lud Wray, who had been a rough, tough lineman and chewed during practice and had rather salty language. But my second year, Marshall, with his theatrical flair, hired about half a dozen Indians to play for us, and he hired an Indian coach, Lone Star Dietz, and changed our name to the Boston Redskins. Dietz himself was very theatrical, very demonstrative. He had appeared in a number of movies, in full headdress. In the movies he would recite poetry and make appeals to the great white fathers. He cooperated with preseason publicity by doing the headdress bit, and for our opening game he put war paint on all of us. Yellow, red, brown, any kind of paint that would show up. No, we didn't object—not as I recall.

Lone Star Dietz was very big on trick plays. Now that kind of thing might have been all right in college ball, where you could maintain control of the defense, but in the pro league you couldn't hold those big guys out of there long enough to run double reverses and bootlegs and fake fumble palys. We had a play where the fullback would pretend to fumble the snapback and then throw a dinky pass over the middle. We had triple reverses and end-around plays and a spectacular thing that we called the squirrel cage. When we received a low, driving, short kickoff—and remember, they didn't kick from tees in those days—everybody would run back to about the ten-yard line and huddle, and the man who had received the ball would hand it to someone else. Then the whole team would scatter in different directions. Our favorite ballcarrier on this play was Turk Edwards, the biggest man on our team. He was the last man you'd suspect would get the ball. So he broke loose at least once or twice that I can recall and ran, oh, forty or fifty yards up the middle of the field before they finally found out who had the ball and caught him. The crowd got a big kick out of it.

Well, as I said, Dietz was very partial to his trick plays, and I discovered that he had bribed the quarterback to call some of them. He encouraged the quarterback by giving him a small bonus. I complained very bitterly about this, because I usually wound up with the ball, and if the play worked, I felt *I* should get the bonus instead of the guy who called the play.

Although Dietz was our coach, George Marshall in a very real sense coached the team, too. He was a laundryman, you know—even when he had the club in Boston, he owned a laundry business in Washington and had promoted it into a very fine linen service. I believe his slogan was "Long Live Linen!" Anyhow, in Boston he would sit on the bench, and if a player went by him on his way into the game, Marshall was liable to tell the player anything. He might tell him to kick or run or pass. After the game he was usually occupied socially, so he would just swing through the dressing room and needle some of us on the way out of the ballpark.

Dietz was gone after two years, and our next coach was Eddie Casey, a Harvard immortal. I guess Marshall felt that Casey would appeal to the Harvard people. He was an extremely cordial fellow, with a Boston accent, but unfortunately, he wasn't much of a coach. I believe we lost eight straight ballgames before we won one. So for the next season, 1936, Marshall hired Ray Flaherty, who had been a great player with the New York Giants and was familiar with Marshall's egocentricities. He had it put in his contract that Marshall would stay off the field. So Marshall had to go upstairs, but he had extensive telephone lines all over the place. He would phone the band and the bench and everything else. Flaherty had a man on the bench who would take Marshall's phone calls, but Flaherty would ignore everything Marshall said. We had our first winning season—won seven, lost five.

That season, as we were approaching our final few games, Marshall was waging a battle with the press, the argument stemming from the failure of Boston fans to show more interest in his great team. We looked like we might win the eastern division, but they still weren't knocking the doors down. We'd draw fifteen thousand or something like that. So in order to pick up a buck or two, Marshall one day raised the price of tickets on the day of the game, "inadvertently." When the fans moved up to the window to get a $1.75 seat, it was suddenly $2.25, or some such figure. So there was a lot of hue and cry, and one thing led to another and darned if he didn't take the team and move us bag and baggage out of town.

For our last game of the season, against the Giants, he moved us to the Westchester Country Club in suburban New York, where we practiced on a big polo field, and he moved the game itself to the Polo Grounds in New York. We won the eastern title, then played Green Bay for the championship, and he put *that* game in the Polo Grounds. The Packers beat us, and then Marshall moved the franchise to Washington. Boston's reaction, I suppose, was good riddance.

Our first year in Washington, Sammy Baugh came along out of T.C.U. and gave us a tremendous lift. Previously we had not had a passer, so our opponents would stack seven- and eight-man lines against us. But in order to defend against Baugh's passing, most coaches felt they had to play a five-man line. In those days, if a back couldn't run against a five-man line, he shouldn't have been playing football. We won the championship that year, 1937, and I led the league in rushing with almost nine hundred yards. Actually, I had led the league once before, in 1933, and had received two or three small raises from Marshall. So now I was making four thousand dollars a season, and I asked for another raise. Nothing exorbitant. Maybe about a thousand dollars.

Marshall and I exchanged letters, and he would say things to the effect that I had better be in camp or I would be subject to a fine. In the meantime, Lou Little, the head coach at Columbia University, offered me a job coaching his backfield. I had played pro ball for six years and probably had several more good years left in me, but I accepted the Columbia job and signed a contract. Marshall was very upset. He became very vindictive. He blasted me in the newspapers and refused to speak to me for ten years. He threatened to sue the university. He sent a strong wire to the president of Columbia, accusing the school of stealing someone in whom he had invested a lot of time and money. As far as I know, the president never acknowledged the wire.

Later on, the New York Giants tried to get Marshall to trade me to them so I could play for them while coaching at

ED HEALEY

Ed Healey as an infant, with parents—1895

Dartmouth football stars Pat Holbrook, Swede Youngstrom, Ed Healey
(left to right), 1919

Ed Healey (extreme left) in the
Argonne, World War I

Ed Healey, Chicago Bears tackle,
1922

JOE GUYON

Joe Guyon at Carlisle Indian School

Joe Guyon today

Joe Guyon as best man
at Jim Thorpe's wedding

Joe Guyon as an All-American
at Georgia Tech

RED GRANGE

Red Grange, 1925, on his first trip with the Chicago Bears. He spent his first $500 on the coat he's wearing— later, while Red was on the West Coast, his brother sold the coat for $50.

Red Grange, the Galloping Ghost

ERNIE NEVERS

The Duluth Eskimos, 1926—an NFL franchise purchased for a dollar

Ernie Nevers: His signature may have saved the League.

CLARKE HINKLE

(Frank Scherschel, LIFE Magazine © Time Inc.)

Above: Clarke Hinkle at Bucknell University, 1931

Upper right: Clarke Hinkle (extreme left) in Honolulu for Green Bay Packers' post-season exhibition tour, 1932

Right: Clarke Hinkle, 1939, a hero to every Green Bay kid

Hinkle carrying the ball, scoring winning touchdown against Detroit Lions in 1937

Ernie Nevers, Bronko Nagurski, and Clarke Hinkle — indestructible giants of their time

Hinkle in Hollywood for screen test

Columbia, but Marshall would not go for the deal at all. In 1940, after the Chicago Bears had beaten Washington in the championship game, 73-0, I visited the Bears' dressing room, because I had coached the Bears' quarterback, Sid Luckman, at Columbia, and was scouting the Bears' offense so we could put it in at Columbia. Marshall came into the dressing room and accused me of giving the Bears the Redskins' plays. Well, that was ridiculous. I hadn't played for the Redskins for three years.

Still, there's no doubt about it—George Marshall belongs with the pioneers of the game, the men who were responsible for bringing pro football out of the wilderness and making it the spectacular show-business operation that it is today. I came back to Washington about 1953 as a manufacturer's representative, and Marshall and I began to see a lot of each other at Touchdown Club functions and things like that. Our realtionship became very cordial. I suppose both of us had mellowed somewhat through the years.

9

ART ROONEY

"What I'm telling you is that we've tried."

Although few but his family, his cronies, and his staff are aware of it, Arthur J. Rooney, millionaire president of the Pittsburgh Steelers, lives in a predominantly black neighborhood. Some thirty years ago, during the Depression, he sent his wife out to buy a house, stipulating only that she confine her search to the vicinity of the low-Irish neighborhood in which he'd been reared. On a fashionable street not far away, Kathleen Rooney purchased a five-bedroom, three-story home for five thousand dollars. The street has long since declined. To the Rooney's immediate right stands a Catholic charity; to their left, an old mansion converted to low-rent offices; across the street, at the time of my visit, a vacant lot piled here and there with rubble. Appearances, however, do not concern the Rooneys. They are comfortable, so they stay. Neighborhood children usually visit them in the evening, each knowing that Rooney will give him a quarter.

Except for a fat cigar (as apt to be a ten-center as a dollar Lozano) that is almost always in the curl of his index finger, Rooney does not look the part of a wealthy man. On a morning when I interviewed him at the Steeler offices, he wore a plain gray suit, somewhat baggy, and beneath it a gray woolen shirt that was tieless yet buttoned at the neck. Stocky and with a ruddy complexion, black-frame eyeglasses, and a great shock of white hair, he resembled an eastern courthouse functionary from the time, say, of Honey Fitz.

He is one of the great contradictions of sport. Perhaps the most successful horseplayer that American racing has known, Art Rooney is professional football's champion loser. He has owned the Pittsburgh club since 1933, yet never won so much as a divisional title. On the other hand, his winnings from a single day at the racetrack have been estimated as high as a quarter of a million dollars. He will neither confirm nor deny it. "That's what the newspapers said," he tells you, eyes twinkling.

Of course, he made his biggest killings in a time that preceded the parimutuel machine—a time when bookmakers at the track gave the player a "price" and paid off on those odds regardless of subsequent betting action. "Bookmakers in those days were such a different brand of people from what they are today," Rooney says wistfully. "They were great people. They had class." He was successful at almost everything he tried. As a welterweight boxer he won both national and international amateur championships. During a brief fling as a minor-league outfielder, he hit .369 and stole fifty-eight bases, then quit because of a sore arm. Besides playing the horses, he dabbled profitably as a fight promoter, acquired a reputation for shrewd stock-market trading, bred race-horses, and bought into racetracks. Across the nation, sports-writers who came to know him as a charitable, completely unpretentious man, rooted desperately for his Steelers, while Pittsburgh's multitudes, increasingly enraged by the team's incompetence or bad luck, grew to think of Rooney as an intolerable bungler. The Steelers—"The same old Steelers," headlines called them—kept losing and losing.

I grew up in what was then the First Ward, but we never called it that. We called it The Ward. All it was ever known as was The Ward. In fact, when I get a taxicab to come to the office, I'll tell the driver, "Well, go down through The Ward." And the old guys, the old cabdrivers, still know where The Ward is.

It was heavily populated. Made up of Irish, mostly. On Saturday nights, when the people congregated, they would speak Gaelic. You would hear pretty much as much Gaelic as you would English, which is unusual because most of the Irish in *Ireland* don't speak Gaelic. There was a smattering of Polish in The Ward, and a few colored, not many, and one Jew. The Jew was an old man named Kurtz, who owned a clothing store and was very highly thought of because he was kind. If anyone ever touched him, it was mayhem.

So that was the makeup of The Ward. The people were poor, and probably the only time a lot of them ever had a ride in an automobile was going to the cemetery when someone died. That was a big event, when someone died. You know, you can go back to the Irish wakes you saw in that movie, *The Last Hurrah*, but compared to the wakes we had in The Ward—well, we had wakes that were tremendous. People would look in the papers to see who died, and they would come from all over town. Of course, some of them were professional moochers, but everyone would be there. It'd last three days, and it would be like a carnival. It was just a gala affair. After those people started in drinking, sometimes they'd put the body outside. One time they put the body outside my father's saloon.

In the horse and buggy days, when I was only a kid, it took all day to get to the graveyard, but in later years we'd borrow a whole string of cars, enough cars for the whole neighborhood. We'd arrive at the graveyard and everybody would scatter all over the place. Everybody would run to the graves where their own immediate people were buried. Then you would hear them hollering the *caoine*, which is the old Irish cry. It was fantastic. It was tremendous. You would hear them hollering the *caoine* all over the graveyard. And in the meantime, nobody paid any attention to the man who was getting buried except his immediate family. Coming back, everybody stopped at least once to get a drink.

When people started taking their dead to funeral homes, that broke up the Irish wake as we knew it. But even today, I like to pay my respects and see the deceased's family. I go to see more dead people than probably anybody in Pittsburgh. I do this because I like to do it. Years ago, in the late 1920s and early '30s, I was a ward chairman, but I'm not a politician now and there's no reason I would be going to visit these people for any gain. But at the office we go through the death notices every day, and when I'm in town it's nothing for me to go to three and four wakes every night.

The Ward was on the north bank of the Allegheny River, across the river from downtown Pittsburgh. I grew up right across from old Exposition Park—Expo Park, we called it— where the Pirates played baseball till they opened Forbes Field in 1909. Later, the Federal League, the outlaw league, played at Expo Park, and all the baseball players loafed in my father's saloon. I knew 'em all. I saw the big fights and top soccer games at Expo Park. It's a funny thing—now they're building a new stadium, Three Rivers Stadium, to replace Forbes Field, and it's on the exact spot that Expo Park was. Which brings to mind the time I almost died there.

In those days, before flood controls, if you spit in the Allegheny River, the flood came up. It wasn't anything ususual for us to leave for school by going out a second-floor window in a skiff. One day there were three of us paddling to school in a canoe—a kid named Squawker Mullen, my brother Dan, and me. We were paddling that canoe right through Expo Park. Right through the outfield.

Squawker was moving around in the canoe, so I said to him, "Sit still, Squawker. You're going to upset the canoe." But he kept moving around, and sure enough, he upset it. Well, we started swimming for the third-base grandstand. Squawker and Dan weren't wearing boots, so they made it, easy enough. But I had on boots and an overcoat. That was the last gasp I had, when I got ahold of that grandstand. You see, I was lucky that I lived to see the new stadium being built. I almost got drowned in it.

I played all the sports. You went on the playground when the sun came up, and you didn't leave till the sun went down. It wasn't anything for me when I was fifteen years old—when I weighed 135, maybe 140 pounds—to be playing baseball against the famous colored teams, the Homestead Grays and the Kansas City Monarchs. All of those barnstorming teams —the House of David, for example—they all came to The Ward. Some years, my brother Dan and I would leave town in the summer with a semi-pro team, and we'd travel through Ohio, West Virginia, Pennsylvania, and New York, playing for ten or twenty dollars a game. We'd play in *chatauquas*. You know what a *chatauqua* was, don't you? It was approximately a week of carnival they'd have in small towns.

A lot of those carnivals had athletic troupes that included fighters who would accept challenges from anybody in the house. You'd get three dollars a round for as long as you could stay. Well, that was made to order for Dan and me, because we could lick all those carnival guys. I mean, what kind of fighters would a carnival have? They could handle a farmer, all right, but they were very ordinary fighters. In The Ward, on the other hand, we had a boxing team—St. Peter's

Lyceum, they called it—that was the equal of any in the world. A lot of us went to the nationals. So in these small towns the first thing we'd ask was did the carnival have an athletic troupe? But after a while they got to know us and they asked us to stay away. It was a reasonable request, so we did, but that was easy money while it lasted.

I remember a guy in The Ward who "did the buck" on the railroad. You know what that was, don't you? It means he was a scab. The railroad men were on strike, but he went to work. Finally people made it so bad for him in The Ward that he had to leave. Later he came back as a fighter for a carnival, the Johnny J. Jones carnival, and as soon as we heard about him coming back, we got ahold of Squawker Mullen. Squawker was a national amateur champion—just a little fellow, maybe 110 pounds, but, boy, could Squawker fight! We had Squawker challenge the guy.

But the trouble was, Squawker was out of condition and he got tired. He run out of gas. The other fellow got Squawker in the corner and he was getting the best of him. So our Dan, who was a heavyweight, he just reached up over the ropes and hit the fellow—he nailed him like you would nail a bird in midair. Right away, someone hollered, "Hey, Rube!," which was the signal for all the carnival hands to come on the run. The next thing, the whole tent came down, and that ended the athletic events of that carnival. Dan's a priest now. He used to be the father superior at St. Anthony's Shrine in Boston. President Kennedy attended Mass at Dan's church once in a while.

The kind of football I played in the 1920s, I suppose you'd call it semi-pro, but our teams were as good as the teams in professional football. We were as good as the teams in the National Football League, which was just getting started. I was no more than twenty-two when I started up a team called

Hope-Harvey. I owned it and coached it and in the important games played halfback. The team was called Hope-Harvey because Hope was the name of the fire-engine house in The Ward and Harvey was the doctor in The Ward. For home games we dressed and got our showers at the engine house, and Harvey took care of anybody who got hurt. So nothing cost us a cent. And a lot of guys in that semi-pro ball got up to a hundred dollars a game—a lot of them got more money than fellows in the National Football League.

I remember we played the Canton Bulldogs and Jim Thorpe in Pittsburgh once. I tried a field goal but it was blocked. Thorpe picked it up and ran for a touchdown, and as I recall, they beat us, 6-0. Oh, I played against Thorpe a number of times. He was certainly very fast, but Thorpe was pretty much at the end of his rope then. Anyhow, the game in those days was just shoving and pushing, compared to what it is now. Not long ago I went to a gathering of some old-timers, just wonderful people. I really enjoy myself loafing with these old fellows that I played ball with and against, but at this gathering they showed a film of one of the football games we played. They thought it was great. They thought it was tough football. But watching it, you know, I thought, "It's strictly shoving and pushing."

In 1933 I paid $2,500 for a National Football League franchise, which I named the Pirates, because the Pittsburgh baseball team was called the Pirates. It wasn't till 1940, when we held a contest for a new name, that we became the Steelers. Joe Carr's girl friend—Joe's been our ticket manager right along—his girl friend won the contest. There were people who said, "That contest don't look like it was on the level."

Anyway, I bought the franchise in '33 because I figured that it would be good to have a league schedule and that eventually professional football would be good. And the reason I bought a franchise at that particular time was that we knew that Pennsylvania was going to repeal certain laws— "blue laws," they were called. You see, until then, Sunday football was illegal in Pennsylvania. This was going to be changed by the legislature. So now I had a franchise, and our schedule was made up. But a couple of days before our opening game, the mayor phoned me and said, "I got a complaint here from a preacher that this game should not be allowed because it's against the blue laws. The repeal hasn't been ratified yet by City Council, and won't be till Tuesday."

"Well," I said, "I never heard of this thing, ratification."

Nobody else had heard anything about it either, until this preacher brought it up. The mayor told me he didn't know what I could do about it but that I should go see a fellow named Harmar Denny, who was director of public safety and was over the police department.

So I went to Denny and I said, "We're in the big leagues now. We can't have a thing like this happen to our opening game." But this Denny was pretty much of a straightlaced guy. All he would say was that he was going away for the weekend. "Good," I told him. "You go away." Then I went to see the superintendent of police, a man named McQuade, and told *him* my problem.

"Oh, that there's ridiculous," he said. "Give me a couple of tickets and I'll go to the game Sunday. That'll be the last place they'll look for me if they want me to stop the game."

So McQuade hid out at the game, and on the following Tuesday the council met and ratified everything. We had three thousand people at the game. Maybe thirty-five hundred.

We didn't draw many people in those days. The colleges got most of the publicity. In Pittsburgh, the University of

Pittsburgh was the big wheel. They'd draw thirty thousand people, maybe thirty-five thousand, while we'd draw three thousand, maybe thirty-five hundred. You didn't make a lot of money but you didn't lose a lot. Maybe you made five thousand dollars a season, or maybe you lost a few thousand. All we paid the players was seventy-five or a hundred dollars a game. Professional football wasn't big league, compared to what it is now. Some people say the newspapers pushed us around, but I don't agree. If I was a newspaperman I would have treated us the same way.

In 1938 I did something I thought would bring a little class to the game. I signed Whizzer White out of Colorado University for a salary of $15,800, which was easily the highest salary pro football was paying. White was very hard to sign. I don't remember what the last eight hundred was for— whether it was for exhibition games, or because he had a Rhodes Scholarship and needed the eight to go to Oxford, or what. Anyhow, the fifteen got pro football a lot of publicity, and of course White *was* an asset to the game, an extremely high-class fellow, as you might judge from his going on to become a Supreme Court justice. But I caught some heat from some of the other owners.

A lot of them thought we were out of line. George Richards of Detroit thought it was terrible. He was very successful in the radio business and a fine man, very loose with a dollar, but he thought this was terrible, paying White that kind of money. George Marshall phoned me from Washington and said, "What are you trying to do?" I told him I thought it was a great thing for professional football to get someone like White to play the game, which I did believe. I did believe it. Everybody on the team respected White highly. If he had been bigheaded, he could have got himself in a lot of trouble, but he fit in right. He was a fine back, and he was right with the boys. So we didn't mind paying him the highest salary in football. But it's a funny thing—because we've never won a title, a lot of people in Pittsburgh say we're cheap. They say we don't do things right. Well, we don't argue about it. We don't say anything. We just leave it go at that.

Actually, the biggest mistake I've made was that, although I understood the football business as well as anybody in the league, I didn't pay the attention to the business that some of the other owners gave it. I was out of town a great deal of the time, at the racetracks. With me, the racetrack was a big business. And generally I'd have a head coach who was like me—he'd like the races.

I let my coaches have a free hand, but it didn't work. The year we signed White, our coach was John Blood. I still believe that John Blood could have been a tremendous coach, if he would have just paid attention. We once played a game in Los Angeles and John missed the train home. John was known to enjoy a good time, of course, so we didn't see him the whole week. On Sunday he stopped off in Chicago to see his old team, the Green Bay Packers, play the Bears. The newspaper guys asked him, "How come you're not with your team?" And John said, "Oh, we're not playing this week." Well, no sooner did he get those words out of his mouth than the guy on the loudspeaker announced a score. Philadelphia 14, Pittsburgh 7. You couldn't depend on John a whole lot.

The only other thing wrong with John Blood was that he didn't believe in fundamentals. Instead he created a lot of nice sayings and expressions. Like if he thought the other team was going to pass, he'd holler, "Air mail!" You know how the players warm up with calisthenics before a game? I don't know if they still count off numbers while they're warming up, but they used to count, "One! Two! Three! Four!" Well, John didn't use counts. He had the ballplayers yell,

"Pirates never quit!" John turned everything into a saying.
The players really loved John. But I remember a game in
New York when they thought he wasn't helping them. John
was a player-coach, you know, and he would put himself into
the backfield every now and then. So we're playing the
Giants and every time we get down to their twenty- or thirty-
yard line, where it looked like we were going to score, John
would put himself into the game to call the plays. But we
wouldn't score. After this happened a few times, our captain
went to the referee and said, "What happens if I don't accept
a player coming into the game?"

"Well," the referee said, "in that case, we won't accept
him."

So the next time John tried to go into the game, our captain
—I don't remember who he was—he refused to accept John.
John didn't argue about it much. He waved his arms a little
that's all, and then left the field. We immediately scored on
a pass and won the game. But after the game, the first thing
John did was call the players together and tell them, "You
called the same play I went in to call."

Professional football in those days wasn't like it is now.
You were much closer to your ballplayers. You loafed with
them, and they were your friends. I don't think I ever had a
ballplayer I disliked. Elbie Nickel, Jimmy Finks, Bill Walsh,
Ernie Stautner—you came to know all those guys. If you
didn't travel by bus, you traveled by day coach in what we
called "the Sullivans." I don't know how they got that
moniker, but that's all I ever called 'em. You'd pull the backs
of the seats down and make beds out of them. You were with
your ballplayers for hours at a time. And after the ballgame,
you might have to wait awhile for the next train, so you'd
have a beer with your players. You got to know all their
problems. Today you meet a ballplayer when you sign him.

Later, when the team flies to a game, you see him on an airplane that gets you there in practically the time it takes to snap your finger.

In the old days I knew newspapermen all over the country. Knew them as friends. A couple of years ago I was spending a week in San Francisco at a time when the baseball season was in the thick of the pennant race and a great many of the newspaper guys were there to cover an important series. I happened to be staying at the same hotel as the newspaper guys. The old ones, I knew. I knew them well, and I was with them every night. They got to telling me their problems, and they said, "Outside of you and George Halas, we don't know the other people in football. You don't get to know them. Even traveling with a baseball club," they said, "you travel so fast that you never get to know the owners like we knew you guys." Now you take the younger newspaper guys. The young newspaper guys today are not really different than those old guys. If they got to know you and you got to know them, it would be a great time all over again. But you don't have the opportunity to know them. It's just an entirely different life today.

The atmosphere used to be more enjoyable among the owners. Although they fought a lot, they were a lot closer to one another than they are now. They were *fans*. The owners today are fans, too, but I think they are also in the game because it does great financially. In the old days you had to be willing to lose your money. Yes, times sure have changed. Today we have nothing to do with making up the schedule. The schedule is sent out to us, and that's it, period. The way we used to do it, we'd have a league meeting and it would last day and night, for maybe a whole week. Everybody tried to get the best schedule. You'd want the teams that drew the biggest crowds. But early in the season you'd want the teams you could beat, so you could start off winning. The owners who had staying power, who were willing to stay in that room day and night arguing, they wound up with the best schedules. The guys who got tired and went home, they got murdered. One time we worked two or three days getting a schedule up there on the blackboard, but when it was just about done, George Marshall got sore. He went up to the board and wiped it all out. We had to go back to work for two more days, because nobody had copied down the schedule.

That Marshall was a man of vision. He probably had more to do with the rulebook and the league constitution, as they're now written, than any other man. He was the father of the player draft. He was the father of the divisions, of the championship game, of player limits. When he wanted to get a piece of legislation passed, he'd get up and talk and talk and talk, but if he saw he wasn't getting anywhere, if he saw he didn't have the votes, he'd suddenly say, "Forget about it. I table this thing." The league meeting would go on maybe five days or a week, all told, and we'd finally be all finished, ready to go out the door, and Marshall would say, "Oh, wait a minute. I forgot about that thing we tabled back there three or four days ago." And everybody would say, "Okay, pass it."

Back in 1938 a fellow named Lipscomb owned the Cleveland club. Cleveland was supposed to play us in Pittsburgh, but we canceled the game because of bad weather. Well, actually we canceled it because there weren't going to be any customers there. Listen, that was nothing unusual. I had other owners cancel games on *me*. This was the only one I ever called off, but this fellow Lipscomb hollered and screamed and yelled that I had to play the game. So then I had to find a place to play the game where it could draw a crowd. Lipscomb said, "Play it in Knoxville, Tennessee. That's my home town." I told him, "People are not going to come out to see *you* play. I'm not about to go to Knoxville."

So I'm looking around for a place to play when a friend of mine named Joe Engle, who was a big shot in minor-league baseball, mentions a guy by the name of Walmsley to me. Coming from The Ward, where you knew politics from the day you were able to speak, I knew who Walmsley was. In The Ward everybody knew about politics, or thought they knew about politics. I knew that Walmsley had been mayor of New Orleans until Huey Long knocked him out of the box. I also knew that a guy named Maestri was now mayor of New Orleans and was a fantastic political leader. Well, as soon as Joe Engle brought up Walmsley's name and gave me his phone number, I got on the phone.

I said to Walmsley, "If we bring this game to New Orleans, will Maestri get behind it?" I knew that if Maestri told the people, "Go!" they went. "Oh, positively. Maestri will positively get behind the game," Walmsley said.

So I gave Cleveland the extra expenses to go to New Orleans and we took the game there. Well, when I got down to New Orleans I accidentally ran into a couple of priests who were teaching at Loyola, and I asked if they were going to the game. They said, "What game?" Then they said, "Nobody in New Orleans knows about it. It must be a secret." Right away I went to Walmsley and told him, "I want to meet Maestri."

So I visited Maestri and I took Whizzer White with me. I figured Maestri might not have heard of me, but everybody had heard of Whizzer White. Well, Maestri and I talked a little bit, but right then and there I knew I was dead, because not only didn't Maestri ever hear of me or know I owned the Pittsburgh club, but he never heard of White either. In fact, he kept getting everything confused. He thought we were a college team that had come down to New Orleans to play

Tulane. He said, "I'll see what I can do." I knew our visit to Maestri didn't do us any good.

So on the day of the game I'm sitting with Walmsley in the Sugar Bowl, and nobody's at the game. Walmsley keeps telling me, "Oh, don't worry about it. Everybody comes late to a football game down here." Well, I'd been listening to that kind of stuff as long as I'd been a promoter. I said, "There's nobody going to show up here." And nobody did. The place was empty. To top it off, Cleveland beat us and the New Orleans police called me at the hotel that night and informed me they'd pinched three or four of my ballplayers for kicking over some garbage cans. I told the sergeant, "We got a train out of here at nine in the morning. You keep 'em till it's time for them to get on the train."

Last season I told the story of that New Orleans game to a luncheon in New Orleans. Ed Kiely, our publicity man, had explained to me that a football group down there wanted me to speak, so I said, "All right. But listen, I'm not much of a talker. These people will be disappointed if you're building me up as something big." Well, the speaker ahead of me was one of the New Orleans Saints' coaches, and evidently the Saints were having problems with their quarterback, Bill Kilmer. The people were on the quarterback. They asked the coach a lot of questions about him. Then I got up.

I told them, "Number one, if you're going to ask me any questions I'm going to disappoint you, because I don't know that I'm able to answer your questions. So, better that you don't ask any." But then I said, "There's one question I *could* have answered, because in Pittsburgh we're *experts* on quarterbacks. We had Sid Luckman, we had Johnny Unitas, we had Earl Morrall, we had Len Dawson, we had Jackie Kemp, and we had Bill Nelsen." I said, "Now those are all quarterbacks you know about, and we traded them all. They were all with our ball club, and we got rid of them."

Right after the war we had Bill Dudley playing for us. I believe Dudley was as good as any football player who has ever played in the National League. As a defensive back he led the league in interceptions. Coaches told their passers, "Don't throw in Dudley's territory." He had intuition. He played tailback in the single wing, and as a runner he led the league. He wasn't fast, but nobody caught him. He couldn't pass, but he completed passes. He was one of the top kickers in the game. The best all-around ballplayer I've ever seen. But our coaches used to say to me, "Well, he don't hit the hole."

I'd tell them, "I don't want him to hit the holes. If he starts hitting the holes, he'll turn the game into such a one-sided farce that nobody will come out to see us play."

Dudley was a great guy, although he had his own ideas and he was strong-willed. Our coach, Jock Sutherland, was pretty much like Dudley that way. So he traded Dudley after some sort of an argument they had. I didn't resist the trade too much, because it looked like Dudley and Sutherland were never going to be able to get along.

In the early '50s we had Jimmy Finks on our team. I think there's no telling how great Finks was. Finks might have been one of the great quarterbacks that ever played football. But he played under Walter Kiesling, and Kies had the funniest ideas. He was a big fellow, he'd been a terrific tackle. He was a tremendous coach, and not only that, a great guy. But he was really stubborn. Kies wanted to select the plays, but there were certain plays Finks didn't want to call. Both of them were stubborn. In other words, there was an argument all the time. We had Lynn Chandnois. There's no telling how great a ballcarrier he was, but Kies never thought that Chandnois put out. On the practice field, maybe he didn't. All I know is when it came time in a game, he was great. So one day we played the Giants and Chandnois ran back two kickoffs for touchdowns, over ninety yards each time. And the first thing Kies said after the game was, "Can you imagine that lucky bum!"

We had Unitas in for a tryout, but Kies let him go. He said, "He can't remember the plays. He's dumb." See, you had to know Kies. He thought a lot of ballplayers were dumb. We were arguing about a guy one day, and I said, "I don't care how dumb he is. He can run and he can pass and he can block. If he can do those three things, he don't have to be a Rhodes scholar." But all Kies said to that was "He's dumb." Kies was a great coach, but everything with Kies was that nobody knew football *better* than Kies.

Our players once went on strike over Kies. They were in Boston for a game when I got a call at home. I flew up to Boston and listened to their beef, which was that Kies worked them too hard. I didn't say a word till the ballplayers finished talking. Then I said, "I just want to tell you this—Kies might be tough and all of that, but I want you to know that you are never going to make a greater friend in your life than you'll have in Kiesling." I said, "He's honest, he's sincere, he gives everybody a square shake. He does have peculiarities, like we all have, and he hollers if he doesn't think you're giving everything you've got. But loyalty? I guarantee you that you're going to make a loyal friend of this man and you'll respect and love him for the rest of your life. That's it. I have nothing else to say, only that he is the coach and he's going to stay the coach, and before you're finished, just what I've told you is what you're going to think of this man." Which they did. The majority of them did.

So over the years it's been one thing or another. It's bad that we've never won a championship. I feel terrible about it.

There isn't anyone in Pittsburgh or anyone in professional football who hurts as much as I do. But what am I going to do about it? I don't know. I just don't know.

We made trades that turned out bad. I let the coaches make the trades. The only trade I ever made personally was one night in 1939 when I was drinking beer with Dan Topping, who owned the old Brooklyn Dodgers. I traded him Sam Francis for Boyd Brumbaugh, one back for another. It turned out a great trade for us. That was the only trade I ever made, and we made it because we were both drinking beer.

I think that was my whole mistake, letting the coaches have a free hand. I'm positively *sure* that had I run my ball club, like George Marshall ran his ball club, we would have won championship after championship. I was *able*. I was competent. Knowing football, knowing football material, and knowing what was what, I'm sure that if I would have said, "We're not gonna do that, and you can like it or get out"— if I'd have said that, I'm positively *sure* we would have won championships. But I can't change now. I'm too old to change.

Have I ever had any idea of selling the club? No, never. My boys are grown now, and they like the business. Losing kept down our crowds, that's true, but money has never been my god—never. I've had opportunities to move the franchise. I've had tremendous offers. Back in the early 1950s I could have moved to Baltimore, and then later, to Buffalo, Atlanta, New Orleans, Cincinnati. The propositions they made were fantastic. So if you didn't have ties, if you didn't care for your city and its people, if you were just looking for wealth, you could have picked up and gone. But that's not you, not if you care for your city. And I believe Pittsburgh is a great city. I believe if we win, we'll do as good as we would in probably any of those other towns.

Well, when you lose you're so dumb you don't know enough to come out of the rain. All losers are dumb. All winners are sharp. When you win, you know all the answers. I don't know all the answers, so maybe we *are* dumb. But we've tried. We hired Buddy Parker, a top coach. He came to us with a big reputation, not many coaches sharper, and he was a good man. But he was here eight years, and still we didn't win. We hired Bill Austin, who came just as highly recommended as could be, by none other than Vince Lombardi, who we know would tell us the right thing. Okay, we didn't win with Austin. Now we come up with a new man, Chuck Noll, who came from Baltimore, a championship club, with a reputation that's just as good as can possibly be.

We *pay*. I think Buddy Parker, when he was here, may have been one of the highest-priced coaches who ever worked in this league. The papers said eighty thousand a year. It was more. When we make trades, we don't ask what does a player get. Until now—and I don't know how long this will continue, because times are changing—but until now, we've never had a ballplayer here who's played out his option. What I'm telling you is that we've tried. But I want you to know, and I want the town to know, that I'm not alibiing. I'm not crying. I've just told you our side. Who's interested in losers' alibis?

10

DON HUTSON

The five-dollar bidding war

In Racine, Wisconsin, twenty miles south of Milwaukee on the Lake Michigan shoreline, Don Hutson's automobile agency sprawls along the edge of the water downtown, row upon row of inventory glistening. As a Green Bay Packer end from 1935 through 1945, Hutson was a pass receiver whose agility and deft hands elevated pass catching to an art that nobody prior to his time had thought possible. But from the moment he entered pro football he regarded the game merely as a means to an end. The son of a Pine Bluff, Arkansas, railroad conductor, he had studied business administration at the University of Alabama and, upon signing with Green Bay, resolved that he would live the year 'round on what money he could earn at off-season jobs, all the while banking his football salary with a view to establishing himself in business. His first years in Green Bay, he lived with his wife, a former Alabama co-ed, in a ten-dollar-a-week hotel room.

When I visited Racine, he had just returned from his Palm Springs vacation home. Lean, tanned, and stylish in a subdued sports ensemble, he walked with a markedly bowlegged, pigeon-toed stride, sort of rising to his toes with each step. One could see that on the football field he had been a figure of considerable personal style. We lunched at his country club, then retired to his office to continue the conversation.

Many contend that to this day there has never been a pass

receiver Hutson's equal, their view being supported by the fact that despite the modern-day obsession with passing, he still holds no fewer than seven NFL performance records as football enters the 1970 season. Throughout his career, opponents assigned two, and often as many as three, men to cover him, yet he would feint them off their feet or catch a touchdown pass one-handed while swinging from a goalpost with the other hand. Against the Detroit Lions he once scored four touchdowns and kicked five extra points for a total of twenty-nine points—all of them in a single quarter.

Curly Lambeau, the owner-coach of the Packers, often wondered if Hutson had a nerve in his body. He approached crucial games as calmly as if they were practice sessions. His wife once remarked that at their wedding one would have thought from his casual manner that he had stepped into the church merely to get out of the rain. Outwardly he appeared unconcerned by the imminence of punishing blows. He wore no hip pads. He stripped down his shoulder pads to the barest simplicity, lest he lose a half-step of speed or an iota of maneuverability. Scarcely padded, his 185-pound frame appeared frail alongside the pros. He was, in fact, too light to play end on defense, but he survived at the position for two years, at last rescued by a decision to transfer him to safety.

As a boy in Pine Bluff, Hutson had been an Eagle Scout (the first in the state of Arkansas, he believes), but he had played only one season of high-school football. A neighbor youth being recruited by Alabama asked that the coaches take Hutson as well, whereupon they agreed to scholarship him on a trial basis. At Alabama he came to innovate new pass-catching techniques and in his senior year, 1934, played for an undefeated team that capped the season with a Rose Bowl victory over Stanford. The pros wanted Hutson, and because the player draft was a procedure that would not come into being until a year hence, there ensued in the winter and spring of 1935 a bidding war for his services that was doggedly competitive and yet, as the reader will see, a far cry from the damn-the-expense battles on which college seniors would capitalize in a later time.

I had offers from all the pro teams to come and try out, but it narrowed down to Brooklyn and Green Bay. Those were the teams that were bidding—if you can call it bidding—for my services. The strange thing is that until I started receiving letters from Curly Lambeau, I had given no thought at all to playing pro football. None at all. I'd never heard of the Green Bay Packers. Down in Alabama there was nothing in the papers about pro football. They didn't even have the results in the papers. It was a whole different country down there. For example, the first tavern I ever saw was when I got to Green Bay.

Anyhow, Shipwreck Kelly, who owned the Brooklyn team, came to see me at Alabama and said, would I agree that I wouldn't sign with anybody else without giving him a chance to bid? I said yes, I would agree to that. So the bidding started —at around eighty dollars per game, or somewhere around that figure. And it rose in five-dollar jumps. Every time Curly would call me and raise his price five dollars a game, I would call Shipwreck collect in Brooklyn, and he would say, "That's all right, I'll meet that offer."

Finally, Curly's offer got up to $175, which was far above anything that anybody was making or ever had been making in Green Bay. I tried to phone Shipwreck, but his office said he wasn't there and they didn't know where he was. So I sent him a wire, thinking they might forward it to him, you know, but I didn't hear from him. I sent him two or three more wires within the next couple of days, but still I didn't hear from him. So when Curly called me to see where things stood, I said, "All right, fine. I'll sign." The next day, I received the contract air mail. I signed it and put it in the mail. About an hour later, Shipwreck showed up.

He said, "What's happening?" He explained that he had been down in Florida and had left word with his office that he didn't want to be disturbed, but finally the office, as I recall, had sent him my telegram or told him about it and he hurried right up to Tuscaloosa. Shipwreck said, "I think the least you can do under the circumstances is to sign the same contract with me that you signed with Lambeau."

"That's probably right," I told him. I said, "I *did* promise you a chance to meet his offer, so I'll sign with you, too, and let somebody else decide where I'm going to play."

That's what I did, and I called Curly to tell him about it. I didn't want to be underhanded about this thing. I told him what had happened and what I had done, and he said, "That's perfectly all right. You just leave it to me."

Joe Carr was president of the league at the time, with headquarters in Columbus, Ohio. And as far as I know, a case like this had never come up, so there was no way of knowing how Carr would settle it. Anyhow, as soon as Curly got my contract he mailed it to Carr. It was delivered to Carr's office the same day that my contract with Shipwreck arrived there, but the Green Bay contract got there just ahead of the other. So on that basis, Carr's ruling was that I would go to Green Bay. And that was a very fortunate thing for me, because in Arnie Herber, Green Bay had by far the best passer in the league and one of the greatest long passers that ever played. He was a honey. And as I was to discover playing against Brooklyn, the Dodgers had no pass offense at all. No passer at all. So it just shows you how things can happen. I weighed only 185 pounds, and on defense I hadn't played very satisfactorily at Alabama. I had made my reputation as a pass receiver. If I'd gone to Brooklyn, I might not have lasted that first year.

Most of the regulars at Green Bay were making a hundred dollars a game in 1935, and the ones that weren't playing regular were making seventy-five. Curly didn't want the players to know that I was making $175, so every week I would get two checks, one for one hundred and the other for seventy-five. The two checks were drawn on different banks. You see, in Green Bay everybody knew everybody's business. The people who worked at the banks might leak the word on the size of my check, so Curly split it up with two banks so that the most I appeared to be making was one hundred dollars.

When I first came up from Alabama I knew nothing about pro football, of course, but I was never one for being nervous —not even in the beginning. There was no question in my mind but what I could play offensive football. But in those days football teams had no use for a one-way player, so I did wonder a little about how I would do on defense. I'd say our pro ends weighed at least 205 pounds, or somewhere along in there, and the pros were generally bigger- and tougher-looking than any football players I had ever seen. They were a pretty tough lot, there's no getting around that.

The players shook hands with me when I reported after the College All-Star game, but they were not overjoyed to see me. They were not at all enthused. Before they accepted you on any kind of a social basis, they were going to see if you could make the team. And in my case, they didn't think I was big enough. No question about it—they didn't think I had a chance.

Furthermore, there was a Green Bay businessman, a butcher named Emmett Platten, who bought fifteen minutes of radio time every Sunday and went on the air just before the Packer games and spent most of the fifteen minutes making critical comments about the Packers. There was tremendous interest in what he had to say, because he was controversial. The players would sit in the dressing room and listen to his program before they went out on the field. Well, we were opening the season at home against the Chicago Bears—I hadn't played in the exhibition games, so this was my first pro game—and Platten spent the entire fifteen minutes of radio time that day saying what a dumb thing Lambeau had done by signing me.

I'll have to admit I didn't like that. It did nothing to improve my frame of mind. But I wasn't nervous. As I said, I was never one for being nervous.

Finally the game started and the Packers brought the kickoff out to the seventeen-yard line. Right there, we lined up for a play that we had practiced for a week. I lined up split out to the left just a few yards. Johnny Blood lined up 'way out to the right. He had been one of the leading receivers in the league for many years, so, of course, *if* we were going to pass, the Bears thought we would pass to Blood. But he was a decoy. He went down as the decoy, and I went down and faked outside to take the halfback out, and then I cut back over the middle and got behind the safety man. Herber let the ball go. It was a forty-yard pass, I suppose, but it was an eighty-three-yard gain, good for a touchdown, and it had worked just like in practice. It was a simple play, but the fact that it was a long pass on the first play made it a surprise. That just wasn't done in those days. At any rate, after that first play, my first pro play, there wasn't any question anymore about my being able to play.

No, I was never very emotional about football, but I loved the game just the same. It's just that I hardly ever lose my temper or become excited about things. There have been many times here when we've had several hundreds of thousands of dollars in used cars outside and the snow was three feet deep, and you wondered what was going to happen with 'em. Well, there's no point in worrying. You can't look out there and make that snow melt, and you can't make people come here and buy those cars when they can't even get out of their houses because of the snow. I'll try something of a promotional nature—I'll do everything I can to alleviate the situation—but after that, I might just as well go home and nonchalantly go to sleep. And I won't have any problem going to sleep because I've done the best I can, and that's all there is to it.

You know, when you said you were coming out here to see me, I wondered what I might tell you that would be of reader interest. Actually, I don't think I'm much of a subject for you. I'm sorry that I'm not, but I can't tell you a lot of things that are particularly interesting, and there's no point in my telling you things that aren't true. Please understand that I was never an especially colorful personality. One story that came to mind, however, deals with how I happened to run on the college track team. It's a little bit interesting.

The man who coached the ends at Alabama was Red Drew, who also was the track coach, and while we were having spring training one year, he said to me, "After we finish practice, I'm going over to work with the track team. I don't have anybody over there to run against my dash man, so I wish you'd come over and run with him after practice."

I said I'd be very happy to. As nearly as I can recall, we didn't have a high-school track team back in Pine Bluff, but I went over to give this fellow some competition and I beat him by about five yards the first time. So Red Drew said, "From now on, you're our hundred-yard-dash man." I ran the hundred in 9.7. Jesse Owens' world record at the time was, I believe, 9.4.

I suppose it's partially right, as you say, that in football I did things that had little or no precedent. I believe that I went in more for the faking—more for the deception—than previous pass receivers had. Until then, catching passes had been, I think, just a question of running your patterns, and of speed. Alabama is where I started the faking thing. It was a question of thinking about fakes and trying, with encouragement from my coaches, to come up with something new as far as fakes were concerned. Now one of the things that I remember deciding was that fakes should be run at sharp angles, not in soft circles or waves. Curly Lambeau once told me that he had been out to California and watched our Alabama team practice for the Rose Bowl—he had got into practice because he'd gone to Notre Dame with our head coach, Frank Thomas—and he said that it was the first time he'd ever seen fakes run at sharp angles. He was very enthused. He thought it was great. You see, the natural thing is to run a fake in a curve—smooth and flowing. But you don't get real faking that way. Yet I still see a lot of receivers running fakes in curves. A lot of 'em aren't, but a lot of 'em are.

You know, I saw Sam Baugh in New York this year, and we started talking about pass patterns and agreed that patterns are one of the few things in football that haven't been changed. The routes the receivers and decoys run are just about what they were when we played. I suppose there's just so much innovation you can come up with and that's the end of it. The only thing that's really different now is the names they give passes. It's amusing—yes, it is. They have a thing they call a fly pattern. In my day we just called it forty-three or seventy-seven, or something like that. We just had a number for it. When we were talking to a fan, a layman, we just described how the pass was run. We didn't give it a nickname. Now they talk about a fly pattern or a swing or a buttonhook, or whatever it is. I don't know why. I don't understand it at all.

My last pro season was 1945, and it was very apparent by then that offense was gaining in popularity all the time. You were getting more great college passers all the time. I welcomed this, and I think the fans did. It's been a great thing for spectators to see offense develop the way it has. Two-platoon football also has been a great thing for the spectator, because the players haven't played all day and you see them at their best, although I don't understand why receivers have to leave the game for a rest after they've run a long pattern. You wonder if they're in shape. You can't help but wonder. After all, they're only playing about fifteen minutes the whole day.

Anyhow, when I quit football I was thirty-one and still on top—I made the all-pro team my last season. I could have played another four, five years, I suppose, but I was in the bowling-alley business by then and it was the right time to quit. In the first place, I wanted to quit while I was still on top. And secondly, I knew I had lost a couple of steps. Also, I was fortunate to have played eleven years without being hurt, and I figured my luck had been stretched far enough. So even before the 1945 season started, I told the club that I was going to quit. I had been trying to for a couple of years, but this time I had built up for it and was going to make it stick.

So that was the end of my playing career, and as I told you, I'm sorry that I don't have more to tell you that would help your book, but I just don't have much that would be of reader interest. You know, one year a fellow visited our training camp to write a story about me for *The Saturday Evening Post.* Cece Isbell was our quarterback at the time, and when the story came out in the magazine it said that Isbell and I played well together but that off the field we weren't speaking. It said we had nothing to do with one another once the game or the practice was over. Well, I was pretty upset about that. As a matter of fact, only that year my wife and I had accompanied the Isbells on their honeymoon. We'd gone to Honolulu together. Cece was furious over the magazine story. He wanted to sue. I telephoned the writer and he said, "Yes, I feel very badly about that part of the article. But see, the first time I turned in the story, the editors sent it back and told me, 'There's nothing there. We can't buy this story.' So I put in that stuff about you and Isbell not speaking and made a sale."

11

TUFFY LEEMANS

"My name is Alphonse . . . but it never took."

In New York, the late 1930s were a time when the pros were becoming familiar sports-page names. Bent on respectability, New York Giant players no longer boarded public transportation wearing football jerseys. They decked themselves splendidly in coats and ties. In 1938 the Giants, with a backfield that included Tuffy Leemans and the dangerous Ward Cuff, met and defeated the Green Bay Packers for the NFL championship before a Polo Grounds crowd of 48,120, the largest turnout yet for a championship game. The advertising industry began to show an interest in pro ballplayers, though it must be said that the players received little more than a taste—literally, a taste—of the rewards that Madison Avenue would shower upon a later generation of Giants. "I advertised Wheaties," Leemans told me, "and was paid off in Wheaties." He also endorsed a line of pipes, but inasmuch as he was not in the habit of smoking one, Tuffy gave his remuneration—fifty assorted pipes—to his father.

An illustrious Giant halfback (1936–43) and a native of Wisconsin, Leemans had come to New York by way of George Washington University. He later settled in the Washington area, where he is in bowling and dry-cleaning businesses. At his Glenmont Lanes in suburban Wheaton, Maryland, I found him now to be a stout man with a heavy shock of gray hair. He appeared somewhat rumpled and unnerved, for a pump had broken down and flooded an area near the snack bar. With a sigh he closed the door of his office and settled behind a broad, cluttered desk. A little silver-gray schnauzer named Ruble—surely a curious companion for a man called Tuffy—settled affectionately at his feet while we talked. The old star said he was surprised and pleased that I had remembered his career and thought to look him up.

The only trouble with being a pro-football player in New York was that you were bored to death. You had too much leisure time on your hands. We didn't have all those meetings they have today. We'd go to practice about 9:30 in the morning and be back at 12:30, and we wouldn't have another thing to do until the next day. Oh, sure, New York was the big city, but your ballplayers weren't making enough money to be whooping it up all the time. And I never was one for a lot of hard liquor. I never did care for it too much.

The Giant ballplayers lived together at the Hotel Whitehall, up at 100th Street and Broadway. Not every player lived there—there were a lot of them that weren't making enough dough. But a number of us lived there, rooming together. My second year, I got married and got a place there with a little kitchen and maid service, but as a matter of fact, my wife also was bored with New York. She said, "My God, there's nothing to do here."

You had no television. You'd got to a movie or go bowling. On Monday, once in a while, we'd get ahold of a businessman who had a boat and we'd go deep-sea fishing out beyond the New York harbor. I imagine that up in Green Bay, with so much more outdoor life available, it must have been wonderful to be a football player, but in New York there wasn't a whole lot you could do. One season I helped coach a high-school team.

Steve Owen, our coach, used to give us his annual talk on the who's and where's and why's of New York City. He would tell us, "Now, listen. You boys are coming in here with your straw hats still tied to your shoulder. There are sharp fellows around who can spot you. Now if you're standing on a corner and a fellow rushes up to you and says, 'I've got to get rid of this thousand-dollar mink coat, and I'll give it to you for forty dollars,' don't buy it. Or if a fellow says, 'I've got a beautiful watch for your wife,' don't buy that, either. I'm telling you this, and I know it to be true, because I got stuck that way myself."

Steve was a tough coach but fair as hell. If you went to him and asked for a raise, he'd say, "I never bother with money. That is not my department. Don't come to me. But if they ask me if I need you, I will tell them I do." Well, this was all he had to do, and you got your raise. Yes, he was a very fair man. His famous saying to the squad was, "I only ask one thing of you guys. I want your ass for one hour of playing time every Sunday." He would tell me, "Tuffy, keep playing out there till you can't keep going any longer, then put up your hand and I'll get you out of there." I'd have that hand up in the air so long that I felt like my arm would fall off.

Oh, cripe!—it was nothing for Steve Owen to say to us after we'd just lost a game, "Well, boys, we're going to work a little bit now." So right there, right after the game was over, we'd practice. One time we went at it for two and a half hours. Knocked heads all the way.

When I was a kid playing ball in Superior, Wisconsin, I probably had a little more heart than the ordinary kid, and I wasn't afraid to stick my nose in where it was rough. As a matter of fact, that's how I picked up the name Tuffy. After I'd dumped a couple of older kids, a couple of big boys, why, they started to call me Tuffy and it stuck. I tried to shake that name because, well, you know how it sounds. My first name really is Alphonse. Naturally you'd want to change that right away, so I kept calling myself Al, but it never took. People would keep calling me Tuffy, and even today I don't know of anyone who comes to this bowling alley that don't call me Tuffy.

I still remember the day of my first professional-football game. I had just played in the 1936 College All-Star game in Chicago and had been voted the outstanding player in the game. The College All-Stars had had beautiful training equipment and five or six trainers. God, I was living like a king. So now I'm with the Giants and we're in New Rochelle, New York, for an exhibition game against, I believe, the New Rochelle Bulldogs, who were a pickup team. We were going to be playing at the local high school, and before the game, in the high-school dressing room there, I piped up and said, "I have very bad ankles and I'd like to have 'em taped."

Well, Len Grant, one of our tackles, said to me, "Oh, you want your ankles taped?"

I said, "Yes. You know, they're very weak, and I'd like to have them taped."

Grant said, "Fine. Just as soon as I get through with this roll of tape I'll throw it over to you." I had to tape my own ankles! We didn't even have a trainer. In those days, if you wanted to get rid of a charley horse, there was only one method they knew of. They would take a broom handle and roll it out. They would lay you down on a table and roll that broom handle over your thigh. You'd have tears in your eyes as big as lemons.

In my rookie year I led the league in rushing, so of course

the front office took pretty good care of me. They signed me to a real good contract, about eight thousand dollars, but with Tim Mara, who owned the Giants, you really never needed a contract. His word always held good. One year I got hurt pretty badly and New York paid my salary in the hospital, which I understand was the kind of situation in which some of the fellows around the league had a tough time collecting. Tim Mara was a white-haired, curly-haired Irishman with a brogue. I don't think he'd gone very far through school. But he enjoyed everything he ever did, and win or lose, there was no long face on him. My best friend was the old man.

But getting back to Steve Owen, *there* was a coach who gave you instructions and expected you to follow them. And in that connection, here's an amusing story that'll be a good thing for your book. We were playing the Redskins at Washington. It was 1942, I believe, toward the end of my career. We did not have a great football team because the war was on and we had some wartime ballplayers. I myself was just playing out my time, waiting to be called into the Navy V-12 program about the fifteenth of November. (As it turned out, several weeks later I was almost killed by a blow to the head in a game with the Chicago Bears, and the injury put me out of kilter real bad and kept me out of the service. As a result of that blow, I have no hearing out of one ear.) Anyhow, we went into Washington and Steve Owen said to me, "I don't want you to throw any passes. I don't want you ever to throw the ball in this game." I was the guy who called the plays, see? I called signals from my halfback position.

Steve said to me, "I want you to play conservative and kick on third down if you have to. This is a pretty good club we're up against, so we've got to play for breaks." He was a great percentage player, Steve was.

Well, we come out for the game, and Jesus! Here over

Griffith Stadium is the darkest cloud you've ever seen. You know from the looks of that cloud that the damn thing is going to let loose and rain all day. So on our first play from scrimmage, I go into the huddle and say to our center, Mel Hein, and a few of the other oldtimers, "Jesus, it's going to rain like hell. I think I'm going to fake a reverse to Cuff and run him wide and see what that Redskin halfback over there does. And if he does what I hope he will, then I'm going to pitch that ball to Willie Walls."

"Geez," Mel Hein says. "Don't start throwing. If they pick one off, Steve will blow his top."

"Mel," I say to him. "It's going to *rain*. We might as well take a chance now."

I told Willie Walls to head straight down and to the outside. Then I ran War Cuff wide on the fake, and this Redskin halfback—Steve Juzwick from Notre Dame, I believe it was —he comes barreling up there to stop Cuff. By the time Juzwick recovers, Walls is out there behind him. I throw that ball to Walls on the Washington thirty-yard line, and he goes the rest of the way. It's a fifty-yard touchdown play that puts us ahead, 7-0. And now it rains. It rains and it rains and it rains.

Washington scores in the second quarter to make it 7-7, but practically the whole game is being played in the middle of the field. And then, in the third quarter, one of our ends by the name of O'Neal Adams drops off on one of their flat passes and picks it off and goes sixty-five yards for a touchdown. We beat the Redskins, 14-7, but now I want you to listen to this. This is almost unbelievable. Our team never made a first down. We gained fifty yards on that touchdown pass I threw, and besides that, we gained exactly one yard. One yard rushing. The Redskins, meanwhile, gained more than a hundred yards rushing and more than a hundred passing, but we beat 'em, 14-7. We didn't do a thing but win. After the game, Steve Owen said to me, "I thought I told you not to throw." He then fined me fifty bucks for throwing that touchdown pass.

12

SAMMY BAUGH

"If they could cripple you, fine."

Although professional football has been intensively souped up since his time, Slingin' Sammy Baugh's name still appears in the record book in more than a dozen places. Starting in 1937, he lasted sixteen years (only one less than Lou Groza, who owed his record longevity to the easy life of a place-kicking specialist), and is held by many to have been the finest passer of his, or any other, time. Over the course of one season, for example, he completed 70.3 percent of his passes. His leg as potent as his whiplike arm, he holds every punting record in the book. But above all, he gave to pro football a radical concept that he had learned from his college coach, Dutch Meyer—namely, that the forward pass could be more than just a surprise weapon or a desperation tactic. Sammy Baugh made the pass a routine scrimmage play.

On a vast plain in West Texas, an hour north of Sweetwater, he lives at the foot of Double Mountain, which in the dusk of late winter wears a grayish cast, rising out of the flatland like two great mounds orphaned from an alien topography. The ranch house, comfortable but inexpensively furnished, belies Baugh's substantial holdings. He came to the door wearing blue jeans and a western-style shirt of country-store fabric, a Gary Cooper quality in his appearance. Six-foot-two and rawboned, he was a leathery man with hips that were remarkably lean. At fifty-five he weighed only 170 pounds—at least five pounds under his football weight. His hands were immense and obviously powerful. But incongruously—and perhaps this was partly because he wore bedroom slippers—he walked with the sort of swishing gait associated with chorus boys. In the mind's eye, one again could see him dropping back to pass, his legs jiggling comically as though controlled by marionette strings.

Baugh seated himself on the living-room sofa and placed a large mug on the coffee table in front of him, from time to time raising the mug to his face and shooting a squirt of tobacco into it. His language was earthy, yet somehow not the least bit harsh or bellicose. On the contrary, he seemed a gentle man, almost diffident, and he spoke in a barely audible voice, although now and then, when a thought struck him funny, his voice would rise, his face would fold into a hundred merry wrinkles, and his mouth would be parted by an almost-toothless guffaw.

The thing that hurt when I first came into pro football in 1937, and it hurt all the boys that threw the ball, was that the rules didn't give any protection to passers. Those linemen could hit the passer until the whistle blew. If you completed a pass out there and somebody's running fifty yards with that ball, well, that damn bunch could still hit you. In other words, a passer had to learn to throw and *move*. You would never see him just throw and stand there looking. You had to throw and start protecting yourself, because those son-of-a-bitch linemen were going to lay you right flatter than that ground every time.

If you were a good ballplayer—a passer or whatever—they tried to hurt you and get you out of there. I believe they did that more so than today, really. See, we had only twenty-two or twenty-three men on a squad, and your ballplayers were playing both ways, offense and defense—so if you lost two good ones, you were dead. Well, every now and then they'd run what they called a "bootsie" play, and everybody'd hit one man and just try to tear him to pieces. If they could cripple you, fine. I don't mean they ran this kind of play very often, but if they came up against a guy that was giving them a lot of trouble, they'd run a bootsie play every now and then and just stay after him.

Like I said, the passers never could relax after they threw that damn ball. Nowadays if a guy is not already in the *act* of hitting you when that ball goes in the air, he's not allowed to hit you. But back there when I started in pro ball, it was just like a boxing match—you were just goddamn dodging and ducking and hitting. It looked awful at times. Some games it wouldn't bother you any at all. But other games, goddang it, it looked awful. For some reason, they didn't stay after you in college football like they did in pro, but in pro the coaches—and our coach had said the same thing—the coaches said, "Put that son-of-a-bitch passer on the ground every time he throws that ball." That was just a cardinal rule all through the league.

My first year, Mr. Marshall talked to me and told me, "If we don't get some kind of a rule in, all the passers are gonna get killed." The first game of my second year, I went down under a pile and got a shoulder knocked out—a shoulder separation. And I guess it was my third year in pro ball, 1939, that we got the rule protecting the passer.

Another thing that later helped men like me was the T formation. I had played seven years of tailback in the single wing, and it about killed me, blocking on that end, carrying the ball a few times, and stuff like that. I weighed only 175 or maybe 178 pounds. After every game my shoulder ached like hell. But when Mr. Marshall decided to go to the T formation in 1944, I didn't like it at first.

Marshall brought in Clark Shaughnessy to teach us the T, and that year we were the most uncomfortable ball club you ever saw. The blocking was all different. In the single wing you had a lot of double-teaming and stuff like that, but in the T you had a lot of single blocking—man-on-man blocking. And taking that ball from center, handing it to somebody, faking it some—that was very uncomfortable to me. But Shaughnessy had been with the Bears and he told me that when he started teaching the T to Sid Luckman, Sid cried over the damn thing. It was hard for him, but he developed into a real good T quarterback. So Shaughnessy told me, "Don't worry about it—it'll come to you gradually where you'll love it under there." Sure enough, after about half that season was gone, I wouldn't have gone back to single wing for anything.

Football was sure changing by then. Back in the '30s it was more of a defensive game. In other words, when you picked your starters, they usually had to be good on defense first. Take the New York Giants. Hell, they had such a good defensive ball club that they wouldn't mind punting to you on the third down from practically anywhere. They'd kick the ball to you 'cause they didn't think by God you was going to move it.

Matter of fact, when I was a boy in Sweetwater, Texas, I used to practice more kicking than I did throwing, really. Punting was a very important thing then. But we kicked different than they do now. We were taught to kick out of bounds all the time. If you didn't, that safety man would run that ball back down your throat, because your offensive line couldn't cover a punt like they do today. We had that short punt formation where you kicked from only nine yards back, so your boys didn't release till they heard the thud of that ball. Today, on that deep punt formation, the center throws that ball back and everybody hits and goes.

Well, in the summertime I used to go up on the football field by myself and kick for hours at a time. I'd kick at those sidelines and then run down and get the ball and kick it back. And especially after I got into college at Texas Christian University and played for Dutch Meyer, I worked at it till I got where I could kick that ball out of bounds inside the five- or the ten-yard line pretty good. In the very first Cotton Bowl game, on New Year's Day, 1937, we played Marquette, and they had Art Guepe, who later coached at Vanderbilt. He was a cocky little boy, Art Guepe was, but a dangerous little boy. Dutch told me, "Whatever you do, don't kick that ball to Guepe. Kick it out of bounds or he'll run it back."

So I was kicking that ball out of bounds, and every time Guepe would pass our bench he'd say to Dutch, "Dutch, tell Sam to kick that ball to me." And all during that game, Dutch would tell me, "Don't kick it to him." But somewhere along the line, I didn't get that ball out of bounds, and that son of a bitch ran it back. We won the game, 16-6, but I remember him going over the goal line with that punt and throwing that ball as high as he could and jumping up and down, and I don't know if we ever laid a hand on that little pisser or not.

I had played baseball all my life, and that's what I wanted to be in the beginning—a professional baseball player. A fellow I played semi-pro ball with was going to get me a baseball scholarship to Washington State University, but I hurt my knee about a month a'fore I was supposed to go. I was sliding into second base and caught a spike and tore up the cartilage. Well, if it'd happened today, they'd operate, but back in those days they didn't know too damn much about knees. The doctor told me to use a mud pack. I put a mud pack with vinegar on my knee. But I couldn't straighten it out, and the scholarship to Washington State fell through.

Dutch Meyer told me he'd get me a job and help me through T.C.U. if I'd come there and play baseball and football and basketball and the whole thing, 'cause I'd played them all in high school. So that's where I went. My freshman and sophomore years at T.C.U., we taped that knee all the time. But I never did have a real good movement, and finally I told them I wasn't going to tape the knee anymore. So we just quit taping the thing, and it never did bother me the rest of the time I was there.

In the spring of my last year, George Marshall brought me to Washington and offered me four thousand dollars, I believe, to play with the Redskins. Down here in Texas, no one knew anything about pro football. Hell, they didn't know what it was. I didn't know if I could make it in pro football, and since Dutch Meyer had offered me a job as freshman coach, I told Mr. Marshall I thought I was going to stay in Texas and coach. Actually, I still wanted to be a baseball player, but I wanted a coaching job to fall back on, because you don't ever know whether you're going to be good enough to play pro. Friend, let me tell you—there's never been a son of a bitch go up there that hasn't had a few doubts.

Anyway, the summer after I got out of college I played third base in a semi-pro tournament in Denver, and Rogers Hornsby, who was scouting for the St. Louis Cardinals, saw me there and signed me to a Cardinal contract for the following year. Now a week or so after *that*, I went to Chicago to play in the College All-Star football game against Green Bay. I talked with the rest of the boys on the All-Star squad and found that a bunch of them were going to play pro football. I found that most of them were just like me—that they hadn't been out of the county too often themselves—and that I could play ball better than 99 percent of them. So I became a little more confident about whether I could or couldn't play pro football. And as it turned out, we beat Green Bay, and then Mr. Marshall got after me pretty hot.

I didn't know how much pro players were making, but I thought they were making pretty good money. So I asked for eight thousand dollars and finally got it. Later, I felt like a robber when I found out what Cliff Battles and some of those other good football players were making. I'll tell you what the highest priced boys in Washington were getting the year before—just a few thousand dollars! Three of them were getting that—Cliff Battles, Turk Edwards, and Wayne Millner. And all of 'em in the Hall of Fame now. If I had known what they were getting, I'd have never asked for eight thousand. But Mr. Marshall never did tell me, "Well, so-and-so is only making so much." He never did say that, and I thought more of him because he hadn't.

Marshall always treated me fair. If he ever told me something, I could depend on it. But he was kind of a ruthless man with other people. He was a businessman, and I guess he had to be that way, but I didn't like the way he sometimes treated other people and I told him so one day. He had fired the trainer a'fore the season was over, although I don't really know why. The trainer was a real fine man who had done a lot for the ball club, so I was disappointed in Marshall and I told him so. He said it was the coach who let the trainer go. I don't know. I imagine it was, but really, I don't know for sure.

Marshall was hard on a lot of players. Cliff Battles led the league in ground gaining a few years a'fore I got there, and when I got there, he led the league for the second time. He was the best damn ballcarrier in the league. He had a knack of following his blockers better than any man I'd seen at that time. He could run punts back, catch passes—he was just a real good athlete. Everybody in the league liked him. They'd knock hell out of him, and he'd just grin at 'em and go on. Anyway, he wanted a small raise, but Marshall wouldn't give it to him. So Cliff said, "Well, I'm quitting then." He had a lot of ball left in him, but he quit pro football.

Well, most men played pro football in those days because they liked football. A lot of players today say they only play for the money, but even now, it's not all money. I don't give a damn if salaries went on back down, they'd still play.

Of course, *nobody* was making a lot of money out of football in the '30s. The owners weren't making money. That's why I'll always think a lot of Marshall and George Halas and Art Rooney and those kind of people—they stayed in there when it was rough. They stayed with it and made a great game out of it. I went with the Redskins the year Marshall moved them from Boston to Washington, and in Boston he had lost money every year—all five years. People weren't making money with football, but it was more fun than it is now. I really think it was, because everything was *growing*.

But hell, I'm not one of those that says ballplayers were better in the old days. I really don't know if I could do as well today as I did then. The best ballplayers are playing *today*, and I'll tell you the difference. Now really, if you want to get right down to it, your big difference is your colored ballplayer. Your colored ballplayers have helped make football a lot better. You just stop and think how many colored boys you got playing pro ball now. So if they can beat out the white boy now, there's some that could have beaten him a long time ago, too.

I told you a while back that I had signed to play baseball for the St. Louis Cardinals even a'fore I signed with Mr.

Marshall. But I wasn't supposed to report for baseball till the next year, and in the meantime, in my first year of pro football, we beat the Chicago Bears for the championship and then went barnstorming with them and played them three exhibition games. We ended up in Miami the last part of January, I guess, and I got a sternum bone torn loose in that ballgame. In the spring I went to baseball training camp, but I couldn't take a cut at the ball. I couldn't really throw like I should have. I played that season at Columbus and at Rochester, but I was just taking about a three-quarter swing at the dang ball. And anyway, I had a lot of trouble with the curve and I couldn't hit the change-up worth a damn. Well, I would have been glad to stay with it if I didn't have a choice, but I could see where I could get further in football.

Of all the years I played for Washington, the early years were the ones when we did best. In the first nine years, we played in the championship game five times. And you know, the best group of boys we ever had was the same group that got beaten 73-0 by the Bears in that 1940 championship game. Dick Todd, Wilbur Moore, Frank Filchock in the backfield, and oh, that Steve Slivinski at guard, and Wee Willie Wilkin at tackle—that group of boys was really the best team I played on. In other words, I figured we were about the same kind of ball club as the Bears were, getting right down to it.

I've got my own ideas about what happened in that championship game, and I don't know whether they'd be right or not, but I think it starts with the fact that we had played the Bears three weeks earlier and had beat them, 7-3. Boy, it hurt 'em. Leaving the field, both teams had to go down the same steps, and I remember some of those Bears were crying. Oh, they were cut to pieces. Their pride was hurt bad. I remember Bulldog Turner coming down those steps and saying, "You just remember one thing—we'll be back in three weeks."

The week of the championship game the weather was so bad in Chicago that I believe the Bears had to work inside all the time. They couldn't get as much work in, probably, as they wished they could have. In the meantime, we had beautiful, sunshiny weather in Washington, where the game was going to be played, and we worked like we were in training camp. We worked like dogs, I'm telling you the truth. But I think we left a lot of our football on the practice field, really. And then, too, mentally we weren't ready for 'em. There's something about football—if you beat a team that's your equal, the next time you meet 'em you're not quite as high as you should be and they're always higher than hell. So they beat us 73-0, but I know we remembered it the next time we played 'em in a championship game. That was two years later, and we won that game, 14-6.

Over the years, George Marshall changed coaches pretty often, as you probably know, and by 1949 I already was playing for my fifth pro coach. We had a few players that were pretty good rounders, so Marshall hired a coach named Admiral Whelchel. He had coached at Navy and was a retired admiral, and Marshall thought he would put a lot of discipline in the ball club. Well, he showed up and he looked like anything but an admiral. He was just a kind of average-looking guy, not very impressive. And the funny thing was, he turned out to be a real nice fellow. All the players liked him, although he wasn't up on his football as he should have been, I guess.

Harry Gilmer was just a young quarterback at that time, and in an exhibition game he quarterbacked the team down to practically the goal line. Then he sneaked the football over for a touchdown. But coming home from the game, the Admiral got out a pencil and paper and must have spent three hours showing Harry why he shouldn't have used the quarterback sneak. He showed him all kind of mathematics about his weight and momentum and everything—I don't know what all. He spent a goddamn long time talking to Harry, and Harry went along with it, although he had scored on that play.

One day—I think it was our first league game that year—the Chicago Cardinals were clobbering the hell out of us. We must have been down thirty points and it was the start of the fourth quarter, and I was sitting on the bench thinking, "At least I'm going to have an easy day from here in." But that Admiral was *fierce*. The Cardinals were just whipping the hell out of us, but he thought that we was still going to beat 'em. He came over to me and said, "Sam, you better get back in there a'fore this thing gets out of hand."

Not long after that, Marshall started trying to coach the ball club. We had two-platoon ball by then, and Marshall told the Admiral that he had his ball club figured out all wrong—that he ought to have the defensive line being the offensive line and that the offensive line ought to be on defense. Marshall told this to the Admiral on the train coming home from a game. Marshall said, "By God, the next practice I'm coming out there and I want to see it done that way!"

Well, the Admiral didn't pay any attention to him at all, and we were out there working one day when here comes Marshall in that big black car of his. He looks at us for a while, then he comes out and stops practice. He said to the Admiral, "I thought I told you what to do."

The Admiral didn't say a word. He just turned around and walked off the field and got in his car and left. Well, that kind of threw Mr. Marshall, I guess. Meantime, we just stood there. Finally Marshall told me and a couple of others—I can't remember who—he told us to get in his car. We were going back to the hotel with Mr. Marshall, and he was madder than hell. "Why could you let this happen?" he yelled at us. He said, "How could you let that man ruin the ball club?"

We said, "Hell, Mr. Marshall. He's the coach. We're just the players."

But George Marshall said, "Hell, I hired him for a *disciplinarian*. I didn't hire him for a goddamn coach!"

I thought that was the funniest thing. Oh, that George was wonderful, goddamn him.

Anyway, he and the Admiral got it straightened out that the Admiral was to stay on till the next ballgame was over. He was going to quit after that. I think we played Pittsburgh or somebody—I don't remember for sure—but whoever it was, we beat 'em. And then we carried the Admiral off on our shoulders.

The whole time I was up there I loved to work with that football, but every year I spent in football I came right home after the season was over. I bought this ranch and the cattle on it in 1941, when it was about sixty-five hundred acres, and now we're running cattle on about twenty-five thousand acres. I always kind of looked forward to the time when I could just ranch altogether. When the football season ended, I never stayed an extra day. I didn't care anything about the city—never have liked the bright lights. In 1939, I imagine it was, I went out to Hollywood to make a picture, and there wasn't a thing there that I was interested in.

That picture was called *King of the Texas Rangers*. Tom King—that was supposed to be my name. Actually, the picture was one of those serials that they used to show in weekly episodes, and I never have known what the damn thing was about. We'd have to be at the studio about six o'clock and get made up. You had a script, but I can't remember very few damn days they ever stuck to it. They'd tell you what to study for the next day, but then you'd get there and maybe the weather wouldn't be just right so they'd go to something else in the script. I got where I never would even look at the thing.

Each day they'd just make whatever they could. I never did know what the picture was about, never could piece it together, because they'd make the start of it one day, then go to the end of it the next day, and then maybe the middle and the side. I saw some of them episodes but never did see 'em all together. I still to this day don't know what I was supposed to be doing in that picture.

I think I was there about six weeks. I rented me a little apartment over there near the studio. Everyone out there was real nice, but as I told you, there wasn't a thing in Hollywood that I was interested in. I didn't care anything about nightclubs. I did go to a few saddle shops and places like that, but I was just glad when the goddamn thing was over.

13

ALEX WOJCIECHOWICZ

The thirty-letter man

The name is pronounced Wojee-hoe-witz. His range as a linebacker was as broad, proportionately, as his autograph, and of the memorable Seven Blocks of Granite who formed an almost immovable Fordham University line in the mid-1930s, the indestructible Wojie enjoyed by far the longest and most illustrious pro-football career—thirteen years with the Detroit Lions and Philadelphia Eagles. His bust rests in the Hall of Fame.

Now a real estate broker and a property appraiser for the New Jersey Transportation Department, he lives with his wife in a spacious house on a wooded three-acre hilltop plot in Highlands, a town on the Jersey shore. His great pompadour is scarcely a few hairs thinner than it was in his rookie year of pro ball, and although horn-rimmed glasses and a somewhat beefy middle give him a businessman's appearance, his thickset build suggests that even in his mid-fifties he is capable of dealing out a punishing tackle. "He was built just like that when he played with the Eagles," I was told by his old Eagles roommate, Steve Van Buren. "I mean, even with the belly." Each morning before breakfast and each night before retiring, Wojciechowicz swims ten laps in his 46-foot backyard pool, weather permitting.

Several years ago he learned that an old Philadephia teammate, Tommy Thompson, had been totally disabled by arthritis. Thompson's misfortune had come to the attention of Jerry Wolman, at the time the president of the Eagles, and Wolman was sending Thompson checks. "But then," Wojciechowicz told me, "I said to myself, 'Why should Jerry Wolman have to help out a guy who played for the Eagles long before Wolman owned the club?' And then I said, 'How many more Tommy Thompsons are there?' It seemed to me that the league should help these people."

Wojciechowicz proceeded to organize the National Football League Alumni Association, a society of ex-pros that in 1969 persuaded the clubowners to create a fund of $80,000 for old-timers in dire need. As president of the Association, Wojciechowicz at this writing is spearheading a campaign to bring all old-timers of at least five years' pro experience into the pension program.

It was a little town called South River, N.J., which was a brick town. That's where I was born. Brickyards and factories, yes. I was born in the tough section of town—The Alley, we called it. A Polish and Russian neighborhood.

My father had a tailor shop, but during the Depression of the 1930s, when I was getting up there in my teens, hardly anybody could afford to have suits tailor-made or even send them out to be cleaned. People did their own. So my father took a job in a factory and my mother worked in a factory and during summers I worked in a factory myself. I made five dollars a week. My father, I think, made eighteen dollars a week, and every evening he would open the tailor shop and measure up a few of the clientele from the right side of the tracks. He would cut the cloth and sew till about midnight. He made suits that looked new for ten or twelve years.

The man who put me where I am today was a high-school football coach and algebra teacher named Bill Denny. When I first reported for football I weighed 113 pounds, because, by God, between the five of us in our family—my mother and father and brother and sister and me—we were barely getting one quart of milk a day. We were very fortunate when we got meat on the table. But in 1930, when I was a freshman, Bill Denny took the entire squad to Ursinus College, a country college over in Pennsylvania. Absolutely without pay, he took us over there for two weeks every summer, and, believe it or not, when we were over there I used to drink twelve or thirteen glasses of milk at every meal. In two weeks, every year, I would put on fifteen pounds.

The way we paid for our keep at Ursinus was that Bill Denny would get each of us a job on a W.P.A. road gang for two weeks previous to going to Ursinus, and we would make ten dollars a week, which was what it cost us for a week's room and board at the college. Oh, it was wonderful there. We'd get up at six o'clock and before breakfast we would take a ten-mile hike through those Pennsylvania hills.

I don't think you'll find many coaches like Bill Denny today. He's retired now, but he's still a god in South River, believe me. He made every boy be in strict physical shape, and he made it a must that you maintain a classroom average of 80 to play football. He said, "All my boys have to go to college." And, believe it or not, in my senior year we had an undefeated team and everybody went to college. Every one of us.

Getting by in South River at that time, it was dog-eat-dog. It was a tough grind, but they were happy days. They were very happy, and I'll tell you why.

You see, the kids today don't really know what fun is. After football practice—say, about seven o'clock—the boys from

The Alley would have races from South River to Spotswood and back, which was about seven miles each way. We were the toughest, roughest bunch of school kids you ever saw. We had hare-and-hound chases through the woods every Saturday morning. We were always doing something. There was never a dull moment. We were building up our bodies, but that wasn't the point. It was fun. We were going and going and going and working and working, and when we played, we played hard, and when we worked, we worked hard. These kids today ride around in cars. If you tell 'em to run five miles —well, don't bother.

I have a son who went to Princeton and studied aeronautical engineering. He had a trick shoulder, so I said to him, "Forget about football. One athlete in the family is enough. Let's have a good student." He finished second in his class at Princeton, and I'm very proud of him, but when he was a kid, in order to get him to run a mile a day I used to have to provide a little incentive—a little cash here and there. You have to *push* these kids. The colored kids, they have the desire the white kids no longer have.

Well, Jimmy Crowley, the head coach at Fordham University, came down to South River in the spring of 1934 and said to me, "Wojie, we want you. We need you. We're driving for a championship team, and I think you'll be great in New York City. You'll be playing before the biggest sportswriters. You'll be a big fish in a big pond." For me, that was it. Fordham was a challenge to me, and I enjoyed the school very much. When I got there, Fordham football was in full swing. Kate Smith, the singer, used to say on the radio, "Fordham cannot lose!"

The press would come around to our practices, and in the beginning they used to call me over and beg me to shorten my name. But Jimmy Crowley finally straightened them out.

He said, "Listen, we believe that Wojie is going to be an All-American. How many Smiths can you name me that made All-America? How many Joneses can you name me that made All-America?" Crowley said, "If Wojciechowicz makes All-America with that name, he'll never be forgotten." My name is Alexander Francis Wojciechowicz, which is twenty-nine letters, but the campus newspaper, *The Ram*, changed it to Alexander Franklin Wojciechowicz, which gave it one more letter, and started calling me "The Thirty-Letter Man." Whenever we played poker, they called me Alex Holdyourwallet.

Jimmy tried to make an end out of me, but I told him I didn't care to play end. I was as fast as some of the great backs we played against—people like Bobby LaRue and Biggie Goldberg of Pittsburgh—but I stuck to playing center and linebacker. I loved the drudgery and the plans and the aches that go with playing up front. In baseball I was always a catcher, the hardest job on the team.

In football I tried to be creative. For example, I didn't like the way the centers in those days were snapping the ball back for punts. They'd have one hand on top of the ball and the other hand on the bottom. Snapping it that way, you couldn't get enough speed on the ball—you'd always get a little curve on the tail. So I worked for two solid months putting both hands on the front and snapping it with a flip of the wrists, and then I started making all my passes that way. From there on, all the other centers followed suit. And another thing— we used to wear heavy woolen jerseys that would shrink when you perspired. The sleeves would tighten up on your arms so that you could almost feel your circulation being strangled. I didn't have the freedom with my elbows and wrists that I wanted. In one game, I got so angry at those doggoned sleeves that I tore 'em off. Then everybody followed suit, especially the centers, and yes, that's how short-sleeved jerseys came into football.

Football was my big love all the way down the line, and although I studied chemistry, pro ball was my ambition. Mel Hein, the great New York Giants center, was my idol. I went to the Giant games and never took my eyes off him. Many times there would be only six, seven, maybe ten thousand people at the Giant games, and most weeks Fordham would outdraw the Giants four to one or at least two to one, but I always went to the Giant games because I wanted to get all the pointers I could and Mel Hein was my man.

Detroit needed a center in the worst way, so Dutch Clark, the Lions' coach, made me his first draft choice. I loved that rock-and-sock Detroit football, which was the brand I had grown accustomed to while playing big-time college ball. The Lions had a terrific fullback, Ace Gutowsky. I had all the confidence in the world, so when it came time for the rookies to play a game against the veterans I told Ace, "If I'm going to get anybody, it'll be you." Well, Ace was a great spinning fullback. But every time he spun, brother, I was right there in the middle. On one play, though, I hit him with my left shoulder and my arm went limp and I didn't have the use of that left arm for about three days. They X-rayed the darn thing but they couldn't find anything wrong with it, so believe it or not, from 1938 into the 1940 season I played with a very badly injured shoulder.

Backing up the right side of the line, you're almost always going to your left, and it gets to be instinctive that bang, you hit with your left shoulder. After the injury, I tried to learn how to tackle with my right shoulder, but it was hard to do and I was arm-tackling. When I made a good tackle with my left shoulder, my arm would go numb and I'd have to center the ball one-handed. So in 1940, after making a very painful tackle with my left shoulder, I became disgusted. I went to Fred Mandel, the Chicago department-store tycoon who had just bought the club, and told him I had had it. Mandel said to me, "Before you say anything more, let me take you to a Dr. Leventhal, my doctor in Chicago." So I went to Chicago, and Dr. Leventhal actually saved my life.

He had me X-rayed for three days, X-ray after X-ray. And he not only found eighteen pieces of bone that needed to be removed from my shoulder but also a blood clot on my artery. At the hospital, when they operated, they told me, "If you had gone on to play another year of football with that blood clot, it would have hit your brain and you'd be gone."

After the operation, football was a pleasure again. All told, I played eight years with Detroit and five more with Philadelphia, and it's a funny thing—even though we didn't have face guards in those days, I went all the way through high school, college, and pro ball without getting a mark on my face. Not even a broken nose. But in my last year of pro ball I lost my two front teeth, and I'll tell you a story about that.

It was 1950. Greasy Neale, our coach at Philadelphia, said to me, "Wojie, we're gonna kind of give you a rest this year. We're gonna break in Chuck Bednarik at linebacker." By now, of course, two-platoon football had come along and I had been playing defense. So now we're going into an exhibition game with the Chicago Bears in Philadelphia, and Bednarik comes down with a fever. And in practice that week, our center, Vic Lindskog, had hurt his knee. So here's old man Wojie, in his thirteenth year of pro ball, and he has to play center and linebacker for sixty minutes against the Chicago Bears.

Now if you'll remember Greasy Neale's defense, you'll understand that on defense I had to play on top of a Chicago end. Let's call him Smith. He was a good, tough competitor who played to win, and I wouldn't want this story to leave anyone with the impression that he was anything else. Anyhow, I had to play on top of Smith no matter where he lined up, whether in the line or at flanker or as an open end. He was a lot of football player to have to hit, so after about two minutes had gone by, I said to Smith, "I've got to play sixty minutes and I'm not going to play very hard. It's only an exhibition game. I'm just going to hold you up—I'm not going to slug you or anything else like that, because I have to go sixty minutes. I'm the only center we have in uniform."

"All right," said Smith, and we made a pact to lay off the rough stuff.

Well, on the very next play, I'm looking up at Smith, just horsing around with him, and all of a sudden I catch an elbow and pop go two teeth. I was knocked cold. A halfback had come right at me and knocked me stiff. Now maybe I was a little too suspicious, but when I came to, I got the notion that Smith might have told that halfback, "Let's get Wojie out of the game and it will be easy pickings from here in, because he's the only center they've got." I was bleeding like a pig.

"All right," I said, "I'll get those guys."

I played the damndest game I ever played in my life! I was a brute out there. All my teammates followed suit, they all got riled up, and we beat the daylights out of the Bears and won the game.

Well, I suppose the point is that you always had to expect a fairly vigorous game from those Chicago Bears. Yes, they came at you with every intention of winning. Back in 1939, my second year with Detroit, Hunk Anderson had come over from the Bears to join the Lions as defensive coach, and he said to us: "Gentlemen, we are playing the Bears at Chicago, and there is only one way you can beat the Bears and that is to outslug them." We had a kicker who always put the ball over the goal line, so Hunk said, "We are going to kick off and the Bears are then going to put the ball in play on their twenty-yard line, and here is what I want you to do."

"I want seven men to line up head to head against that Bear line," Hunk said. "And when that ball is snapped, I want every man to slug the man in front of him. The worst we can get is a fifteen-yard penalty. Whether one slugs or seven slug, the most we can get is fifteen yards."

So on that first play from scrimmage, what you heard all the way down the line was bang, bang, bang. And remember, nobody wore face guards then. Joe Stydahar, the Bears' great tackle, walked off the field. He was bleeding at the mouth furiously.

The officials, of course, penalized us fifteen yards, which moved the ball to the 35. Now it so happens that Hunk's instructions were to slug them not just on the first play but on the first three plays. So that's what we did on the next play and the next. Everybody just socking away. Penalties moved the ball to the 50 and then down to our 35. And do you know, that's the farthest the Bears got all day. The Big Bad Bears were stunned. Instead of being the meek Lions, we were the Big Bad Lions, and we beat those Bears, 10-0.

Well, the way the pros play today, they *have* to wear face guards, because gradually the blocking came around to where your offensive linemen on pass protection were simply backing off the line and fending off their man with elbows and forearms, so with all those arms coming up, why, they broke a lot of jaws and noses. This is where the face guard came into play. But to tell you the truth, I don't care for the kind of blocking I see now. We blocked with our shoulders. Good, solid blocks, where a man really drives his opponent out of his position.

And the most remarkable thing to me is that you see these

fast receivers coming off the line without even being touched. Greasy Neale would have hit the ceiling if we were not on top of them and slugging away at them while they were going out. Especially on a sure pass play. The way they let these ends and flankers go downfield on a short pass play, it's amazing to me. In our day it couldn't possibly have happened. And don't forget—we had to contend with Don Hutson. Don Hutson of Green Bay was fantastic. Even today, with all the specialists, I don't see a Don Hutson. If you didn't knock Hutson down, he'd score four or five touchdowns a game. If I didn't knock down those ends, I don't know where I'd have ended up. In my last year we were beating a team by about six touchdowns so I relaxed toward the end of the game and let the end get inside me and catch a pass. Now if you were a linebacker for Greasy Neale, it was sinful to let an end go inside you. Greasy reran the film of that play where I relaxed—he reran it five times. He wouldn't lay off. He said, "How the hell can a man who's played almost thirteen years of pro football let that happen?"

Greasy had a dual personality, which to me is what a successful coach must have. He's got to be a no-good son of a gun on the field and a great guy off the field. On the field Greasy was God Almighty. Off the field, a terrific man. He'd play pinocle or gin with you, have a drink with you, play a round of golf with you. He liked to play golf with our quarterback, Tommy Thompson. Tommy could see out of only one eye but was a par shooter and once beat Byron Nelson in an exhibition. Anyhow, on the field Greasy would chew Tommy's tail out, but you had to forget the things Greasy said on the field. Greasy was in his fifties then, about thirty years older than most of the ballplayers, but he was like a brother or a pal to them.

ART ROONEY

Art Rooney as an international amateur boxing champion

Art Rooney as owner of the Hope-Harvey football club while in his early twenties; he is shaking hands with a rival clubowner before the opening kickoff

SAMMY BAUGH

Sam in grammar school in Texas—he's in the front row, extreme left

Sam (front, right) with George Raft

Sammy Baugh, game and date unknown

Mr. and Mrs. Sam Baugh, newlyweds on first ranch at
Sweetwater, Texas, 1939

Sammy Baugh in Hollywood, 1940. He played the lead in the serial *King of the Texas Rangers*, Republic Pictures

Sam and Kelly Miller, Redskins' equipment manager, during the later part of Sammy's career

BULLDOG TURNER

Bulldog Turner Day, 1966, at Sunland Park in New Mexico, just outside El Paso

Publicity photo of Bulldog Turner made during build-up for All-America at Hardin-Simmons in Abilene, Texas

Bulldog and Ray Bray, Chicago Bears guard

Bulldog Turner as a rookie in 1940 with Chicago Bears

Bulldog Turner, No. 66 in second row

CHICAGO BEARS
NATIONAL CHAMPIONS
1940

BOBBY LAYNE

Bobby Layne, 1948, as rookie with Chicago Bears—young fan is unidentified

1950—Bobby Layne's first year at Detroit. Left to right: Layne, halfback Doak Walker, head coach Bo McMillin, center Joe Watson, end Cloyce Box

Bobby Layne with coach Buddy Parker and teammates after Detroit defeated Cleveland, 17-16, in 1953 NFL championship game

Three years running—1947, '48, and '49—we won the eastern division title and played for the championship. The first time, the Chicago Cardinals beat us on an icy field, by one touchdown. The second time, we beat the Cardinals in a blizzard. The third time, we woke up the morning of the championship game—it was in Los Angeles, against the Rams—and it was pouring. In those days people in Los Angeles did not buy tickets in advance. There are 100,000 seats in that Coliseum, so the fans waited till the day of the game. Well, we'd been expecting about 90,000 people, which would have meant a payoff per man of about three thousand dollars, which of course we'd already spent. And now we wake up and it's raining.

We phoned Commissioner Bert Bell—that is, we the players phoned him—and we said, "Postpone the game for one week. Play it next Sunday and we'll pay our own expenses to stay out here the extra week." But Bell turned us down, as I recall, because of a commitment to radio. Only 27,000 fans showed up and it was still raining, a downpour. Steve Van Buren, my roommate, was so upset, he was so furious, that he went out in that mud and gained 196 yards, which was, and still is, the record for a championship game. We beat the Rams, 14-0, and collected only $1,000 and change per man.

Then we were told by the club that no one was going to get a raise the next year. One reason they gave us was that we had been making extra money on championship games. They figured we were going to keep winning championship games forever, you know. Then, too, the owners were not making much money. We played in Shibe Park, which held only 35,000, and we had no television then. So we went to training camp that year, 1950, agreeing to play the season without a raise, but after we got out there to that camp in Minnesota we found there were six ballplayers who hadn't signed. There were six looking for raises. They were in camp but they didn't suit up. So Greasy Neale telephoned Jim Clark, who was the big stockholder and ran the business end. "Listen," Greasy told him. "You either sign these six or send 'em home. They're standing around here leaving a bad taste in everybody's mouth. You told everybody that nobody's going to get a raise, and here are six guys that want raises!"

Jim Clark hopped a plane to Minnesota, and what did he do but give those boys raises. He gave the rest of us a flat raise of three hundred dollars, but what he gave the other six, we didn't know. It was a bad situation. It was the downfall of the Eagles. Greasy called Clark all kind of names, and later, after a game we lost in New York, they almost went into fisticuffs. Clark came into the locker room and Greasy said to him, "Stay away from these lockers. You take care of your office and I'll take care of my boys!" They almost went at it right there. At the end of the season, Tommy Thompson quit and I quit and so did a lot of the other fellows.

Well, thirteen years was a long time. But when we went through the transition from sixty-minute football to two platoons I became strictly a defensive man, and if I hadn't, I don't think I would have been able to last the five years that I had with the Eagles. Did you read that book *Instant Replay*, the one that Jerry Kramer wrote? Now there's no doubt about it, Kramer was a great offensive lineman with Green Bay. But he speaks of how hard the game is, and the next thing you know, he tells how he's going out hunting or golfing on Monday, the day after the game. When I used to play sixty minutes on a Sunday, I couldn't possibly go hunting on Monday. I'd be in a whirlpool getting rid of my aches and pains. I don't want to appear critical of modern football, but I'm simply saying that if these follows had played the sixty-minute game, they would not have been walking around on golf courses or tramping through the woods on Monday.

You may hear otherwise, but we oldtimers did know how to play football. Danny Fortmann, the Chicago Bears guard, was like a cat. He had all the moves in the world. Do you remember Stan Mauldin? Another cat. A tackle with the Cardinals and a great one. We played sixty minutes against one another, and he was complaining of a headache. He said, "My head is getting worse and worse. Gee, my head is bursting." Meanwhile, I threw my sacroiliac out of place. They rubbed some hot stuff on my back, and I stayed in the game. After the last play of the game Stan helped me up and said, "I know you've got a bad back. I'll help you off the field." I said, "Well, I know you've got a headache." But he helped me off the field, and just as we hit the dugout he suddenly dropped me and ran off. I thought he was just going off to vomit.

I was taking a shower when I got the word that Stan Mauldin was in the Cardinal locker room unconscious. I hurried over there, and when I entered that locker room, my God! Stan was stretched out on the rubbing table and they had oxygen on his face. Some of the ballplayers were in the nude and some were completely dressed, and all of them were kneeling around that table. They were praying. There was not a sound in the room. Half an hour later, Stan died of a blood clot. There was none better than Stan Mauldin.

And if you're talking about guts, how about Whizzer White? We played together at Detroit in the early 1940s. Whizzer, he had all the guts in the world. He was a man's athlete. He loved the game all the way. He ate it up. A real down-to-earth guy. Whenever I go down to Washington I give him a call and we get together and talk about the old times and about what the boys are doing today. All he asks is that you call first and make an appointment. Right there in his chambers we have lunch, and he comes down to earth from his justice. What's wrong with remembering the past?

14

BULLDOG TURNER

The raconteur of Cowhouse Creek

It was mid-March, a crisp, sunny day in the rolling green countryside of central Texas. Out by the stable Clyde (Bulldog) Turner asked if I cared for a beer. Then he went behind the stable and plucked two cans of beer from the cool ground under a shade tree. The beer was not cold but was sufficiently chilled to be refreshing. Owing to a touch of sugar that afflicts him, Bulldog had been warned by his doctor to abstain from alcohol, and so in order to escape recriminations from his wife, he had found it convenient to store an occasional libation in the outdoors. He recalled that a few years before, a newspaperman had come down from Dallas to interview him, and while they were chatting at the stable he asked the newspaperman if he would like a drink of vodka. "That'll be fine," said the visitor, whereupon Bulldog plunged his arm into a large bin of oats and fetched up a bottle of vodka. "I'll be damned!" said the newspaperman.

A big, beefy man, Bulldog had paid the price that Texas summers extract from those who labor on the land. His skin was burnt, his thick, straight hair faded silver at fifty, and the backs of his hands, scaled. He explained that mainly he breeds racehorses but that he also owns cattle, sheep, and goats, though "not many of each." Agriculture, he went on, had not been prosperous in recent years. His modest 1,200-acre ranch had dwindled to 250 acres.

People in the countryside and in nearby Gatesville, a town of five thousand, in some cases knew him to have been a professional athlete, but they surmised that he had been a baseball player. The fact is that in 1941, only a year after he had turned pro with the Chicago Bears, he became the first man in nine years to unseat the great Mel Hein of the New York Giants as the National Football League's all-league center. Men who played against him say that he brought exquisite stealth to the art of holding. Although on defense Bulldog Turner played linebacker, not cornerback or safety man, he once intercepted eight passes in an eleven-game schedule, a performance that over the fourteen-game schedule of 1969, for example, would have ranked him second in the league in interceptions.

On summer weekends, Bulldog told me with a sense of resignation, townfolk and soldiers from Fort Hood park their cars along the road running past his property and go wading in Cowhouse Creek, which in part lies on his land. They frighten his cattle, and when he asks that they give the cattle a bit of room to water, they jeer him. "I don't blame the people," he said heavily, "but I'm trying to make a living off the place."

In the living room of the old house, built in 1900, he joined his wife Gladys, a handsome blonde from the Panhandle who in her youth surely must have been a great beauty. He chose an armchair, soberly forewarning me that he was certain his voice would sound ludicrous on my recording machine. He suggested I reconsider. Actually, his voice had the depth of a general's. His posture was ramrod straight, and his forearms rested authoritatively on the arms of the chair. I knew, of course, that I had wandered into the presence of a master storyteller.

I'll *tell* you how I come to be called Bulldog, but along that line I'll have to explain a few things. First of all, I come from Yoakum County 'way out in West Texas, where my dad was a cowboy. He worked for big ranches. Hell, they had to be big to make a living, because that wasn't too good a country up there. No trees or nothing. I was born in a little cabin on a ranch, in 1919, and when I was three or four, we moved into a town called Plains. That was the only town in the county at that time, so naturally the courthouse was there. Two fillin' stations and two stores and a post office and the courthouse is all I remember being in Plains. There wasn't even any town square. There wasn't enough town to go around.

Up there in Plains, you went all the way from the first grade to graduation in the same school building, and of course there was no such thing as a football team. The only football I ever saw there was in the Sears Roebuck catalog. To me, it was an odd-shaped ball, and that was all. I didn't know anything about football till after we moved to Sweetwater. In 1932 my dad came over there and traded for some property and started buying and selling cattle, and then he came back and got us.

It was my junior year when I first went to Sweetwater High. I noticed that some of the boys there had a big "S" on a knit sweater they wore, and that those boys got all the attention. In the fall there'd be pep rallies, and people would go down to the station to see those boys off on the train. So I decided that maybe I ought to get me one of those knit sweaters. Finally I learned that the boys wearin' 'em were football players.

But I didn't go out for football right away, because in the fall of the year people started to gather cotton, and that's what I did the first fall. We lived in town but it wasn't but a couple of blocks till we went into the country. Out there—

oh, maybe a mile—was a cotton farm. So I used to run home from school and change my clothes and grab a cotton sack and run out there. I'd throw a few rocks in the sack to make it weigh a little heavier, and between school and dark I'd make about thirty-five cents. Of course, I'd give my dad part of it. The Depression was getting real tough then, and as I look back now, I can't see how my dad was making a living. Yet we were living good. We were eating simple things, but all them things are still my favorite foods. We were probably poor, but I didn't know it.

I picked cotton all that fall, and then I told my dad, "I'm going to quit picking cotton. I'm going out for football." He asked why, and I said, "I want to get me a sweater." That's all I wanted was that ol' slip-on knit sweater with a big ol' "S" on it.

Well, man, I went through many a rough hour to get that sweater. The first day I went on the field was the roughest day I ever spent on a football field. That includes college through pro. I had cleat marks all over my shins. Right then I was nothing, and that season I was just a shock trooper. They'd use me anywhere. There were fourteen on the squad, the Sweetwater Mustangs, and I was number-one substitute. I played every position except quarterback, I guess. Sammy Baugh was two years ahead of me at Sweetwater High, so that makes two of us from one school that made the Pro Football Hall of Fame. But Sammy had already gone when I started.

That year we had a lousy team. We won maybe a game or two out of the whole season, but I got my sweater and in getting it I developed something that I didn't anticipate. I found that I loved to play football. I found I loved any kind of competition. So I was real fired up and looking forward to the next football season, but then they said I couldn't play anymore for the high school.

I was fifteen then, see, and I was supposed to graduate. My older brother Jay actually was fourteen when he graduated. A lot of boys down here in Texas graduated young. Why, I don't know. Nobody ever asked me before. Maybe the schools were letting them jump grades or something. Anyway, I was supposed to graduate, but the move from Plains to Sweetwater was such a big jump that I failed my first year at Sweetwater and when I was supposed to graduate at fifteen, I didn't. I had to go another year. But they said I was ineligible for football, because I'd already had eight semesters of high school. So at fifteen I was ineligible for high-school competition.

That nearly run me crazy. I said, "Heck, I can't stand this." So I ran off from home. I ran off to see if I could get me a place on a college team. And now I'm getting to why I'm called Bulldog.

At that time I had an old cow, as I recall, and cows brang about eight dollars. I sold that cow and bought me some new gloves and a new coat, and I think I still had a good bit of money before I left. I hitchhiked around for a while and then I went to Fort Worth and checked into a hotel. In those days you could get a room for $1.50 a week, so I stayed there and went around to more colleges within hitchhikin' distance and told them, "I want to be an athlete." Every damn one of them turned me down. They said, "Well, we're all filled up." See, I had no reputation as a football player.

After a while my whiskers started to grow a little bit, but I'd forgotten to take a razor with me because at home I had been using my brother's razor. Yet I do remember shaving at Fort Worth, and what I did, I pulled out an old dresser drawer in that hotel room and found old razor blades in there, and I'd soap up my face with the regular hotel soap and hold an old razor blade against my comb, and then shave.

I was getting along all right in Fort Worth, but after I had been turned down by about seven or eight colleges around the countryside, I was pretty near out of money, and then I remembered I was a musician. I had played stringed instruments. Banjo and guitar. So I went down to this big theater, although as I looked back on it now it was a little ol' burlesque striptease place, and asked to see the manager. I told him I played the banjo. He said, "Well, we don't use the banjo." I said, "I think it would add something to the show, to have a banjo with the piano." So he said, "Well, it might work out all right at that. You got a banjo?" I said, "No," so he said, "Then we can't use you," and I didn't get the job.

So I headed for Lawton, Oklahoma—for Cameron State Agricultural College at Lawton, Oklahoma. I had heard they kind of took tramp athletes, so I said, "I'll make it to there." I had a dime and a candy bar in my pocket when I got out on the highway.

A guy came by in a great big ol' yellow roadster-type car, and said, "You got any money to help me buy some gas?" I said, "No, sir, I got ten cents is all I've got left." He said, "Oh, well, I'll give you a ride anyway." So we didn't drive but about forty or fifty miles till he pulled in a gas station and says, "Well, if you ain't got any money for gas, I believe I'll let you buy me a cigar." I thought, "You dirty son of a bitch." I told him, "I ain't got but that one dime, and if you want it I'll buy that much worth of gas." Then he said, "No. I believe I will let you buy me a cigar." And he spent my last dime for a cigar, and that candy bar was the last bite I had to eat for five days and five nights.

I'll tell you how country I was at that time. I got up to Lawton, Oklahoma, and I went in there and met the athletic director and the coach and all. I had been better than two days getting there. It was wintertime, and I was half frozen. The coach looked me over and said, "Son, why don't you come over to the cafeteria with us and have lunch?"

Well, that word *cafeteria* scared me to death. Never heard of it. Didn't know what the hell a cafeteria was. So rather than expose my ignorance, I said, "No, thank you. I just ate before I came in." Which was a damn lie, because I hadn't eaten in two days by this time.

So I waited there in that room and sat down on a cane-bottomed chair, and I was so tired that I went to sleep and fell into a big ol' stove and burned myself. I didn't burn myself bad, but I'm telling you how tired I was. The coach and the athletic director came back and asked me to stay the night, but by then I was feeling so ignorant that I said no and got back on the road.

Wichita Falls is not too far down from Lawton, yet it took me a couple of days to get there. See, I noticed these Mexicans coming by me on the highway in big new cars, and I said, "I'll be damned! Down there where I live, the Mexicans don't many of them drive cars like these." But directly one of them came by without a hat on, with just a band around his head, and finally it dawned on me—"Goddammit, these are Indians up here!" They had struck oil and they was all driving these big ol' cars, but the difficulty was, they wouldn't pick you up. So I was two days getting to Wichita Falls, and then I spent the night there, which made five days and five nights without a meal.

In the morning I hitchhiked down as far as Throckmorton, not far south of Wichita Falls, and I was starving to death. I walked into a filling station, which also was kind of a grocery store, and I asked, "How much them apples?" The man had some green apples there, and as I told you, I had bought me some new gloves when I left home and I wanted to find out what I could get most of for my gloves. I said, "I want to trade my gloves for something to eat."

The man said, "I'll trade you a sack of them apples for your gloves. They're twenty-five cents a sack."

That was a big old sack—I'd say half a bushel in there. But I was so hungry I needed that. So I traded him them gloves, and I tied into them apples. But I ate only about half a apple and I'm full. My stomach starts cramping. I hadn't had anything to eat in so long, my stomach just drawed up. I ate about half a apple and I'm plumb full, and here I got the whole sack. So I was out there hitchhiking and carrying that sack of apples with me, and I thought, "I could have traded for something a hell of a lot easier to carry."

Finally a guy stopped and said, "Where you trying to go?"

"I'm trying to get to Sweetwater," I said. I wanted to get home.

"Well, I'm going to Sweetwater," this guy told me, "but I'm a salesman and I got to stop several places, so I won't get in there till tonight. You could probably beat me there." But I said, "No, I believe I'll just stay with you, if you don't mind."

So we come into a little ol' town called Rule, Texas, and it's getting about noon. I know it's time to eat. I'm thinking, "If this guy's a nice guy, maybe he'll buy me a lunch." He was a pottery salesman. He had a lot of pottery in his car. So he parked at the curb and took some pottery into a store and filled an order or something, and then he pulled down the street and said, "I've got to run in here and see a guy." I watched him go into a café and he was in there an *hour*, and I said, "That dirty son of a bitch. He ain't gonna buy me no lunch." Man, I wanted to get home, 'cause I knew Mama's got something for me to eat if I ever get there. So finally the pottery salesman come back out, and we stop at every little town on the road while he sells a few pottery. Finally about 8:30 or 9 o'clock that night, he got me to Sweetwater. I had been gone three weeks. I walked in the house and Mamma started crying.

I guess I looked real bad. I had lost a lot of weight and my eyes were sunk back. My brother Jay was sitting in there with my dad, and Jay was laughing and slapping his leg. "Oh, you finally decided to come home," he said. My dad laughed and said, "Well, it wasn't so great out there, you seeking your fortune." But I had been out there trying to get myself a scholarship, because I wanted to compete in athletics. And that leads up to the story where I got the nickname Bulldog.

I went back to high school and really knuckled down. Meantime, we had a fullback in Sweetwater High that was a pretty good fullback—a big ol' boy named A. J. Roy. He was a good buddy of mine. Frank Kimbrough, the head coach at Hardin-Simmons, was interested in A. J. Roy. Kimbrough already had turned me down when I was on the road hitchhikin', but he had said to me, kind of off the cuff, "Come on down next season. We'll try you out." So A. J. and I thought we'd both get an invitation down there together when the time came. During the summer we started training. We'd run sixteen miles out to Lake Sweetwater and sixteen miles back. We didn't know anything about getting in shape, but we figured you had to be running.

So while we'd be running along them damn highways we decided that if we got into a scrimmage at Hardin-Simmons and one of us wasn't looking too good, why, here's how we'd handle it. If it was A. J. looking bad, I'd say, "Hey, Tiger! You're not acting as tough as you did back home." And if it was me looking bad, he'd say, "Hey, Bulldog! Get in there and hit 'em like you did at home!" We'd kind of make out like we were just having a bad day. There in 1936 Hardin-Simmons and all them schools had tryouts, just like a pro camp. You made the team, you got a scholarship. If you didn't make the team, you didn't stay. We wanted to stay in school.

Well, as it turned out, A. J. got an invitation to come down there to Abilene, but I didn't. So finally he went to the coach and said, "You promised Clyde Turner that he could come down here and try out." And the coach said, "Yes, that's right. Well, we have *this* group of boys here now, but we have another group coming in next week. Have him come down here and report Monday." That first week they had a hundred or two hundred boys—make a better story if you say two hundred, I guess—and out of those, they were going to keep twenty-two. Then they had ninety of us come in the second week. And I'm the only one of that bunch that stayed. You betcha.

What happened was that on the first day the freshman coach said, "Now all you boys who think you're tough, step up here." So I stepped up. Everybody laughed, and that kind of embarrassed me. But I wanted to make the dern team.

"What position do you play?" the coach said to me.

"End," I said. Like I told you, in high school I played all of them, but *none* of them really, and that had been two years ago. So I didn't know much about football. But I knew I could run a little bit and I could catch the ball. So I said, "End." And he said, "Okay, get over there."

Nobody else volunteered, so the coach appointed a few guys to step out and we started scrimmaging right then and there.

Well, I had learned one thing—if you just hit everybody that you can hit, the coaches will look at you. So I started doing just that. I started hitting every guy that come close to me, and the coach got a little bit impressed.

Now they had an all-state center down there from up in the Panhandle somewhere—fella name of Hump Campbell. He was kind of humpbacked, so they called him Hump. He was a good football player, but what happened, I had been there about a week, I guess, and Hump got hurt. So the freshman coach—his name was Theo Rigsby—he went to Kimbrough and said, "Our center is hurt. Hump Campbell is hurt."

"Well," said Kimbrough, "do you got anybody you could make a center out of?"

And Rigsby said, "We got this one kid out here that is damn sure tough and will try anything. His name is Turner."

"Can he center the ball?" Kimbrough asked him. Remember, we played the single wing at time, so you didn't just hand the ball back to the quarterback. You had to center it. So Kimbrough said to Rigsby, "Find out if he can center the ball, and if he can, make a center out of him."

Well, Rigsby came out the next day and asked me can I play center, and I said, "Yep." Which I thought I could, because from the day I started high-school football till I finished playing pro, I always listened to everything the coaches ever said. I think I can name you verbatim every lecture that I ever attended. I was suited for football. I loved it. So I had remembered the high-school coach showing the center how to put his hands on the ball. "Okay," Rigsby said to me. "You know where the ball is. Let's take a look at you." That's the first time I'd ever tried it in my life, but I snapped that ball back pretty good. I made the dern team, and a week or two later A. J. Roy told everybody the story that we had cooked up about him going to call me Bulldog and me going to call him Tiger. Of course, we never did have to use it, 'cause both of us did well and made the team. But everybody got a big kick out of that story, and some of them started calling A. J. by the name Tiger and all of 'em started calling me Bulldog. From that day on, by golly, "Bulldog" just stuck with me, and that's the only name a lot of people know me by. Nobody calls me Clyde except my wife. And that's when she's mad.

At Hardin-Simmons we had a real good publicity man that came in there from Illinois named Hershell Schooley. Hershell was teaching journalism and he was handling publicity for the school, and he was also writing stories in the local paper. We got to be good friends, and I found out that his journalism course was pretty easy to pass, so I started doubling up on that journalism and I finally had more hours in journalism than I did in physical education. As a matter of fact, many times Hershell would be working down at the newspaper office, and I'd conduct class for him.

He was a wonderful fellow. He started sending out these stories about "there's a little school down in Texas that's got a big bull there," and he had the famous photographer Jimmy Laughead take pictures of me. You ever hear of Jimmy Laughead? He takes pictures of all the pros now, but at that time Jimmy wasn't taking pictures of nobody. So he came over to Hardin-Simmons and took a picture of me holding a live calf over my head and running to that dern camera, and that got in a football magazine where Hardin-Simmons had never been before. So a few people started watching us, though we still weren't any rich school. We traveled in a Pullman car that they'd park on the side of the damn track while we played the game. Seniors got an upper berth by themselves, but juniors and lower classmen had to sleep double in the lowers. That's right—two guys to a lower.

In 1939, my senior year, we rode out to play Loyola of Los Angeles in Gilmore Stadium, Los Angeles, and it held about eighteen thousand people. Well, we had a sellout crowd. I mean, I never saw so many people in my life. They were setting on the *walls*. Anyway, I had a super game against those Loyola guys, and, boy, we smoked 'em. I played linebacker on defense, and I was making tackles from one sideline to the other. They had a big star out there and I hit him so hard that he looked up and said, "I don't know your name, but you're the hardest hitting son of a bitch I ever saw in my life." Boy, that impressed me, 'cause he was All-American, see? Can't remember his name, but he was a big star. And his telling me that really fired me up, so when I got another shot at him I hit him good again. I'm telling you, he's laying out there and blood's running out of his ears. I had later on heard that any time blood runs out of your ears, you're gonna die, and I've always wondered if that boy ever got over that. I never did know.

Now at that time, George Richards, who owned the Detroit Lions, had a house out there in Los Angeles, and what happened, a guy phoned him at halftime and said, "George, you better come out here to the game. There's a guy out here you ought to be here watching." So when the game was over, George Richards was right there and he said, "Would you be interested in playing pro football?"

I said, "You bet." By that time, see, I'd already seen a newsreel on the Green Bay Packers on pro football, and I saw how big them ol' boys were and liked it. And so George Richards said, "Well, I'd like to have you on my team, the Detroit Lions." I'd never heard of the Detroit Lions or anybody else, except I had seen that film on the Green Bay Packers. "We're going to see that you get with the Lions,"

George Richards told me, and later on, after I played in the East-West game in San Francisco, he asked me to come on down to Los Angeles as his guest.

He had a whatever-you'd-call-him—a guy that was working for him named Church. Church picked me up in a big limousine and took me out to George Richards' house to have lunch with him. We went into a big ol' dining room, and there was a great big ol' table. And Richards sits down at one end and I sit at the other, and there's Church kind of in the middle. There's nothin' on the table—nothin'. But servants brang you each course. They brang you the service that you were going to use for each course. Well, back home when I sat down to dinner all the food was on the table. You'd pass this and pass that and everybody's up close and you eat. But here we didn't do it that way. Me and Mr. Church, I think maybe we had pork chops, and George Richards had some kind of game bird—quail or something. They'd get a little ol' dried-up pork chop and set it on a big ol' white plate, you know, and serve it off a big ol' silver service tray. I thought that was a hell of a way to eat, but anyway, that's the way we ate.

Then George Richards asked me, "Would you like to go to the track?" I said, "No, I don't know anything about that." The pros were in town to play what was then the Pro Bowl —the champions played an all-star team made up from the rest of the teams—so I said, "I thought I'd like to go out and maybe watch the pros practice." So George Richards said, "Fine. Mr. Church will drive you." He handed me forty or fifty bucks and said, "Here. If you had gone to the track I'd have bet this for you, so you might as well put it in your pocket." Man, that was the most money I ever saw in my life. And I'm being drove around!

So we watched these big hogs practice, and I said, "They're

not bad. They probably come pretty close to me." See, I
never was *taught* to play center, but I developed my own
style. Most guys would get down over that ball like an ol' hen
over a nest o' eggs, their elbows all bent, and you could knock
them back if you hit them up high. But I started keepin' my
shoulders and head up. And now I noticed that these pros
kept their arms straight, which I was the first one to do. And
I said, "Well, I'll be derned. Maybe they've been playing a
little center."

I was able to meet a few of the people around there, and
I was real impressed. I met one of the coaches, ol' Hunk
Anderson. We went to the hotel room with Hunk. I remember ol' Hunk had to go back to the hotel about two or three
times a day and change shorts. He had a bad case of hemor-
rhoids or something. He was the line coach for Detroit, and
I was pretty impressed with him. See, he'd pull off his clothes
there, and, man, he really had muscles in them legs. He said,
"We're going to be happy to have you with the Lions. But we
got to keep all this quiet till after the draft."

The thing was that George Richards had told his head
coach, Gus Henderson, to draft me number one. And he told
me that if any of the other teams wrote to me about playing
football, I should tell them I'm not interested. So when the
draft came up, Detroit was about the third pick, but instead
of picking me, Gus Henderson picked some quarterback that
nobody ever heard of. Some guy named Doyle Nave from
Southern California that never even showed up. Harry Wismer, who was the broadcaster for Detroit games at that time,
told me later that he was the guy that ran to the phone right
quick and called George Richards and told him, "Gus Henderson didn't pick Bulldog Turner, and the Chicago Bears
picked him." So George said, "I can't get anyone to run
things the way I want them to," and he fired Gus Henderson.

Meantime, George Richards didn't give up on me. He said, "You're still going to be with the Lions. You just tell the Bears you're not going to play pro football." He said, "I own three radio stations, a glass factory, and a bunch of other things—I don't know what all. I'll make you a coach at a high school out here in California for the first year, and after George Halas gives up on you, you go with the Lions."

So I went along with that, but then Halas invited me to Chicago on an expense-paid trip to fly up. Being the country boy that I was, I had never been on an airplane before, so I couldn't say no. You know, it took all day to fly to Chicago then. I left Abilene in the morning and landed in Oklahoma City and I don't know how many places, and got into Chicago that night. George and his wife met me at the airport, which George Halas don't do normally. But I didn't sign a contract. I was grateful for the trip, but I kind of strung George along, you might say. However, Richards found out I went up there, and he was mad.

He came down to Abilene, Mr. Richards himself did—he and Mr. Church. They came to the hotel there, and they registered incognito. Now as I told you, me and Hershell Schooley were getting along real good, so I told Hershell, "George Richards that owns the Detroit Lions is in town and he wants to talk to me tonight." Well, goddamn, you can't tell a newspaperman secrets. Hershell said, "I'm going with you," and carried a pad and pencil.

We went up there to the room and Mr. Richards came out of the shower with a towel wrapped around him and he said, "Who is *this?*" I said, "This is Hershell Schooley, a reporter." Richards said, "A reporter!" And man, he hit the ceiling. He said, "I've come all the way from California incognito, and what are you doing with a goddamn newspaperman here?"

Well, now, ol' Hershell was just about as thick as one of

those fireplace pokers over there. He was about six feet tall, and I guarantee you he wouldn't have weighed a hundred pounds. He wore about a twelve collar and it's 'way too big for him. But he jumped up and he drawed back and said, "Why, you old son of a bitch, we think more of this boy here than you *ever* will in your life! We're not going to take this kind of talk!"

I thought they were gonna fight, ol' man Richards with a towel around him and ol' Hershell with a suit and a tie on. They were just drawed back like, and neither one of them could have whupped nobody. But I was proud of ol' Hershell, and that one thing that happened kind of kept me thinkin', "You know, maybe this Richards don't think so much of me." Anyway, Mr. Church and me cooled the smoke down, and I thought, "If he's so hot for me, maybe it's time to see if he means it and cash in." I said to Mr. Church before I left, "I need about fifty or sixty dollars." He said, "Fine. Mr. Richards said to give you whatever you need." So I said, "Say, it's wintertime and I don't even have an overcoat." He said, "Fine. Mr. Richards will buy you one." And the first thing I know, I got to really putting it to him, and finally I worked out a deal, they was going to send me a hundred a month until something happened on the high-school coaching job. But real soon after that, I think maybe I asked them to quit sending me the hundred. Mr. Richards promised me the world and I'm sure he would have kept his promise, but I signed with the Bears. I didn't want to lay out a year.

Then the league found out that George Richards had been trying to get me, and they fined him five thousand dollars for tampering with me after I was drafted by the Bears. They said Mr. Richards had spent five hundred dollars getting my teeth fixed. Well, that wasn't the truth. He never spent a nickel on my teeth. But he must have been a heck of a swell guy, because he never even denied anything. He sold his ball club and got out of football, and it was an injustice, because he had never spent a nickel on my teeth.

Here was George Halas's method of operation in practice. First, he'd say, "Give me a center!" Then he'd say, "Bausch!" He'd say, "Give me two guards!" Then he'd say, "Fortmann and Musso!" Well, the first time I heard George say, "Give me a center!" I didn't wait for nothing more and ran out there and got over the ball. I noticed he looked kind of funny at me, but I didn't think anything about it. I found out later that Pete Bausch was the center—a big, broad, mean ol' ballplayer, a real nice German from Kansas. But all I knew was George had drafted me number one and I had signed a contract to play center, and I thought when it come time to line up I should *be* at center. From the beginning, I was overendowed with self-confidence. I feared no man. So I just went out there and got over that ball, and I was there ever since. They didn't need Pete no more.

I was such a good blocker that the men they put in front of me—and some of them were stars that were supposed to be making a lot of tackles—they would have their coaches saying, "Why ain't you making any tackles?" They'd say, "That goddamn Turner is holding!" Well, that wasn't true. I held a few, but I was blocking them, too. I used to think I could handle anybody that they'd put in front of me.

Bob Suffridge that played with the Philadelphia Eagles, he beat me for one half of a game and then I beat him the rest of our career. I learned how to block him. Heretofore I had always beaten everyone to the punch, but this man was quicker than me. Man, it was getting embarrassing. So finally I got to retreating—I'd take a step back and then I'd see him and I could react quick enough to get him. And after that, he was soup in my hands.

Those little guys that tried to outcharge me, or the big ones either, they was my soup. Like there was a guy named Tarzan White—oh, *goddamn!* He'd get so mad! And the madder he'd get, the blockered he would get. I'd have him on his back before he could ever hit me. Goddamn, it was funny. Another guy I met was this big Ed Neal. There in the late 1940s he played at Green Bay, and by this time they had put in the five-four defense, and they put the biggest, toughest guy they had right in front of the center. And I was expected to block him either way, according to which way the play went.

Well, this Ed Neal weighed 303 pounds stripped. His arms was as big as my leg and just as hard as that table. He could tell when I was going to center that ball, and he'd get right over it and hit me in the face. You didn't have a face guard then, and so that Ed Neal broke my nose seven times. Yes, that's right. No—he broke my nose *five* times. I got it broke seven times, but five times *he* broke it.

Anyway, I got where I'd center that ball and duck my head, so then he started hitting me on top of the headgear. He would beat hell out of my head. We had those headgears that were made out of composition of some kind—some kind of fiber—and I used to take three of them to Green Bay. Those headgears would just crack when he'd hit 'em—they'd just ripple across there like lightning had struck them.

So there one day, every time he went by me I'd grab him by the leg, and I began to get him worried. He said, "You son of a bitch, quit holding me!" I said, "You bastard, if you'll quit hitting me on the head, I'll quit holding you." And Ed Neal said, "That's a deal. By God, I want you to quit holding me, 'cause I ain't making no tackles." So the second half of that game we got along good, and later I got Halas to trade for him. I said, "The toughest damn guy in the league is that Ed Neal." And Halas traded for him, but he got his leg broke 'bout our second game and never did do much for the Bears.

Actually, the first guy that ever convinced me that I couldn't handle anybody I ever met was Bill Willis, who played on Cleveland, and I was on my way down then. They called him The Cat. He was skinny and he didn't look like he should be playing middle guard, but he would jump right over you. Now he might not enjoy my saying this, him being colored and maybe taking it the wrong way, but I'll tell you —the only way I could block him was I'd squat, and when he tried to jump over me, I'd come up and catch him. Every time, my nose would be right in his armpit—and later I'd tell my wife, "Goddamn, Gladys, that man perspires. I can't stand it." But that guy was a football player, and don't think he wasn't. Oh, he was a war-horse, that Willis.

To show you how I got off to a pretty fair start in pro ball, in 1940 when I was a rookie we won the championship, and that was the famous time we beat Washington, 73-0, in the championship game. And I'll tell you how that got started.

Clark Shaughnessy was one of our coaches, see, and Clark Shaughnessy to me is the most brilliant football man that ever lived. He was a genius to the extent that he was lacking in personality, and so a lot of people didn't like him or were jealous of him. We had guys that'd sleep while Clark Shaughnessy was lecturing. Every once in a while ol' Shaughnessy would hit one with an eraser or something. But he was such a brilliant man that as a rule he didn't have time to see if everybody was listening or to wake 'em up. Myself, I could listen to that man by the hour.

Anyway, Washington had just beaten us a couple of weeks before, and so when it came time to play the championship game, Shaughnessy gave us a little lecture. He drew up a play and he said, "This play's gonna work." He told us his reasons, and we were convinced that play was gonna work. Then he said, "Now, then, if it *don't*, here'll be the reasons why. And I'll give you another play that *will* work." Well, by the time he finished, all you had to do was open the door. We were ready, 'cause, really, he done had us convinced that that first play was gonna do it and if it didn't the other one would. It was an off-tackle play, the first one, and you know, the funny thing about it, the damn play didn't work.

Bill Osmanski was carrying the ball, and there wasn't no hole anywhere. So he started backing up, and he slipped 'way out around the end and started down the sideline. And he started picking up some blockers coming across from the other side. Ol' George Wilson, who later was head coach for Detroit and Miami, he was an end coming from the other side real slow. He was a real slow end, but, man, he could block. He hit one guy and knocked him into another, and when that happened, ol' Bill Osmanski was home free. That was the second play of the game, and it went sixty-eight yards for a touchdown and we went on to kill those guys. We got so much publicity from that game that later all Bill Osmanski wanted to do was run up into the line and then slide out and go around end. I got where I was disgusted with him because he wouldn't run Clark Shaughnessy's play the way it was supposed to be run.

But in that Washington game, after he scored that first touchdown, we scored so many times and kicked so many extra points that we started running out of footballs. The extra points were going into the stands, see? Well, after one of those touchdowns, Bob Snyder comes in from the bench and says to me, "Coach said to make a bad pass from center. He said we don't want to kick any more points because we're losing too many footballs." I think it was Snyder who was going to hold for that next extra point, but anyway, I said to him, "You go to hell. I'm going to put that ball right back in your hands, and if you don't want it, drop it. But I'm not going to make a bad pass." So I centered it back there, and he just turned it loose and let it lay on the ground. I don't remember who was kicking—we had a lot of guys kicking extra points that day—but whoever it was, damn if the guy didn't kick it up through there and lose *another* ball.

The reason I wouldn't make a bad pass from center was I had never made a bad pass yet—not in all the time I'd played center. As a matter of fact, in my whole thirteen years of pro football I never made a bad pass. One time we put in a running play off of punt formation, and on this play I was supposed to center the ball wide so as George McAfee could catch that ball on the run and have a fast start. Well, we tried that fake punt play and it failed. I laid that ball right where I was supposed to, right in George McAfee's hands, but they caught him for a loss. The next day the newspapers said, "Due to a bad pass from center, McAfee had to run the ball." It didn't seem to me like there was much justice there.

We won the western division the first four years I was up there in Chicago, and three of those times we won the championship. Of course, one reason we had a good team was we had an awful smart quarterback. Sid Luckman was smart and he could move. He was a great runner in college, you know. And he had a lot of guts. I've seen Sid take some fierce beatings out there and just keep dancing. But a lot of people called him lucky, and it did look like he was lucky. Like on third-and-ten or third-and-fifteen, he'd make a terribly bad pass but a guy would reach back and get it or scoop it off the ground. So it did look lucky, but after seeing it happen week after week, year after year, I can't call it luck. That was a talent there, because Sid kept doing it. He couldn't throw too good—he kind of palmed the ball and threw them soft, sloping type of passes—but he'd complete 'em.

Sid was kind of a prima donna. If we were going to leave a hotel on a bus at 10:35, well, we'd all be down there on the bus at 10:30, but then we'd have to wait for Sid. Finally, right on the money, here he'd come at 10:35. Course, everybody would gripe at him and they'd cuss him, but Sid didn't care. Actually, you couldn't blame Sid, because Halas kind of discouraged him from fraternizing with the players. Halas felt that if a quarterback buddied up with the players too much, he would lose some of his authority on the field. So Sid stayed with the coaches most of the time or by himself. He worked hard, which I liked and he didn't claim he was perfect. One time we had the ball on the other team's one-yard line with one second left. I gave Sid a pass play to use, and it worked and we won the game. Sid said, "Bulldog Turner called the play. I didn't know what to call."

You know, I was captain of the Bears for about seven, eight years. I was never appointed captain but I made myself captain. See, George Wilson was appointed captain, but a lot of times George would be a little bit slow in making a decision, so when a decision would come up that had to be made that took some thought, I would go up there with him and I'd say, "George, you get them in the huddle. I'll tell the ref what we want." And George would go back there in the huddle, although, of course, he'd been on the team several years before I was.

After Wilson quit, I still was never appointed captain. We just didn't have an official captain for about five years while I was doing it all myself. One day finally, something come up in a meeting and Halas said, "Turner's your captain. Talk to him." But up till then he had never appointed me, 'cause to be a captain you didn't only have to be a good player and a leader of men, but your off-the-field activities had to be real good, too, which mine weren't too good. So he never would appoint me captain.

Those men followed me, even up to the quarterbacks, who in many cases asked me what plays to call. One time in 1949 we were playing a prison team up in Michigan or somewhere. It was an exhibition game to raise some money for charity, and we furnished the prison team with a certain number of players. Anyway, George Blanda was just a rookie then and the coaches were fixing to cut him. But he was in the game and we had a fourth-and-one situation inside the fifty-yard line, which it looked like a pretty good call to go for the first down. Blanda came back to the huddle and he couldn't think of a play. He said, "I don't remember those plays. Wh-wh-what plays we supposed to call to make one yard?"

I said, "I'll tell you one, it's called twenty-nine direct cross buck." Now that was one of those plays where you're gonna go all the way or you're gonna lose ten yards. But Blanda didn't know that. He said, "Yeh, okay. We'll run the twenty-nine direct cross buck." Well, our halfback took off around the end, and he had gone forty yards when he remembered that he was supposed to hide the ball behind his back. So there, where it didn't matter, he put the ball behind his back and went the rest of the way for a touchdown. The coaches thought that was a damn smart play to call, and they kept ol' George Blanda on that account.

I don't know if you want to put this in your book, and I damn sure don't care if you do, but I originated the draw play, along with a lot of other plays. Sid Luckman was our quarterback then. Buckets Goldenberg, who played for Green Bay, could read Sid real well. Somehow he could tell when Sid was going to pass. And damn, as soon as that ball was snapped,

Buckets Goldenberg would pull back and start covering the pass. So I said, "Let's fake a pass and give the ball to the fullback and let him come right up here where I am, 'cause there's nobody here but me." The next year we put that play in, and it averaged thirty-three yards a try. The fullback would run plumb to the safety man before they knew he had the ball.

Remember my telling you how ol' Ed Neal would beat my head off? Well, I said to Halas one day, "You can run somebody right through there, 'cause Ed Neal is busy whupping my head." I suggested that we put in a sucker play—we called it the thirty-two sucker—where we double-teamed both of their tackles and I would just relax and let Neal knock me on my back and fall all over me. It'd make a hole from here to that fireplace. Man, you could really run through it, and we did all day. But later, ol' Ralph Jones—he used to be a Bears coach and was coaching a little college team—Ralph told me had brought his whole team down to watch the Bears play the Green Bay Packers that day, and he had told them, "Now, boys, I want you to see the greatest football player that ever lived, it's Bulldog Turner. I want you to watch this man on every play and see how he handles those guys." But see, ol' Ralph didn't know about that sucker play, and later he said to me, "Goddamn if you wasn't flat on your back every play!"

Did you know I got a forty-eight-yard average running with the ball? Damn right I do. I knew everybody's assignments and could play every position on the field. One time in Pittsburgh we got in a fight and two or three of our players got kicked out, leaving us shorthanded, and Halas let me go in and play halfback, which was all right because he knew I knew the plays. I loved to do it. Anyway, ol' Gene Ronzani, our quarterback that time, called a real fancy play named twenty-two behind. It was a play that hadn't been run since training camp. Yet I come on up through that line with the ball and got through that damn line. Ol' Abe Croft, a good Jewish boy that was from Texas and a hell of a nice guy, is downfield fixing to block for me, but I run right over him and over the guy he was trying to block and everybody else. I just kept plowing my way and finally got out in the open. They had a little ol' kid, I can't remember his name, that saw me coming and saw that I was coming full steam. So he started getting lower and lower and lower, getting himself ready for me. And I started lowering down like I was going to run right over him. But the funny thing, he froze. He froze there, and I just sidestepped him and ran on in for a touchdown, and he was still standing there froze. It was a forty-eight-yard run, and that's the only time I ran from scrimmage. Matter of fact, I was running so hard I couldn't stop and I ran right into the grandstand wall.

Big ol' Walt Kiesling was the Pittsburgh coach at that time, and he was mad. He thought we were making jest of him by using me at halfback, but we weren't. We had run out of players, that's all. Then after I had scored that touchdown, Halas put me back in safety to field a Pittsburgh punt, and I caught the ball and did a little dee-do and started up the sidelines. I went right over next to their bench and got tackled there. And as I was laying there, ol' Walt Kiesling come up and kicked me right in the butt just as hard as you ever saw. He thought we were making fun of him, and, boy, he let me have it. I thought it was a very unsportsmanlike thing to do.

You want me to talk about George Halas? Well, George Halas was a very brilliant man. He was a fair man. Never have I heard any of the great football players that he had say anything bad about Halas, have you? Have you ever heard of a man named Harlon Hill? His rookie year up there in Chicago he was going great guns, and one night we were coming back home on the train. I was on the coaching staff then, and this Hill was going great guns as a receiver. But on the train some of the boys said to me that Harlon Hill was about wanting to quit the squad. They said, "Harlon don't like Halas, and we'd like you to tell Harlon what *you* think about Halas."

So I said to him, "Harley, I'll tell you. I've been with Halas now about sixteen, seventeen years, and of all the time I've been with him, damn near every year I'd get in a little bit of financial trouble, and I'd need money during the off-season. I'd get in pretty bad trouble. But I would do two things. I would pray and I would call George. And you know? Every damn time George Halas came through first."

Ol' Harlon Hill said, "By God, that's good enough for me. I'll just go along with that."

Most of the criticism that you heard about Halas was that he wasn't paying. Oh, man, he had me believing all my career that I was the highest paid man in the league. But I argued with Halas a lot and I never signed until I'd gotten what I wanted. My first year up there, 1940, I signed a three-year contract for $2,250 the first year, $2,500 the second year, and $2,750 the third year—a $250 raise every year. I went on an interview once and I said I got $2,250 my first year, and a kid there said, "Oh, that's not much money, is it? How much did you get for playing?" I said, "That's what I'm talking about —I didn't get *nothing* for signing, I got $2,250 for playing the whole season."

After we won the championship in my first season, we went out to Los Angeles to play an all-star team in the Pro Bowl there, and Halas got sick out there and went in a hospital. I went up there and said, "George, I hate to call on you in a time like this, but I'm going back home to Texas. I'm *un-happy*."

He said, "What's the matter, Bulldog?" I said, "I play too cheap." And George said, "Too cheap? What do you want?" I said, "I want a bonus for what I've done. I want a bonus of $250."

Well, his secretary and his wife and his boy was there, and George said, "Make Bulldog out a check for $250." Then he gave me the check. I thanked him, shook his hand, went down the elevator, and started walking out, and then I thought, "I'll be damned!" I turned right around and went back and got on the elevator. I said, "George, goddamn it! That ain't enough!"

He screamed at me. "What do you mean, it ain't enough?" he yelled. I said, "I want another bonus." And from that hospital bed there, he screamed at me again. He said, "What do you mean, you want another bonus?" I said, "I want $250 more."

Well, he raised hell with me. He give me a big fight. But I said, "I play too cheap." So finally he said, "If I give you another check, are you going to be happy?" I said yes, I would, and he said, "Give him another check for $250." So I took it and I went away.

Now as I told you, I had signed a three-year contract. But I learned that Danny Fortmann was George's favorite boy and that Danny Fortmann was making more money than anybody else, outside of quarterbacks. I had become quite a star. I'd done shown them a thing or two up there myself. So when I went back up there to Chicago for my second season I carried my contract with me. I walked in and said, "George, I ain't gonna play for this contract." I tore it up in front of him and threw it in the wastepaper basket.

George acted real impressed. "What do you want?" he said. Well, actually, I'd rather have had a verbal agreement with George than a written one anyway, because if you've got a written one he'll show it to you too much. The owner had all the advantages in them contracts. But anyway, I said, 'I want to see Danny Fortmann's contract." He said he couldn't show me Fortmann's contract, so we argued around for about a week or ten days, and finally I just insisted. So he brought it out. "Okay, there it is," he said. But he had folded over the top of it where he used to type in bonus clauses. I couldn't see what he had typed in there, but I looked on that contract and Danny was making $4,500 salary. That's almost double what I was making. I said, "I ain't gonna play unless I get one just like it." So George wrote me one up.

Well, me and ol' Halas used to squabble a lot, but he was always fair to me. In the last few years I got up to fifteen thousand dollars a year, which was big money then. We argued a lot about contract, but once I signed I never said another word. Oh, George is the greatest guy that ever lived! If there was ever a human being could walk on water, he'd be one of them. I love him. I just love him.

You know, George Halas always liked to try new things, especially if they had to do with doctoring injuries. If he'd hear of some quack or someone that could cure a pulled muscle or a wrenched ankle, he'd send for him. He used to fly in a certain doctor from Detroit to work on the boys, and they couldn't stand it. Goddamn, I just hated to see him coming. I've seen guys cry with him working on them, he was that rough. Anyway, Hamp Pool got this shoulder injury one time, so Halas called in this doc from Detroit and told Hamp, "Go over and see the doc."

Hamp went down there and the doc said, "What's your trouble, son?" Hamp said, "I've got a little trouble with my shoulder." "Which one?" said the doc, and Hamp gave him the wrong shoulder. So the doc worked on the wrong shoulder, and he worked on it and worked on it and worked on it. Then he flew back to Detroit.

But ol' Hamp couldn't keep his mouth shut. He told a few guys what he had done. Well, Halas got word of this and he fined Hamp two hundred dollars for having the doc work on the wrong shoulder.

George Halas instilled a championship attitude in his players. He used to tell us, "Now when you go on that field you're the champions." He'd make us go out there and line up plumb across the field and then run down that field so that we'd run the other team plumb off it while they're out there warming up. He'd make us use more than our part of the field to warm up. "You're the champions," he'd tell us.

He was a fanatic on weight. I had to weigh 232 for all my thirteen years. During the off-season I'd get up to three hundred pounds, but then I'd have to come down to 232. George used to weigh us in once a week, and he'd fine you fifty dollars for every pound you was overweight. In order to lose weight we used to take laxatives, and one kid said one time that he ate so damn much of that Ex-Lax that he got fat off the chocolate.

Today, the bigger you are in pro ball, the better they like it. When they went to the four-man line, they wanted big men. I probably could have played at 240 or 250. Joe Stydahar played at 255, but he could have played at three hundred. He went to three hundred as soon as he quit playing and he wasn't fat at three hundred. Of course, in our time there wouldn't be but two or three in the whole nation that would weigh three hundred pounds. Now it's full of them.

Well, I hate to compare today's players with yesterday's. I'd rather not even get into it. Whether they could beat us or not, I don't want to say. I feel like maybe they couldn't, but I don't want to be quoted too much on that, because I could be wrong. But one thing we had that they don't was loyalty to the club. To me, the Bears was number one. I had some off-the-field activities that were questionable sometime, but they could never question my loyalty to the Bears. There's nothing like that today.

I never did save any money out of football. I never could save enough money to buy a place. I'd buy one, then have to pay it out. I always owed a lot of money. Some of our guys had good jobs in the off-season. They'd go to work for somebody that wanted to hire them because they were players. But I never did capitalize on being a player. I always came back to Texas in the off-season and practiced poverty. But I liked it here and got happiness out of coming back. I can't regret doing it. And if I'd have stayed around Chicago and made a lot of money, I probably wouldn't have kept it.

Anyway, I had me some great times, and along that line I'll tell you just one more story. I believe this was about 1946 or '47. We were playing in Washington against Sammy Baugh, who was in a class by himself. I think Joe Namath is the first that's come along that can sling that ball like Sammy. But anyway, Sammy fired that ball and I intercepted it on our three-yard line. I started weaving up that field and picking up blockers, and goddamn!—first thing I know, I'm about out in the clear and I got up a head of steam. I'm coming down that sideline, right by our bench, and as I went by I asked George Halas, "How am I doing?" I went on down that field and still had a couple of blockers in front of me, but I had a couple of opponents in front of me, too. I was kind of playing them. It was good running, I'll have to admit it. It was a good broken-field run.

But I finally decided I'll just dart over to my left, and I did.

And about that time somebody hit me in the back of my head. Somebody jumped on me. Well, it was ol' Sammy Baugh. He had jumped on my back and I was carrying him. I carried him for about seven yards, and I got the ball over the goal line and I looked up and said, "Sammy Baugh, I can outrun you, I *know* that. How in the hell did you get back there?"

And he said, "Well, Bulldog. You just cut back one time too many."

Now that's the truth. It shows in the films. I went ninety-seven yards for a touchdown, the last seven with Sammy Baugh on my back.

15

BULLET BILL DUDLEY

The time the Steelers might have won

From the time of their creation in 1933, the Pittsburgh Steelers have failed to win a single championship, or even a divisional title. Pittsburghers understandably do not accord Steeler management much sympathy, yet any dispassionate accounting of the club's misfortunes must acknowledge that an evil cloud seems to hover above the Steelers, defeating their best intentions. Bullet Bill Dudley's fleeting career with the Steelers was a case in point.

Immediately following World War II, clubowner Art Rooney hired one of the nation's foremost coaches, Dr. Jock Sutherland, a tall, dour Scotsman whose iron-fisted coaching —first at the University of Pittsburgh and then with the old Brooklyn Dodgers of the NFL—had turned out singularly bruising football teams. "His teams would hit you with everything but the junk man," says Tuffy Leemans, the old New York Giants backfield star. "The next day, all you could do was make your way down to the corner for a *Trib* or a *News* and then spend the day soaking in a hot tub." Sutherland's acceptance of the Steeler coaching job in 1946 was made doubly propitious for Steeler fans by the fact that Bill Dudley, the greatest of all Steeler backs, had come home from the war. Here, then was a combination—Sutherland and Dudley —that appeared to be the beginnings of an electrifying change for the better. But true to the calamitous pattern of

Steeler history, a hitch developed. Sutherland and Dudley discovered almost at once that they could not abide each other.

In 1938 Dudley had enrolled at the University of Virgina, a "gentleman's school" of the South. He was sixteen, stood five feet, eight and one half inches, and weighed 148 pounds. He had come from Bluefield, Virginia, just across the state line from the West Virginia coal fields, and it was on the strength of a lengthy, impassioned plea by his high-school coach, Marshall Shearer, that Virginia had granted Dudley an athletic scholarship.

"Right before I went down there they told me it was a coat-and-tie place," says Dudley, now a successful insurance executive, a member of the Virginia legislature, and resident of a fashionable section of Lynchburg. "So I went to a Bond's store in Bluefield that had a sale on. The suits were priced, I think, at nineteen dollars, twenty-nine, and thirty-nine. But whichever suit you bought, you could pay a dollar more and get another suit. So I bought the twenty-nine-dollar one and paid an extra dollar, and now I had two suits. Then my older brother, Jim, said to me, 'Now, Bill, you must wear garters at Virginia.' I said, 'Why?' And he said, 'To hold your socks up! That's the way you're supposed to do when you go to college.' So off I went to college with two suits and a pair of garters holding up my socks."

Four years later, in 1942, the Steelers exercised their right as a last-place team to make the first selection in the pro-football player draft, and they chose Dudley. By now he stood five feet, ten and one half inches, and weighed 168 pounds. His nickname, Bullet Bill, was a misnomer, merely a product of the sports world's passion for alliteration. At college he had been dubbed the Bluefield Bullet, and from that calling card grew the nickname Bullet Bill, but in the training camp of the College All-Stars at Chicago, he consistently had finished dead-last among all backs in sprints.

Poised to run a play, he effected a comical stance, his toes pointed outward, ducklike. He threw passes with an awkward sidearm motion. And when he place-kicked extra points and field goals, he stood directly over the ball; without moving forward an inch, he would bring his kicking foot downward like a pendulum. But what he lacked in classic form, Dudley made up in fiery attitude, flawless instinct, and a brilliantly analytical football mind. As a rookie, playing both offense and defense, he led the league in rushing and lifted the Steelers from last place to second.

"It was literally a vacation with pay, the most fun I ever had playing football," he says of that '42 season. "You'd stick your head in the huddle and the smell of alcohol would hang there till hell froze over. But you'd just raise up and go, 'Ahhhhh,' and get a breath of air, and then go to work. We had a lot of fun." The season over, Dudley enlisted in the Army Air Corps and went off to pilot a bomber in the Pacific theater.

John Bain Sutherland, himself an officer in the war, long before had forsaken dentistry to coach football. Wearing steel-rimmed glasses, his lips set tightly, his command uttered in a Scotch burr, he had disdained the advance of the T formation, doggedly turning out single-wing teams that ripped through opponents with the precision of a military drill team. In Bill Dudley (who could run, pass, and kick— "the best all-around ballplayer I've ever seen," says Art Rooney), Sutherland would have the perfect tailback for his offense. Rooney handed Dudley a blank contract on which Dudley entered the salary of thirteen thousand dollars. And as the 1946 season approached and the smoke-blackened mills along Pittsburgh's rivers swung into peacetime enterprise, the dawn of a new age seemed at hand for the Steelers.

Actually, Dudley had returned from service at the tail end of the previous season, and now he was to surpass his sensational rookie performance of 1942 by leading the league again, not only in rushing but in interceptions as well; and the Steelers, who had fallen back to last place, would muscle their way into the thick of the eastern division title race, playing to sellout crowds week after week. Yet as the players reported to training camp that season, no one could know that before another season rolled around, Sutherland would trade

Dudley, and that in less than two years' time, the dour Scotsman would be found wandering aimlessly along a Kentucky road, the victim of a brain tumor that killed him in a matter of days.

═══════════

We were supposed to report in on a Monday morning—eight o'clock or nine o'clock, I don't remember. Frankly, the exact time hadn't made an impression on me. You see, the only training camp I'd ever been to was the one in '42, and because of the College All-Star game in Chicago that year, I didn't have to be in camp in the beginning. So I didn't realize you had to be right on time the first day. I got up at six o'clock Monday morning and drove to the camp at Hershey, Pennsylvania, but I did not get there till the afternoon's practice.

Well, nothing was said. I just broke right in. It never entered my mind that the Doctor was a little miffed. Later on, I found out that he had been. At least that's what I was told, and maybe that's where the trouble started.

Of course, the Doctor was a taskmaster, no doubt about that. But at the same time, he was a man who knew what it took to win. Something like Paul Brown, you see, or Vince Lombardi. There's a lot of coaches don't know what it takes to win. They can say, "Oh, well, give me a six-foot-five fullback and give me a good quarterback," and you could give them everything they want and they'll still lose. But there are certain coaches who know what they want and know that if they get it they'll win. The Doctor was this type of coach.

Anyway, about two or three weeks into training camp we were out on the practice field one day and I was having trouble hitting people with my passes. I never was the greatest passer in the world, but I felt that it wasn't helping me any in practice to have the defensive men wearing the same color jerseys as the offensive men. I couldn't understand why clubs wouldn't go to the trouble to put different jerseys on the defense. Even today, a lot of high-school teams don't go to the trouble, and it's one thing I don't understand.

Well, we were scrimmaging and it was hot and it was late in the day, and I wasn't hittin' anybody to speak of. So the Doctor said, "Dudley, what's the matter with you? You haven't hit *anybody*."

I just looked at him and then I said, "Well, sir. If you had put different colored jerseys on the defense, I might be having a little bit better results."

And with that, you could have heard a pin drop. Evidently the Doctor wasn't used to being questioned. He stopped practice and came up to me and said, "Dudley!" I said, "Sir?"— because I always had the utmost respect for everybody I ever played football for. I always had respect for authority.

The Doctor said, "Are you coaching this football team?" I said, "No, sir." And he said, "Well, then, till you are, you keep your mouth shut. I'll make the decisions around here."

We went back to practicing, but I was a little teed off. That little scene had been embarrassing to me and I think embarrassing to the other ballplayers. But that night I went to Dr. Sutherland to apologize. Yessir, I went in to say I was sorry. But I ended up asking to be traded, with tears in my eyes. You see, when I tried to apologize he said, "Well, you know, Bill, there's a lot of ballplayers on the club who don't particularly like you." I don't remember his exact words, but they were words to that effect. And then he said that I wasn't blocking and tackling the way I should be. I was upset, and I said, "Sir, if you feel this way, and if the ballplayers feel this way about me, then maybe you'd better trade me, because if I'm not wanted I don't want to stay around here." I told him, "From the time I was in high school I've always played all-out. No one ever has accused me of not doing my job." And that was true. I had *never* been called anything but a team player, by *anybody*. I was hurt, you bet I was. The Doctor kind of passed over my suggestion that he trade me, but I said, "I'm serious. I'll talk to Mr. Rooney about it tonight." I went to Mr. Rooney—he was in camp that night—but he just glossed over it, too.

Then I went to Chuck Cherundolo, our center, and asked him if some of the ballplayers looked upon me the way the Doctor said they did. Chuck said, "Oh, hell, Bill. You know that's not true." I asked others and got the same answer. Maybe the Doctor was just trying to prod me, but I'd never been the kind you had to prod. I loved the game too much.

Well, the season soon was under way, going along into late October, and in one game I caught a helluva boot in the ribs. On Monday morning I could hardly get out of bed. On Tuesday we reported to start getting ready for a game with the Redskins, but I could hardly walk. So the Doctor didn't make me do a single thing in practice that week. He sent me over to the Jewish health center, the YM&WHA, where a young fellow gave me heat treatments and massages and did a great job with me. But in the first quarter of the Washington game I caught another terrific blow in the ribs and went down. I finally got up and played about fifty-one or fifty-two minutes of the game. I intercepted one of Sammy Baugh's passes and went eighty yards for a touchdown, and we beat the Redskins, 14-7, to go into a four-way tie for first place with Washington, New York, and Philadelphia. It was a big win for us, but on Monday I was right back where I'd started. I just couldn't do anything.

This time, though, the Doctor made me stay out on the practice field. He made me stay out there and run. But before I get on with the story, you ought to know what the Doctor's drills were like. There wasn't a team in the league that drilled the way we did. Two steps, cut! Four steps, cut! Six steps, cut! Eight steps, cut! One step, pivot! One step, pivot! One step, pivot! It was drill, drill, drill—the same things over and over. And the result was that you could execute the Doctor's plays no matter how damned tired you got in a game. It was something like Pavlov's experiment, you see. You heard a number, you reacted. It didn't matter what the score was or how tired you were, you automatically reacted.

I'm not complaining about those drills. As I said, the Doctor knew what it took to win. There's no doubt that he was the one who made me the Most Valuable Player in the league that year. Besides, I *wanted* to excel, and I was willing to spend the time needed to excel. Yet at the same time, if a man's injured, if he can't practice properly, I don't see why a coach should make him stay out there on that practice field. You see injured players standing around at practice, and pretty soon they're telling jokes or gossiping with newspapermen or bumping one another to keep warm. They're not helping themselves. They could be getting treatment or studying films, you see. And even if they're able to run somewhat, it doesn't do a bit of good to run a play at half speed. If you can't run it full speed, you can't get your timing down.

Now to get back to the story, we went out to Detroit to play the Lions, who hadn't won a ballgame hardly, and I told the Doctor's assistant, John Michelosen, "John, I can't *run.*" I hadn't had a chance all week to get well. Yet I started the game, and not surprisingly, I gained only six yards the whole game. On defense I let a boy named Johnny Greene come by me and catch a pass and go ninety-two yards for a score. Well, the Lions beat us, 17-7. So on the train coming home that night, I said to Chuck Cherundolo, "Chuck, I won't be back next year. I just can't take it. I love the game, but when I've got to play like this, there's no point to it." It wasn't that I objected to playing with an injury. I played with many an injury. The point was, if you can't get ready properly to do your job, why keep playing?

We beat Philadelphia the next week, so we were still in the running. The way it stood now, the Giants were in first place and we were in second. We were going into New York to battle it out with the Giants for first place, and with only two games left on our schedule, we had to win if we were to stay in the race. Anyhow, in practice that week the Doctor put a new play on the board and told me to take X number of steps and then cut. When we went on the field I did just as he'd told me, but all of a sudden he came up and said, "Bill, who told you to run that play like that?"

I said, "Sir, you did." He said, "I did?" And I said, "That's right, sir." You see, the Doctor was beginning to have lapses of memory. I don't think there's any doubt that the sickness that killed him more than a year later already had begun. But of course he didn't realize it. He called an assistant over and said, "Now how about this? Did I tell Dudley to run the play that way?" The assistant coach said, "Well, no. You didn't." A lot of people *feared* Jock Sutherland.

I respected him but I didn't fear him. I said, "Now wait a minute!" I called over another assistant coach, Mike Nixon, and I said, "What about it? Who's right here?" I'll always admire Mike Nixon, because he said, "Doctor, Bill's right." The Doctor turned around and walked away, leaving everybody standing there.

I had a good ballgame against New York, but we lost, 7-0, and then we lost our final game, which dropped us to third place. Then I went home and wrote a letter to Dr. Sutherland and sent a copy of it to Art Rooney. I told the Doctor that I admired and respected him but that we simply had conflicting personalities. I did not ask to be traded. I simply said that I thought it would be best if I didn't play any more football. When football gets to be all work and no fun, it's time to quit. So I signed on to coach the backs at the University of Virginia.

As far as I'm concerned, Jock Sutherland was the best coach I ever played for. But it's a strange thing, and I've witnessed it among other coaches and players. If you're a football coach and you can't get along with a good football player, something's wrong.

(After Dudley took up his new duties at Virginia, coaching the backfield in spring practice, he received a visit from Gus Dorais, the head coach of the Detroit Lions. Explaining that the Lions had obtained the rights to him from the Steelers, Dorais offered Dudley a three-year contract and ultimately persuaded him to resume his pro career. Dudley played three seasons with Detroit and three more with Washington before he retired for good. Meanwhile, the year after Dudley left Pittsburgh, the final season of Jock Sutherland's career and of his life, the Steelers finished in a first-place tie with Philadelphia for the eastern division title. In the ensuing play-off, the Eagles won. At no time in the Steelers' history had they come so close to winning a title, nor have they since come that close. Art Rooney and Steeler fans can only ponder what might have been had Jock Sutherland and Bullet Bill Dudley been able to coexist.)

16

STEVE VAN BUREN

"Money meant nothing to me. I was stupid, that's why."

His chin tucked to his chest, his great shoulders lowered to batter aside anyone in his path, his knees pumping violently, Steve Van Buren was a sight never to be forgotten by Philadelphia football fans of the 1940s. Who among them would argue that he does not continue to stand as the greatest Eagle ballcarrier of all? Having made his way through the heavy traffic, Van Buren baffled the next wave with instant changes of direction climaxed by a burst of speed that, in the time it takes one to wink, carried him beyond reach.

Still keeping his hand in pro ball as a scout for the Eagles, Van Buren lives in surburban Philadelphia. He is a soft-spoken man, very nearly shy with strangers. He hastened to caution me that I would find him no raconteur. Yet if the ability to view one's talents and shortcomings with equal candor is an appealing quality, Steve Van Buren wears very well indeed.

I guess the reason I made up my mind to make the high-school football team was that I wanted to go to L.S.U. Down in New Orleans I used to listen to the L.S.U. games on the radio and knew all the players' names. So I went out for the high-school team in my junior year, and I remember that they knocked the hell out of my nose. Blood was *pouring* out. I thought I might die. That was the first time I'd ever had a nosebleed. Sure, I'd been in a few kid fights, but I was always too fast for anyone to give me a nosebleed.

Anyhow, I wasn't able to make the high-school team. I weighed 135 pounds, and they said I was too small. When I tried out, I think I scored a touchdown every other time I ran the ball, but they still thought I was too small. So after my junior year I dropped out of school and went to work in the ironworks in order to build myself up and make the team. I worked there for a year and went up to 165, and then I went out for a halfback and made the team. But they put me at end.

By the time I got to L.S.U. the next year, 1940, I weighed 205. Bernie Moore, the coach, made me a blocking back in the single wing. I didn't care for the position and told Moore I didn't, and between seasons each year he would tell me that he was going to move me, but not until my senior year did he put me at running back. He later became commissioner of the Southeastern Conference, and when I ran into him about ten years after I'd been gone from L.S.U., he said, "Steve, I did you a terrible injustice." I said, "Well, everything turned out all right." He was a nice old man.

I was fast. Moore called me about the third-fastest man in the country at fifty yards, but I was out for track three years in college and never won a race. That's right. Never won a race. I ran the hundred but I was a quitter. I could run fifty but not much farther. Well, either you have it or you don't.

I didn't. It's just like racehorses, you know. Some of them are quitters. And when I bet on a quitter I don't curse, because I was that way. You have it or you don't.

I studied mechanical engineering and didn't work too hard at it, but in my last year I got some kind of award for being, I think, the athlete with the best scholastic record in the Southeastern Conference. Yeh, I used to walk around with a slide rule and all that stuff. But I never did use the engineering at all, and I've regretted that. I'd be doing a lot better. Anyway, we beat Texas A&M in the Orange Bowl, and I had a couple of long touchdown runs and threw a touchdown pass and on another play ran seventy yards but passed out at the ten-yard line because I had a bad ankle. I set an Orange Bowl ground-gaining record that lasted more than twenty years, but I didn't know I had that record till eight years later when my brother, Ebert, came up to Philadelphia to play for the Eagles and told me. I didn't care much about things like that.

The Eagles made me their first draft choice. Their general manager, Harry Thayer, came down to New Orleans and offered me four thousand dollars. Well, I had never heard of the Philadelphia Eagles. I'd heard of the Chicago Bears and Green Bay Packers, but not the Eagles. Anyway, I told Thayer I wanted ten thousand. He thought that was ridiculous and left. Then I went to Chicago to play in the College All-Star game, but about two or three days before the game I had to have my appendix taken out, and I thought I was through for the year. I watched the game from a wheelchair. Thayer came up to me and again offered me four thousand, and I thought I'd better take the four. Because of the appendicitis, the Eagles had a corset made for me.

The Philadelphia sportswriters called me the Barefoot Boy from the Bayous, which I didn't mind, although later on, when I was getting an award at a big banquet, I put my foot up on the table and told 'em, "Look. I wear shoes." It's true, though, that I didn't wear socks too often in those days.

When I set out to report to the Eagles I took a train to Philadelphia, but I didn't find out that I had passed Philadelphia till the train got to New York, and I had to turn around and come back. Well, when I finally got to town, Greasy Neale, our coach, came up to my room and told me about a great play of his—a long end run where nobody blocked the defensive end at all. The end was supposed to be faked inside, and I was supposed to go around him. A quick pitch is one thing, but I'd never head of a long end run where nobody blocked the end. I thought it was stupid. But it worked. We won with it. We went with it year in and year out. Greasy was creative, but once he created something he stayed with it. It was *his*, you know, so he stayed with it.

My rookie year I made all-pro, and even in later years when I'd lead the league in ground-gaining, Greasy would keep trying to teach me how to run the ball. He'd keep after me, make me run plays over and over. I'd finally holler at him, "For Christ's sake, why don't you trade me to a semi-pro team? Why don't you trade me to Bethlehem?" He'd laugh like hell. He kept asking me, "Why don't you keep your head up so you can see where you're going?" I knew why. You had no face guards then, so if you ran with your head up you wouldn't last long. In college I ran that way, but I learned my lesson my first year of pro ball. I got cut so badly under the lip that when I drank beer the beer ran out through the cut. I had to have sixteen stitches to close it.

One week we worked all week on a pass play to use against Cleveland. I had to take exactly six steps, then cut out at ninety degrees for the pass. By the end of the week I was sick of the play *and* Greasy Neale. Anyway, we used that play and Cleveland intercepted and went all the way for a touchdown. Greasy said I went out one yard too far, and he raised hell with me. Tommy Thompson, our quarterback, who was Greasy's boy, wasn't catching any hell, so I said, "I didn't throw the goddamn pass, you know. I only ran out to catch it!" Well, Greasy kept me hustling. Every year he had me feeling like I might be cut from the squad. Really.

One season I was sick the week of a game, and Greasy knew I was sick. He told me he was going to come up to my hotel room Sunday morning, the day of the game, to see how I was. Well, I was up an hour before he got there, and I had a thermometer so I took my temperature. It was 102, maybe 103. Now Greasy comes along with *his* thermometer and takes my temperature and studies the thermometer. I say to him, "I just *took* my temperature. I *know* what it is." But he keeps looking at his thermometer and finally says, "Gee, you got a little fever. Ninety-nine," he says.

What did I say to that? Nothing. I'd known what he was going to say.

I was weak as could be, but I think I scored three touchdowns that day. That's all I ran was three times. I ran one touchdown around end where nobody was within ten yards of me. Anybody could have run it. And I remember catching a pass over the middle, about a twenty-five-yard pass that anybody could have caught.

In the exhibition season of 1949, I had a bad back—not real bad, but just something that lasted three or four days or a week. In practice I'd go into the huddle and bend over to put my hands on my knees, and my back would give way and I'd pitch over flat on my face. I missed an exhibition game because of my back, and Greasy gave me all kind of hell. Jim Clark and a syndicate of new owners were just taking over, so Greasy gave me a lot of stuff about what I owed the new owners. Jesus! I never heard more crap in my life. But all I ever said to Greasy was, "Why don't you trade me?" I never got mad at him. Never.

Alex Wojciechowicz and I, we used to get in our cars and race to the stadium. If he was ahead of me and stopped for a light, I'd go up on the sidewalk to pass him. In those days I was in as many as three accidents in one day. Pretty good ones, too. One day I had my car towed in after an accident, and the wrecking company loaned me a car. A half hour later I wrecked that one. Then I borrowed a car from a player and had a fender torn off that one. All within twenty-four hours. But most of my accidents weren't my fault. I was wild but not real wild. I'm telling you, most of 'em weren't my fault. I was going only five miles an hour when I got hit by some of them, you know. I never got in an accident for going too *fast*.

Money didn't mean a whole lot to me. One time, all I had to do was go ten blocks and sign my name, and I would have picked up a thousand dollars. It was for endorsing something. But I didn't go. I think we were playing cards in the hotel at the time, or something like that. Money meant nothing to me. I was stupid, that's why. After I played the 1944 season for four thousand dollars and made all-pro, Greasy came to my apartment—and this is the honest-to-God's truth—and he said, "Steve, I want to sign you for next year, and here's what we would like to pay you. We can pay you $7,500. Whatever you ask for we're going to have to give it to you, but $7,500 is what we want you to sign for." And I signed. I wouldn't have argued if he'd have said five thousand.

I liked the Eagles organization. It was the only one I knew. A few years later—1949, I think—I was making fifteen thousand and the All-America Conference offered me twenty-five thousand. But I wouldn't have left the Eagles for *any* money. They treated me good. Early in 1952 I hurt my leg in practice. It was torn up so badly that one of our coaches came over and looked at it and turned around and threw up. The ball club told me not to worry, that I had a lifetime job with the Eagles. I was on a four-year contract for fifteen thousand a year, but I knew I couldn't play again so I cut my salary that season to $7,500. I never did play again. I left the organization. If I hadn't, I would at some time or another have been head coach, you know, but I never gave a darn. I went into the automobile business and went bankrupt.

The Philadelphia fans had been great to me. I used to go to the racetrack a lot, and then on Sunday, when I'd go out on the football field, I'd hear the fans yell, "Hey, Steve! What's going to win the double tomorrow? What's going to win the daily double?" I'd wave to 'em. They were great.

In the days before television, you played harder at home than you did on the road, because at home was where your fans saw you. Today, with television, more home fans see you when you play on the road than when you're at home. It used to be that when you were on the road, if an opponent was running down the sideline you'd just push him out of bounds. But at home you'd knock hell out of him. Your friends would be there to see it.

When I first came into pro ball I played both ways, offense and defense, but later we went to platoons and I played only offense. I don't agree that today's game is less tough than the old game. I think it's tougher. Well, it's tough one way and not as tough another way. If you're playing just offense, say, you're going to play harder than if you're playing both ways. When I played both ways I'd loaf a little on defense. And everybody else loafed at times, too. They paced themselves. See, you knew when to loaf. If a play went away from you, and you were a little tired, you just weren't going to chase it as hard as you would if you were only playing one way. And if you were looking good—if you'd just run for a couple of touchdowns—you knew you were going to loaf a little on defense.

But, of course, the amount of money you make has something to do with how hard you play. When I was making four thousand dollars I was out there playing only three weeks after having my appendix out. But if I'd been signed for big money, I wouldn't have showed up at the ballpark in that condition. Some years, I played with twelve shots of novocain a game, for very little money. If I'd have been making $600,000 on a no-cut contract, like some players got in the 1960s, I wouldn't have done it. You don't take that kind of punishment when you're rich.

17

MARION MOTLEY
AND BILL WILLIS

The color line is broken

Even in the minds of senior sportswriters and persons actively working in the game, the origins of the black man in pro football are surprisingly murky. Any reasonably knowledgeable baseball fan knows without having to think twice that in 1947 Jackie Robinson broke the color line in baseball and that Branch Rickey, general manager of the Brooklyn Dodgers, was the enlightened mogul who decided it should and would be broken. Yet both the public and the experts are badly mistaken, or at the least foggy, about events leading to pro football's social transformation.

Very early in my research on this book, I heard at least three Negroes mentioned as having been the Jackie Robinson of pro football. Many of my own generation, having been in their teens in 1946, when a shifty black halfback named Kenny Washington put on a Los Angeles Rams uniform, somehow remember Washington as the first of his race to play pro football. On the other hand, an old-timer told me that Ray Kemp, a mulatto who played tackle for Pittsburgh in 1933, was the first Negro in the game. Others went back still further to Fred (Duke) Slater, a splendid tackle who spent a decade in the NFL and later became a judge in Chicago. Slater's pro career dated clear back to 1922, the third year of organized pro football, when he played for the Rock Island Independents. Yet even Slater had predecessors.

Hanging in clear view on a corridor wall in the Pro Football Hall of Fame at Canton, Ohio, is a squad photo of the 1921 Akron Steels of the American Professional Football Association, the forerunner of the NFL. Among the squad stand two black men. One was Paul Robeson, whose pro-football career came to be dwarfed by his career as a brilliant actor and great basso, as well as by his controversial role as a Marxist. As an end at Rutgers he had made Walter Camp's All-America team two years running, and according to his biographer, Edwin P. Hoyt (*Paul Robeson: The American Othello*), he received as much as a thousand dollars a game playing pro ball while attending Columbia Law School. But he "shared a public revulsion against professional-football players that existed in the 1920s," Hoyt has written.

The other Negro in the photograph is Frederick (Fritz) Pollard, a beaming halfback sporting the sort of coiffure that almost fifty years later would come to be known as the natural Afro look. A former Brown University student, Pollard actually had begun playing with Akron in 1919, a year before the American Professional Football Association came into being, and there may have been other blacks, too, who were in on the very creation of pro-league play. But pro football, having made a biracial beginning, gradually became lily-white. The handful of Negroes that had speckled the NFL in the 1920s vanished, and few others took their place. By the middle 1930s, the Negro had disappeared from pro ball; some say that a few clubs employed light-skinned mulattos, passing them off as Indians, but the notion is unverified. The game was going to have to turn up a Branch Rickey and a Jackie Robinson of its own in order to tap the great pool of black football talent that was going to waste in America.

Paul Brown, though he never has been accorded the distinction, probably was the Rickey of pro football. A largely forgotten lineman named Bill Willis probably was the Robinson.

The year was 1946, and the nation was vigorously exercising her appetite for peace, having just come through another world war. A new league—the All-America Football Conference—was ready to challenge the NFL. In Cleveland, Paul Brown became head coach of the new AAFC franchise to be known as the Browns. He quietly gave Bill Willis a tryout and signed him. A week or so later, he tried out another Negro, fullback Marion Motley, and signed *him*.

That same year, it is true, the Los Angeles Rams, owned by Dan Reeves and coached by Adam Walsh, signed UCLA star Kenny Washington and a UCLA end named Woodrow (Willie) Strode, bringing the NFL's unwritten racial barrier crashing down. But if, for the purpose of simplifying football history, a Jackie Robinson and a Rickey must be designated, Willis and Brown probably deserve the distinction on the ground that the Cleveland experiment produced the more lasting effects. Kenny Washington, troubled by injured knees, played only three years, and Strode lasted but a season. Willis, a middle guard who weighed little more than two hundred pounds but had the reflexes of a mountain cat, played eight years (four of them after the Browns were merged into the NFL) and seven times made all-pro. Marion Motley, as a fullback and a truly fearsome one, established the Negro's place in the pro-football headlines. But most important, by helping to make the Browns champions, both in the All-American Conference and in the NFL, Willis and Motley placed the black man in demand and made him a pro-football fixture.

I visited Motley at his modest but comfortable home on the east side of Cleveland. A bulky, mustachioed man weighing in the neighborhood of 260 pounds, he wore a Browns sweatshirt and held a stout cigar in one hand and a glass of ale in the other. Physically he looked the part of a ward politician who has everything well in hand. A good host, he saw to it that I, too, had ale. But as he told his story, his mood occasionally darkened. For in the years since 1955, when his playing days ended, he has moved from one dreary job to another, finally settling into a management position with a construction company, a job that resulted from publicity attendant to his 1968 induction into the Hall of Fame.

My meeting with Willis took place in the den of his ranch-style house on the outskirts of Columbus, Ohio. He is deputy director of the Ohio Youth Commission and in that capacity heads up the state's network of juvenile corrective institutions. As the reader will observe, the two men—Motley and Willis—have been left with somewhat disparate views of pro football's Branch Rickey, Paul Brown.

===

Motley

In 1946, after the war ended, I was getting ready to go back to college, but in the meantime I had wrote Paul Brown and asked him about trying out for the Cleveland Browns. He wrote me back and told me that he had all the backs he needed. So I forgot about trying out for the pros. Matter of fact, my coach at the University of Nevada sent me a train ticket and I was all set to go back to school. But then one day I heard where Bill Willis had went to camp to try out for the Browns and was doing very well. And then one night I got a call from one of Paul Brown's assistants.

He asked me how would I like to come up and try out for the football team. Willis had made the ball club, see, and they had to have someone to go along with him. They wanted another colored fellow to room with him. I learned about this later. After my first season I got the word from a man who had heard it through the front office. I was only supposed to be a roommate for Willis.

In a way, Paul Brown and I went all the way back to high-school days together. I played three years for McKinley High in Canton, Ohio. We lost only one game each year I was there, and the one game we lost every year was to Massillon. Paul Brown was the Massillon coach. He was one of the great high-school coaches of the 1930s. In Canton we highly respected Paul.

The way I first came to play for Paul, and this was long before pro ball, was just one of those lucky things. I came here to Cleveland in 1945 to be inducted into the service. I don't know how many guys were standing in line in front of me— must have been a hundred guys. The people in charge never asked 'em what branch they wanted. They'd just tell 'em, "Army! . . . Navy! . . . Army!" But when I got up there— and this shows you how fate worked things for me—they said, "What branch do you want?" I'd heard that in the navy you'd get to see the world, plus I'd heard the navy was much cleaner than the army and had the best food. So I said, "Navy." If I'd said army, I never would have played for Paul Brown and probably never would have played pro ball. This is why I say fate worked in a peculiar way there.

The navy sent me to the Great Lakes Training Center outside of Waukegan, and when I found out that Paul was coaching the football team there, I phoned him to see if I could get on the team. He said, "Yes, I remember you, Marion. Why don't you come over Monday and talk with me?" His main logic was to see if I had gotten real fat and out of shape. I was about twenty-four or twenty-five by then, but when he saw that I was down to about 220, he immediately said, "Well, yes, I'd like you to play for me." So after I finished my twelve weeks of boot training they moved me into ship's company, which put me in safekeeping.

But one day in August, all of a sudden, I got orders to move out. I was going to be moved out right away with a unit going to Port Chicago, California. The trains came right up to Great Lakes to pick you up, and I was right there at the train when I phoned Paul and told him what was happening. He told me, "Don't you move. You stay right there at that phone."

Then he called the commandant and told him, "If you want me to coach this football team, you better stop that player and any other player that comes through there." Then Paul called me back and said, "You get your gear off that train and bring it back to the barracks."

I was elated to be playing under Paul, because I knew what a great coach he was. There was nothing complicated about his football, although he was a stickler for detail and a disciplinarian. Matter of fact, Paul was sitting on a train one Sunday afternoon at the same time that I and another player —a young kid—were sitting in another train on the next track. We were going out on liberty. This kid I was with didn't see Paul, but Paul saw *him* from the window of his train. The kid had a cigarette in his hand. On Monday morning Paul fired the kid. They sent him to Iwo Jima, I think.

You know, I'm probably the only player who ever knocked Paul down, or at least the only one who got away with it. Up at Great Lakes I had a toe that was real tender. I'd broken it badly in a game. Well, Paul had the team around him in a circle one day, and he was talking to the players, and while he was talking he backed up on my foot. Boy, I just hauled off and hit him with an elbow that sent him clean across that circle. He *flew* across that circle. He said, "What'd you do *that* for?"

I said, "You stepped on my foot. You stepped on my poor foot."

He just laughed and turned around, and after that he always told people, "Don't step on Marion's feet, 'cause he'll hit you."

Well, as I said, Paul later was coaching the Cleveland Browns in 1946, and I got invited to camp for a tryout. A cousin of mine drove me from Canton over to the camp in Bowling Green, Ohio, and I made it there in time to go straight out to the afternoon practice. That first day, we ran wind sprints and I was out in front of everybody. I beat all those guys—the fullbacks, anyway. So the next day Paul put me all the way up on the second team and I immediately saw resentment from the players.

As Bill Willis and I were going to our room after practice, I said, "Gee, I sure hate Paul putting me on that second team today, 'cause some of those backs was just acting awful snotty." They hadn't *said* anything, but I could feel the tenseness around me. I said to Bill, "I just wish Paul would put me back somewhere and let me *work* my way back up. Then I'll straighten some of them out up there."

I think Paul saw the resentment, because the next day he threw me back to the fourth team. But it didn't take me long to move back up. They had a scrimmage and I played mostly on defense, at linebacker, and I had 'em all standing on their ears. After the scrimmage was over, one of the guys asked Willis, "What the heck was eating Motley today? Was he trying to kill somebody?" Willis told him, "No, he's just trying to make the ball club." So from then on, there seemed to be a change of feeling toward me. I had the best times in the sprints, I ran the ball as well as any of the others, and after they saw that I had the ability, their attitude toward me changed.

Of course, Paul was very strong for fairness. In those early years that I was with the Browns, whenever any rookies from the South reported to camp they came right over to meet Willis and me. They'd come and find us and shake hands and make friends with us. Somewhere along the line they were told that when they got to camp they would have to do that or they couldn't play. I'm sure they were told, before they signed, that we were part of the ball club and that they were going to have to play *with* us. So best to make friends with us. But our opponents were something else.

In the very beginning, Paul warned Willis and me. He said, "Now you know that you're going to be in many scrapes. People are going to be calling you names. They're going to be nasty. But you're going to have to stick it out." It was rough, all right. If Willis and I had been anywhere near being hotheads, it would have been another ten years till black men got accepted in pro ball. We'd have set 'em back ten years.

I still got many a cleat mark on the backs of my hands from when I would be getting up after a play and a guy would just walk over and step on my hand. Look. You can see the scars. I couldn't do anything about it. I'd want to kill those guys, but Paul had warned us. The referees would stand right there and see those men stepping on us, and they would turn their backs.

The guy that finally broke it up was a referee out of Buffalo —one of the older referees. Oh, what the hell's his name? I shouldn't have forgotten it. Anyway, this is what he started doing. When he caught a guy stepping on us, he wouldn't tell him nothing. He'd just pick up the ball and start walking off fifteen yards. They'd ask him why, and then he'd say, "For stepping on that man." The other referees saw what this ref was doing, and they looked around and saw that we were bringing in the crowds as well as the white guys, so they started to protect us.

Of course, the opposing players called us nigger and all kind of names like that. This went on for about two or three years, until they found out that Willis and I was ballplayers. Then they stopped that shit. They found out that while they were calling us names, I was running by 'em and Willis was knocking the shit out of them. So they stopped calling us names and started trying to catch up with us.

We had a close-knit ball club, and I think this was why we won. Many times the guys wanted to fight for Willis and me. They'd want to take care of the guy who was playing us dirty. But I'd say, "What the hell, just let him go, because I'm going to run over him anyway." Actually, I loved the game.

Paul worked his psychology on everybody. The thing about him that used to irk me was that when I'd come out of the game for a rest—and maybe I'd been both playing offense and defense, working hard as I could, but maybe I hadn't done something I was s'posed to—when I came out of the game, Paul would walk up to me and in a low voice, almost like he was hissing at me, he'd say, "Do you know that you're *killing* our football team?"

Then he'd walk away from me, like nothing had happened. Boy, I could have walked up behind him and choked him. I'd go back out there, and the first jersey that got in front of me, I'd try to kill the guy wearing it.

(Although he never gained as much as a thousand yards in one season, there are some who say that Motley in his peak years was a more valuable fullback than Jim Brown, the man who signed with Cleveland two years after Motley's final retirement and came to be generally recognized as the greatest fullback in pro-football history. Motley lives but a few blocks from the small house in which Brown resided until his departure for Hollywood and an acting career; Motley knew him as a friend, and I recalled seeing Marion at the Brown home when in 1963 I had worked with Brown on a book. I wondered which of the two men was the better fullback in Marion's opinion.)

I can't answer that. The thing I probably would have had on Jim was the fact that I could block better. I had a knack for it. Blocking was no task for me. But I don't think Jim had anything on me as a runner, either. I was bigger than he was. I don't know who was faster, it's hard to say. I couldn't tell you. Of course, when I was a rookie I was twenty-six already, and when we went from the All-America Conference to the National Football League in 1950, I was an old pro by then. I was thirty. But the thing was, I didn't have the running plays Jim had. I had one wide play, the end run, and that was it. Just an ordinary ol' end run. See, I didn't have the flips. I often said to Paul, "Let me get them out there and scatter 'em. Let me take a few of 'em out there with me." But he'd say, "No, the flip wasn't designed for you." I had to make my yardage up the middle.

You know, during half of my eight years with the Browns —in fact, the whole four years I played with them in the National Football League—I had bad trouble with my knees. Geez, did I have trouble with them. And the way Paul handled the situation, he really shortened my career. In 1951 we were in training camp, getting ready to play the College All-Stars, and Paul was giving us fundamental drills in blocking and tackling. In one of these drills a player's knee hit my knee, and as soon as he hit me, well, I was *hurt*. By the time practice was over, my knee was like a balloon.

The trainer told Paul to give me a couple of days off, but Paul said, "No. No, he can come out and run a little bit. If he can't run, he can hop around." So that's what I did. I ran on one leg. The ground at that particular time was like cement, and running on that one good leg, I wound up with *both* knees full of water.

Our team doctor was on vacation, so they sent me to see a doctor in Cleveland who's now one of the top surgeons in the country. A Dr. Lambright. He took two pans of water off my knees, and then he called the training camp and told our trainer that I shouldn't run for three or four days. So I went back to camp thinking I'm going to get a rest, but after I'd stayed off the field for one day, Paul Brown told me, "You get your suit on and be out here." I put on my equipment and stood around out there for a while, and then Paul said, "All right, Motley, Get in here. I want you to run some." I tried to, but my knees locked up on me and swelled up on me big as a balloon. I had to have the water taken off again.

I went to Chicago and played in the All-Star game, and after the game I couldn't walk out of Soldier's Field. I had to lean against a wall while they brought my car to me. I couldn't move. I always had knee trouble after that, and football became a job.

The thing that burns me up is that the other ball clubs give their players a break when they're all through, but Cleveland didn't do anything for me. I didn't think Paul *owed* me anything, but I thought that I should have gotten a job or something. I felt I deserved a chance. Oh, I *asked*. I asked Paul for a scouting job, and then in 1964, when Blanton Collier was coach, I asked Collier and Art Modell, the owner. I told them, "I know that the white scouts are having trouble getting information from the Negro schools, and I think I'm well enough known that I could help you." This was a beautiful idea. Modell thought this was a beautiful idea. But I waited half the football season and never heard from them. Dante Lavelli was scouting for the Browns at that time, so I said to Lavelli, "What the hell's happening? Nobody's called me. If they don't call me soon and send me out to scout, I'm going to call the newspapers." I guess Lavelli told 'em right away, because that Friday they called me and told me they wanted me to go to Wilberforce.

But Wilberforce had nothing. Neither one of the teams in that game had anything. The Browns were just sending me there as an appeasement, to keep me from saying anything. I made two or three trips that year, but all this was appeasement. One day I caught Modell at the practice field. "Modell," I says, "what about the scouting thing that we talked about?" He's kneeling on one knee, looking at practice. He doesn't even look around. He looks out on the field and tells me, "Well, Motley, you know what? The only thing you can help us with is signing the ballplayers." I says, "Is that what you think?" He says yes, and I tell him, "Well, I thank you." And with that I walk off that field.

At the end of the season they hired a guy named Nussbaumer, who coached at Detroit, who hadn't ever given Cleveland a single day—they hired him as a coach and scout. So I blew my top. I wrote a statement. I blasted 'em. I don't know what all I said, but I really gave it to them. I had a newsman, a colored writer, put it on UP, AP, and all the rest of them. Later, I'm watching practice one day and Modell came over and said, "You did me an injustice." He said, "I'm not prejudiced. I always tried to help the Negro. I give to their community fund." I said, "I don't know nothin' 'bout that. It doesn't bother me what you give. But what you give *me* was nothin'."

I still wear my Cleveland Browns jacket. A lot of times somebody will mention it or make some kind of playful remark about it. Well, my answer is, "I earned it. I earned the right to wear this jacket."

Willis

From 1938 at the latest, and on into the early '40s, college football had some truly outstanding Negro players, but none of them ever made it into professional football. The National Football League seemed to have an unwritten law against them. It was therefore inconceivable to me that I could play pro ball. Even though I had made All-American as a tackle at Ohio State, no team drafted me. So in 1944, after I had played my last season of college ball, I accepted a job as head football coach and athletic director at Kentucky State, a Negro school. I coached there in 1945, and the way I like to describe that season is that we lost only two games out of ten. I usually don't mention that we tied four. At any rate, it was shortly after that season that I got the urge to play pro ball. The reason I felt that I might have a chance was that a new league, the All-America Conference, was being formed and Paul Brown was going to be one of its head coaches. I knew Paul well.

I grew up here in Columbus, where I attended East High School and participated in football, basketball, and track, but I almost did not enroll in East High because my brother, Claude, was a great fullback there and I did not think I could measure up. They nicknamed me "the Deacon" but Claude was the original Deacon, and really, he was the outstanding athlete in the Willis family. At any rate, my high-school coach was trying to get me a scholarship at the University of Illinois when Paul Brown was hired as head coach by Ohio State. That changed everything. Ralph Webster, my coach, advised that I go to State. Even then, Paul had a reputation for fairness, because he had used many Negro players while coaching high-school ball at Massillon. So I went to see Paul and he said yes, he would like to have me play for Ohio State.

I never had any difficulty with any teammate while playing with State or, later, while with the Browns. One reason was because I always attempted to show respect and conducted myself in such a way as to demand respect from my fellow players—I never told ethnic jokes, never called a teammate by a nickname unless I was certain that I was in bounds, never rubbed a teammate's hair for good luck, as some players did. Then, too, Paul set the tone—"the thread follows the needle," you know. Paul treated every man alike.

Consequently, early in the spring of 1946, after Paul had become coach of the Cleveland Browns, I drove over to Cleveland to ask him if there was a possibility of my playing in the new league. He told me he knew of nothing whatsoever in the league's constitution or bylaws that would keep Negroes out. He said he was going to a league meeting soon and would be in touch with me later. I felt encouraged.

Now it so happens that at that time the Canadian League was beginning to compete for American football players, and not long after I visited Paul I heard from a coach named Lew Hayman, who invited me to play in Montreal. That very year, Jackie Robinson was breaking into organized baseball in Montreal, and I had read that he was being accepted for the great ballplayer he was. So I made up my mind that if I couldn't play for Cleveland, I would play in Canada. Early that summer, in order to get ready for the season, I underwent surgery on an old knee injury and had the cartilage removed. Time was slipping by, and I had heard nothing further from Paul Brown, but Lew Hayman came to visit me and left me a plane ticket with instructions to report to the Montreal club in two weeks.

It was a Sunday, I'll never forget, and I was just about to pack up and go to Canada when I received a phone call from a fellow named Paul Hornung, a Columbus sportswriter. He had covered the Ohio State games and thought an awful lot of me, and now he was calling from the Browns' training camp at Bowling Green and wanted me to come to camp and try out. "I can't do that," I said. "I wouldn't feel right walking into camp without being invited."

Hornung said to me, "Now wait a minute. You just get over here." He said, "You just take my word for it that you can make this ball club, and as a matter of fact, I'll stake my reputation on it." Well, I said to Hornung, "Look—I have a plane ticket to go to Canada. If I go to the Browns' camp it's going to cost me expenses." Then Hornung said, "Never mind about that. You just be here." He was so insistent that I finally said okay. I phoned Lew Hayman and told him what I was doing, and he bet me a new hat that I wouldn't make the Cleveland club.

Practice was just ending when I arrived in camp. When Paul Brown spotted me, he came across the field to greet me, and it seemed obvious from his manner that he had been expecting me. I imagine he'd put Paul Hornung up to phoning me. Why? I don't know why. Nor do I know if Paul knew anything about my surgery, but he asked me if I felt I could play football. "I don't know," I said. "I think so." I said nothing about my knee. I had been exercising it some, but the thing was still kind of gimpy. "Well, go get a uniform and be out here tomorrow," Paul said, and the next day, toward the end of scrimmage, he put me in on defense at middle guard.

The five-man line was popular then, and as middle guard I played directly opposite the center, who on the Browns happened to be a player named Mo Scarry. He had gone over to the Browns after playing a couple of seasons in the National Football League and was very quick at snapping a football. In fact, he had the reputation of owning the fastest hands in pro football.

But the first time he snapped that ball back to Otto Graham, the quarterback, I hit right into him and drove him into Graham and broke up the play. As a matter of fact, I broke up four straight plays. Scarry couldn't believe I was getting through him legally. He yelled, "Hey, check the offside! Check this guy for offside!"

But what I had been doing, you see, was concentrating on the ball. The split second the ball moved, or the hands tightened, I charged. And I charged him a different way every time. I would go under him, then over him. I would bang off his left shoulder, then I would bang off his right shoulder. I caught Graham every time, usually before he had even begun to pull away from center. My knee was still a little weak, but I figured I had to make the club that day.

"Yes, I had better check this for offside," Paul said when Scarry started complaining. Paul got down in a crouch in the linesman's position, and he stationed one of his assistants, Blanton Collier, right behind me. The offense ran three more plays, and all three times I charged through and caught Graham. Paul called off practice and told me to see him at his office that night. He signed me to a four-thousand-dollar contract and told me to say nothing to anyone. An announcement, he said, would be made at the proper time.

So that's how it all began. Although I was the first Negro player in the league, my arrival in training camp caused no commotion as far as I could tell. You see, in contrast to most professional football teams, Paul had gathered most of his players from the Big Ten, and there were about six men I had played with at Ohio State. After I had been in camp for a week, as I recall, Paul announced that he had signed me, and again there was no commotion. And maybe that's why Paul decided to sign Marion Motley. He asked me one day if I would like a roommate. I said that would be nice, and he said, "Well, Marion Motley is going to be reporting."

At Ohio State I had played against Marion when he was playing for the Great Lakes Navy team. Some might say he was so great a fullback as to be the equal of Jim Brown, who came after him in Cleveland, but there is really no fair way in which Motley can be compared with Brown. Jim Brown was perhaps the greatest running back in pro football. In my opinion, however, Motley was a better all-around ballplayer than Brown—a great runner, great blocker, and a threat as a pass receiver. Also, Motley was a great defensive ballplayer. Those famous goal-line stands we used to make were due to a very large degree to the effectiveness of Motley as a line-backer. He was not quite as fast as Brown, but he was fast. He wasn't as shifty as Brown, but, brother, he could shed those tacklers. In a scrimmage one day I dived over the center and while I was in midair I saw Motley coming straight at me. I must have looked like Pluto in a movie cartoon, because there I was, trying to turn around in midair, churning my legs. Marion hit me head-on, and I saw stars.

Remember, Marion several times gained at least eight hundred yards in a season despite the fact that the Browns at that time were almost strictly a passing team. We were a passing team because we had a great passer in Otto Graham, a great blocker for him in Marion Motley, and great receivers in Dante Lavelli and Mac Speedie. Our halfbacks hardly ever carried the ball, so our opponents knew that if Graham didn't throw, Motley ran. Marion made his yardage pouring through that line, especially on trap plays. He would run the ends only once in a while, just to keep the defense honest. Yet he would gain more than eight hundred yards in a season and average almost six yards per carry during his pro career.

In the beginning I played both ways, offense and defense, and up there in the line I'd hear the opponents getting ready for Marion—especially the Brooklyn Dodgers, who had quite a few bigoted players on the team. That is, there were many players who tried to create racial tensions while playing. You would hear them yell, "Get that big black blankety-blank!" or "Look out over this way! That black so-and-so is coming around here this time." They also had some choice words for me. When they stopped Motley, they would hold him up, keep him on his feet, so they could take shots at him. They would keep coming, taking whacks at him.

The first time we played the Dodgers, just about the whole lot of them piled on Marion. I started pulling guys off, saying, "Okay, boys, the play's over! Let's go!" Well, they had a five-by-five type, a guy about 260 pounds, and he wheeled around and said, "Keep your black hands off me!" I stepped back a pace in case he tried to reach me with a punch, but I was angry and I kept my hands on his shoulder pads. Before anything more could happen, some of our players—Lou Rymkus, Lou Groza, and some of the others—raced over and broke it up. Then Rymkus told me there was no point in my getting into fights and risking being thrown out of the game. He said, "If anyone gives you a bad time, you just tell us. *We'll* take care of him."

However, I soon won the respect of my opponents. They

learned that I could take it and dish it out, and I didn't really have to play dirty ball to hold my own. Speed was my greatest asset, but I could unleash a pretty solid forearm block and a rather devastating tackle. Besides, we had to play each team twice during a season, and by the second time around, my opponents and I had convinced each other that it would be to our mutual advantage to play the game clean. Then, too, there were officials in the league who soon learned who the dirty players were and stayed on top of the situation. By the second year my biggest problem simply was keeping some of my opponents from holding. Of course, this is not to say that every once in a while someone didn't let an elbow slip accidentally on purpose. However, these incidents were cleared up without too much trouble after a few retaliations. By the way, when the Browns played in Miami, Paul Brown gave Marion and me the weekend off (with pay) to prevent our being subjected to any possible Southern hostility.

I had some unpleasant moments in pro football, but the experience was much more pleasurable than unpleasant. I never had a run-in with a teammate. I did not have the problems that Jackie Robinson experienced when he broke into the big leagues. Perhaps I was fortunate that I had played with or against many of the pros in college. And don't forget, we were a Paul Brown team. It has generally been overlooked, but I think it is accurate to say that Paul Brown was the Branch Rickey of professional football.

Oh yes—Lew Hayman, that fellow from Montreal who bet me a new hat I'd never make the Browns—he bought me a very nice Stetson.

18

BOBBY LAYNE

"I sleep fast!"

With the possible exception of his coach, Buddy Parker, it was Bobby Layne, more than any other man, who made the city of Detroit one of America's hotbeds of pro-football enthusiasm. Television riches as yet had not begun to engulf the game when, in 1950, Layne arrived in Detroit, his third stop in the National Football League. Briefly in the mid-1930s, the great tailback Dutch Clark had attracted huge crowds in Detroit, even leading the Lions to a championship in 1935, but the club lost its momentum and did not really establish itself as a major spectacle until Bobby Layne had taken a foothold in the city. Blond and blue-eyed, a fast-living young Texan with an infectious grin and a rasping drawl, Layne not only quarterbacked the Lions to four first-place finishes and three league championships but also brought to the drab, industrial metropolis a flamboyant presence. He was flamboyant not in the sense that he *strove* to attract attention but in the sense that he was constitutionally propelled toward it. He never required more than five hours' sleep to be at his best. "I sleep fast" was the way he once put it. A jazz buff oversupplied with nervous energy, he loved to lead forth his teammates to a night on the town, and so he became a night figure, fair game for gossip columnists and hecklers. His temper complicated matters. He could not abide intruders. He experienced run-ins with fans, and although some of his best friends were cops, he occasionally clashed with the law. The combination of his good looks, his love of a good time, and his combustibility made him the most glamorous football figure of his day. Yet sadly, it was that aspect of his career that he hated. He speaks of it with great reluctance.

I came to know him on the downhill side of his career, having become a sort of marginal member of his circle. Buddy Parker had quit Detroit and become coach of the Pittsburgh Steelers and in 1958 had brought Layne to Pittsburgh, my lifelong residence. Layne soon began frequenting Dante's, a restaurant where I, too, spent many hours. Striving to make the best of a sorry team, he would gather his offensive linemen around him and work his psychology upon them endlessly. He would buy another round of drinks and restate his position that offensive linemen, in contrast to defensive linemen, were artists. "Hear! Hear!" the giants around him would shout. Blocking he would get.

He attempted to invest the Steelers with an *esprit de corps*, and to a modest degree succeeded. He railed at them on the field. Off the field, he led them in fun. Some players, to be sure, resented his autocratic ways, but it is noteworthy that defensive lineman Ernie Stautner, the club's greatest and most competitive player, at once became his fast friend and remains one to this day.

Fifteen tempestuous years after he had traveled north in 1948 from the University of Texas to join the Chicago Bears, Bobby Layne retired on the advice of his coach and friend, Buddy Parker. "I hadn't realized it," he says, "but I was a hell of a lot slower. It's what they call that one step. Yeh, that one step in getting back to pass." He went home to Lubbock, Texas, and except for brief stints as an assistant coach in St. Louis and Houston, he left the bright lights of the football circuit behind him.

At the end of my first season of pro ball, George Halas, who you'll recall was both owner and coach of the Chicago Bears, called me in and told me that he thought for sure that Sid Luckman was going to retire. He said, "My plans are for you and Johnny Lujack to be my quarterbacks from here in." Mr. Halas was being honest with me, I'm sure, but after I got back to Texas he called me and said, "I've got to trade you. Sid has served me well over the years, and he's decided he wants to play some more."

Mr. Halas said, "Here's another thing—Sid's Jewish and Johnny Lujack is Catholic, which means they're a hell of a drawing card in Chicago. And besides, I cannot afford to pay you three the type of salaries you're making."

I imagine the three of us together were making somewhere in the neighborhood of seventy-five thousand, and in 1948 that was a lot of money for a pro club to pay one position. A lot of pro clubs at that time were suffering. Mr. Halas was sold out every game and probably made money, but he didn't make a lot of money. So what he did was sell me to the New York Bulldogs, which was the beginning of quite an experience.

Ted Collins, who managed Kate Smith, the singer, owned the Bulldogs. He was bringing the club down from Boston, where it had been the Boston Yanks, and he hired a new coach, Charley Ewart. Ewart was a Yale guy, so they made the team colors blue and white and called us the Bulldogs, just like Yale. But the names on that team were not exactly Yale names. Those names amazed me. Sabasteanski! Domnanovich! Barzilauskas! Jarmoluk! Batinski! Slosburg! Phil Slosburg didn't weigh but 150 pounds and was our diving halfback. His daddy manufactured pants.

We played six exhibitions and twelve league games, and outside of tying the Redskins and beating the Giants, which

I guess was the upset of the century, we lost them all. We didn't have a cut dog's chance. Charley Ewart was a nice young guy who had been coaching over in Philadelphia, and he believed in that Steve Van Buren type of football. But the trouble was, we didn't have any Steve Van Burens. "Run it!" Ewart would tell me. He liked a running game. But Collins would tell me, "Throw it!"

I'd throw it, what do you think? I listened to the man who owned the club.

Well, it was just a horrible year. Collins was always changing coaches. He'd tell Ewart that he was still the head coach but that he couldn't come to practice or do any coaching. Collins would have Ray Nolting coach the team one week or Joe Bach another week. We had fines for fumbles. In order that we wouldn't get fined, we got to where we'd just pass the ball every down. But our pass protection wasn't what it should have been. Hell, I think I carried the ball more than anybody on the club—but not from being *supposed* to, but from *having* to.

A lot of clubs, the Philadelphia Eagles in particular, had great teams at that time, and some of those teams would be beating us 40-0 and they'd still be clawing to get at us. Greasy Neale had all kind of bonus deals for the Philadelphia players. He'd pay a defensive lineman ten dollars for every time he got to the quarterback. An interception was worth twenty-five. The Eagles had all those kind of bonus offers, so, hell, they'd be whipping us by forty points and still fighting to get at us. It was some year, I'll tell you.

We made up pass routes in the huddle and used hideout plays and anything we could think of. In a game at Detroit, a receiver named Ralph Heywood hid out in front of one of the benches. I think it might have been the Detroit bench, right near Bo McMillin, the Detroit coach. Anyway, nobody saw him. Then he ran down the sideline and I hit him for a touchdown. The Detroit fans threw snowballs at Bo McMillin.

At our home games in the Polo Grounds, lor-*dee*, you'd look up in the stands and there'd be about thirty people huddled together up there. And that'd be our wives. If anybody hollered you could hear an echo. Collins put on circus acts to get people out to the games—he hired tightrope walkers and all that. But he couldn't get anybody out. To cut losses, the club fired so many players that by the end of the season we had only nineteen players suited out. Guys were playing positions they'd never seen before. I think that's the year the league put in a rule where you have to have a certain number of people suited out. Lord, I'd weighed two hundred pounds or maybe a little more at the beginning of the season, but at the end I weighed 169. I drove into Dallas to see my old high-school buddy, Doak Walker, who was in his last year at SMU, and Doak didn't know me.

I promise you, I would not have gone back to that club. I would have given up football first, 'cause it was just too tough there. But I had learned one thing playing with the New York Bulldogs—I found out that I wasn't gun-shy. I could stay in the pocket and get hit, and it would not bother me. I think you've seen quarterbacks that you'd say were a little gun-shy —quarterbacks that are expecting to get hit. I learned I could take it. But I wasn't going to go back there to the Bulldogs.

Now in the meantime, Buddy Parker had quit the Chicago Cardinals and gone over to Detroit as an assistant to Bo McMillin. Buddy had tried to get me for the Cardinals when I was still with the Bears, but there was no way Mr. Halas would let me go to the Cardinals. At the time, they were the Bears' crosstown rivals and were in the same division. Mr. Halas didn't want me coming back with the Cardinals and beating him, and anyway, he got Ted Collins to pay him a bunch of money for me. But when Buddy Parker got over to Detroit he still wanted me, and so one night while I was at a basketball game in Austin I got word that Buddy was trying to reach me. I'd been traded to the Lions. And that was the greatest thing that ever happened to me, because that same year everything just seemed to fall into place.

Detroit drafted Doak Walker. They drafted "Fum" McGraw, who turned out to be a fine tackle. Leon Hart, the Notre Dame end, was the club's first pick in the draft. Somehow McMillin got Bob Hoernschemeyer, a fantastic back, from the Chicago Rockets in the other league, the All-America Conference, which had just folded. Oh, gosh, we had some great players come up that year. So actually 1950 was the start of something big in Detroit, but it was a pretty confusing year because we were six and six and we had a better team than that.

I liked Bo McMillin, but he was getting up in his years and was very outdated in his methods. For instance, he never would kick a field goal. Doak Walker was a darned good kicker, and I remember many games that we could have won that year by kicking field goals from inside the thirty or inside the twenty. But McMillin wouldn't kick a field goal.

In those days, baseball and hockey were the big sports in Detroit. Football players were recognized around town by very few people. We didn't average but twenty or maybe twenty-two thousand a game. Early in the season we'd have to play our home games at Detroit University because the Tigers were still playing baseball at Briggs Stadium, and we had to work out at a place called Jayne Playfield, which was a public playground out in Hamtramck, a tough part of town. We'd go out there to practice and Bo would try to clear the neighborhood kids off the field and they'd tell him, "Go screw yourself!" Oh, lor-*dee!* Bo couldn't do a thing about it. Those kids stayed right out there while we practiced. 'Course, the players could have run them off, but we didn't care.

That was the coldest year you'd care to go through. Bo used to come out to practice in one of those flying suits—a real warm suit—and he'd be wearing flight boots and a flight cap and gloves. There wasn't anything to break the wind on that public playground, but he'd keep us out there three hours, maybe three and a half hours, and we wouldn't accomplish anything. We'd just freeze to death while he stayed warm in that flight suit. Lord, I used to hate those practices with him. You'd try to save yourself all through practice, 'cause you knew that at the end of practice he'd make you run. And *that* was just drudgery.

Furthermore, your opponents could drive right up to the playground and park there and watch you put in your formations. I remember one time we were getting ready to play the Bears. We'd already beaten them, *bad.* The second time around was going to be a big game for them because they needed it to win the division. Well, Bo came up with a Y formation and an X formation at the public playground, so now we're playing the Bears and he sends in word to put in the Y formation. We did, and all the Bear players yelled, "Y formation!" Oh, God a'mighty, it was funny. They knew everything we were doing.

Well, there were eighteen guys who owned the Lions, and what finally happened was that even before the season ended they called a group of us down to the Book-Cadillac Hotel for lunch. Doak Walker, Cloyce Box, and Les Bingaman were there. So was Johnny Greene, who was our captain, and I believe Hoernschemeyer was there, though I'm not positive. We sat down and the owners said, "How can we get a winner? What does it take?"

To a man, we said that we thought Buddy Parker could win with the team we had. So the owners fired Bo McMillin and gave the job to Buddy.

(In the years that followed, a firm and constant relationship was to flourish between Layne and Parker, both Texans, both willful men. Enjoying Parker's full confidence, Layne came to run the Lions on the field with absolute authority, and with a disdain for enemy blows. Except for a helmet and a set of almost wafer-thin shoulder pads under a loose-fitting, short-sleeved jersey, he wore no protective paraphernalia—neither a face guard nor pads on his ribs, thighs, hips, or knees. "I like the freedom," he says. Both he and Parker were equipped with a genius for strategy; the mating of their minds produced significant change in coaching theory.

Principally, Layne's burgeoning reputation for derring-do sprang from his ability to march his team long yardage to a game-winning touchdown or field goal while with utterly nerveless aplomb he ate up practically all the remaining time, thereby depriving his opponent of a chance to strike back. It was a talent that Parker exploited to the fullest. All along, it was Parker's conviction that many games were won or lost in the final two minutes of the first half or in the final two minutes of the game. So Parker became, in all probability, the first coach to devote large segments of practice time to what came to be known throughout football as "the two-minute drill.")

When Buddy took over in 1951 we became the happiest group of ballplayers I have ever seen in my life. Buddy was young at the time, and although he believed in performance, he also believed in having fun. For example, you could go to Buddy in training camp and say, "We're getting sick of all this," and he'd say, "Well, all right. We'll skip tonight's meeting. Take the night off and go to the track."

The players were crazy about Buddy. We worked our asses

off to win all the exhibition games that first summer under
Buddy. We were trying to get those fans fired up to buy
season tickets and get the club going, so we even worked hard
getting ready for exhibitions. But the result was that we hit
our peak too soon. And in the next-to-last game of the season,
although we beat Los Angeles, we had four or five key injuries. The next week we just didn't have enough people available to beat San Francisco, and so the Los Angeles Rams
backed into the divisional title and we finished second. But
we had gotten the city of Detroit excited that year. And in
the next three years—1952, '53, and '54—we finished first in
the division all three times and in the first two of those years
we won the National League championship. I don't think
anyone will ever have the type of group that we had those two
years.

I'm not saying that was the greatest team that ever played
football. I'm talking about the kind of *people* we had—the
individuals. It was the most amazing thing that's ever happened to me in sports. Not long ago I got out the pictures of
those '52 and '53 squads and looked them over, and I'm
telling you, we didn't have a single bad fellow on those
squads. Well, maybe one. But he was young.

Lord, we had got us some ballplayers. Doak was a winner.
Hoernschemeyer could run and block and think—he was just
one hellacious ballplayer. We had Les Bingaman, who
weighed about 340 pounds and was so big that when Buddy
finally retired him he told him, "I want you to quit, because
I don't want you dying on the football field." Bing couldn't
lose weight. He had little bitty feet—I'd say he'd wear a nine
and a half or a ten shoe—and he had to tape up his arches
because of that tremendous weight that he carried. But the
guy was quick as a cat and a brilliant middle guard. He was
captain of our team, yet he came to camp every year with a

fear of getting cut. In scrimmages he was all eyes. He looked at everything. He'd spot something—he'd see someone in our offense tipping off the play, and just before the snap of the ball, he'd say, "Six hole!" And the defense would pile into the six hole and stop the play. I'd say, "Bing, goddamn it, tell me who's tipping the play. Tell me so I can get him straightened out." But he wouldn't tell me till after training camp was over —till he'd made the team. He was all-league practically every year, but he never did stop worrying about being cut.

We had a team of leaders. The fellowship between our players was practically legendary. We all thought the same way—you could have all the fun you wanted to, but when you went out to play you had to win. We looked forward to practice. We looked forward to games. We even looked forward to training camp. Goddamn, it was like going on a vacation when you went to training camp. Guys got there *early*, just to get up there and get their hands on a football.

After 1953 I saw this spirit start dwindling away, and today it's gone. I think the reason is money. When I was playing at Detroit in those early years, no ballplayer ever heard of the goddamn stock market, and they didn't have any money to put into it anyway. But now you see guys sit down on the edge of a secretary's desk and pick up her phone and say, "What's General Motors doing today?" I'm not saying this is good or bad, but I'm saying that we had just one interest in Detroit and it was football. Every son of a bitch on that team was all football.

We brought up our rookies much different than they do now. During training camp, if we went to a tavern for a beer and a rookie came in—well, he just didn't *dare* come in. Rookies found their own joints. There were good reasons for rules like that. Say, for instance, that a rookie came up from Texas and got cut. Well, if he could, he might come and try to cry on my shoulder. But I didn't want to hear that crap. After the season began we let the rookies come to team parties and we had them perform for us—we had them sing for us—and it added a lot to the closeness of the team, but still, we had a rule that you were a rookie until the exhibition schedule ended in your second year. Joe Schmidt, who of course later went on to become head coach of the Lions, had played about six games in his first year when he was at a party one night and heard everybody calling a tackle named John Prchlik "Jolly John." So Joe called him Jolly John. But Prchlik turned on him and told him in no uncertain terms that he was *Mr.* Prchlik. He really let Joe have it. He scared him to bits.

It was just terrific the way everyone became a part of the team. In 1953 chlorophyll had come out and you had it in chewing gum and in everything. It was chlorophyll this and chlorophyll that. So we had a slogan that year—"Chlorophyll will put more sock in your jock!" We went on to beat Cleveland in the championship game, and all our wives sat up there in the stands wearing hats that they'd made from jockstraps dyed green. Some tied a bow in 'em, some of them wore them as a band. They wore those jockstraps just every possible way you could wear one, and it was pretty cute. The wives were real close in Detroit, you see, and that was a big part of our team, too. That was one of the things that Buddy Parker always insisted on, closeness among the wives, 'cause you get a bunch of wives scrapping and you got hell.

Well, I guess I can't explain what it was that we had those two years. It's an intangible thing. It's just the most difficult kind of thing to explain. But not long ago I went up to New York to be inducted into the College Hall of Fame, and I looked around and Bob Smith had come there from Tulsa and Cloyce Box had showed up from Dallas and Harley Sewell from Arlington, Texas, and Doak Walker and Dorne Dibble from Detroit, and I mean just a whole bunch of guys I'd played with. Guys I didn't expect to see. They'd gone there to be with me. It was fantastic. Men who played on those Detroit teams still get together around the country, they still look each other up. I don't know if you're going to see that happen with the teams you've got now. I don't know. I don't think so.

(In the company of his teammates he was always the big spender. At that time, he may have been the biggest in sports. He had not come from affluent beginnings, having been reared from the age of six by an aunt and uncle because his widowed mother could not support him. But at the conclusion of his college-football career, he found himself in the enviable position of being bid for—by the Chicago Bears in one corner, and by the Baltimore Colts of the short-lived All-America Conference. George Halas handed a blank contract to Layne's college coach and adviser, Blair Cherry, and told him to write in a figure. So from the beginning, Layne was paid well by the standards of the times—a $10,000 bonus and $22,500 salary—yet actually he had signed for a figure somewhat lower than the offer Baltimore had made him. It was Cherry's feeling that the Bears, as a going concern that had won championships, offered values that could not be measured in dollars and cents. "That was great advice Blair Cherry gave me," Layne says appreciatively to this day, even though he lasted but a year in Chicago.

In college he had married well. Carol Krueger, a pretty and delightful brunette, was the daughter of a brilliant, wealthy Lubbock surgeon, Dr. J. T. Krueger. So between Layne's own substantial income and his wife's background, he felt no pressure to hoard his dollars. When I revisited him in Lubbock —in a sumptuous three-room suite of offices from which he now manages his investments and the estate of his late father-in-law—I recalled to him the trail of smiling waiters that he left in his wake.)

You're talking about something now that was always exaggerated. You ask me, did I slip fifty dollars to headwaiters? Did I toss a hundred-dollar bill to the band? Yes, I've done these things, but not to the extreme that people say. I've tipped good but I've gotten good service. Where I didn't get good service, I didn't tip. I never owned a Cadillac. I never owned a boat. I have a hunting lodge, but I never had a diamond ring in my life and never wore any rings or stickpins or crap like that. I don't think I dressed fancy. But I did carry around a little spending money, because I felt I had to spend a little extra money around the ball club. I felt like I was supposed to.

For one thing, I was making more money than anybody else on the club. So I always allocated a certain part of my salary to spend on the players. I called it play money. I mean, I didn't try to pick up *every* tab, but I tried to pick up more than my share. Some of the guys just couldn't afford to go to nightclubs and hear good music or go to nice places to eat. They just didn't have the money. So I tried to see that they did a little of this. I wasn't trying to be a big shot, and I don't think any of them ever thought I was trying to be one. Lot of times I tried to pick up tabs in a way that they wouldn't know about it.

See, I was making good money—a heck of a lot more than probably most of the guys on the team. Whenever I went in to sign a contract with Nick Kerbawy, our general manager in Detroit, we never had an argument. We didn't spend thirty minutes signing a contract, *ever*. In 1955 our team did poorly —Lord, we lost the first six games coming off a great team in '54. We had some injuries and I knew in my own mind I'd had a bad year. So I went to see Nick and told him, "I feel like I ought to take about a $2,500 cut." Taxwise, with other income and me being in a certain bracket, it made only about a four-hundred-dollar difference to me. Well, I think the club appreciated it. The next year I had a real good season and led the league in scoring, and I got a nice raise.

I was very fortunate, because in pro football if you start high it's hard for them to get you down, but if you start low it's hell to get up. In the 1950s it was a difficult thing for even a Joe Schmidt or a Yale Lary to go from seven thousand, say, to ten thousand, and then from ten to twelve thousand. The general manager's job is to get the guys signed for as little as possible. But Nick Kerbawy was a tremendous person, and he was responsible in a lot of ways for those great teams at Detroit. He put us up in first-class hotels. When we'd go to the West Coast on a two-game trip, the club would slip us a hundred or two hundred dollars for spending money. Nick got boys out of financial jams and never said anything about it. And when the team was going through a letdown, I might go to Nick, or our captain might, and say, "Nick, we need to have a beer party or something." He'd be all for it, and at the club's expense. He was *for* the football players. A lot of them didn't think so for a long time, but they finally realized that he was for 'em.

(At Dante's, the restaurant in Pittsburgh, Layne continued to spend well, although he usually avoided the front cocktail lounge, confining himself to a table in the darkened rear dining room. Surrounded by teammates and cronies, he enjoyed telling a story or hearing one, but there was one surefire way to plunge him into an ugly mood. One needed only to mention the press.

The blood would rush to his face, and he would launch into a tirade that rambled on and on, while those around him waited silently for the storm to spend itself. Although he had a scattering of close friends among the sportswriting frater-

nity, he saw the press as one great mass of gossip-mongers
waiting to feed on his traffic tickets and nightclub celebra-
tions. His argument was that the press had no consideration
for the feelings of his wife and two sons. On one occasion,
while the two of us sat in a parked car outside his apartment
at 3 A.M., he stated his argument plaintively, keeping a grip
on his temper. But at the table in Dante's, he sometimes
would turn on me, remembering that I was a member of the
press, and denounce me in the strongest possible terms. I
would leave the table and go to the bar. The next night he
would beckon me to his table, and when I refused, he would
insist. Finally I would approach the table. He would utter the
beginnings of an apology, but then his pride would stop him
and again he would explode with a denunciation of me. I
would return to the bar.

Even at those times, I always liked him. One does not
expect even temperament from genius, whether it be in the
field of painting, letters, or quarterbacking. Another time,
shortly after he had treated me to another blistering, he over-
heard a tipsy belligerent giving me a hard time at the bar,
whereupon he appeared as if from a puff of smoke and with
a finger wagging under the man's nose warned him that he
had better settle down "or mister, I'll tie your tongue to your
shoelaces."

Usually he appeared to be in hale spirits. But his bursts of
anger came more frequently toward the end of his five years
in Pittsburgh—partly because the fans had gotten on him for
his failure to deliver a championship, and partly, I suspect,
because he saw that time would run out on him before he
could taste another one. There would never be another Detroit. He knew he would never recapture the good years with
the Lions.)

Well, I was in Detroit long enough. In football you can't stay
at one place a long time. It's kind of like a car dealer being
in a town for a long time—sooner or later he's a son of a bitch.
Have you ever noticed that? Well, it's the same in football.

I don't care where you are, sports fans get tired of you. It's the damn truth, they get tired of you. I can't put my finger on the reason, but the only time a guy in sports really truly becomes worth a damn is after he quits. I got booed in Detroit when we were winning championships. But I went back not long ago and was introduced at halftime of a Lions game, and I got an ovation.

· Looking back, I don't think I'd want to change many things, but it *is* something I've thought about an awful lot. Some of the past I don't like. The glamour image? Yeah—that type of thing. If I had it to do over, I would probably try to do something about that part of it. It's not good when you have kids growing up. I don't think it's hurt my two boys, but they've probably been conscious of some of the publicity I got. I used to be real happy when the Detroit papers would go on strike. I had a lot of experiences—sad experiences— with writers.

How would *you* feel if your name was in headlines and you weren't within miles of the incident? "Bobby Layne's Car Caught Doing Sixty in a Thirty-mile Zone!" That was the headline. But it was Hunchy Hoernschemeyer and Harry Gilmer that had my car. I was in bed. But when people see "Bobby Layne's Car," they know damn well that if it's his car he was there. How would *you* feel?

Listen, I've known some wonderful guys who were sports-writers, but the press can crucify you and get away with it. If I had those years to do over, I probably wouldn't expose myself to that kind of treatment. Mantle learned how to handle it. In his later years he did a fantastic job of avoiding exposure. You've got to have some fun in football—it can't be all business—but I would make an effort to avoid the exposure.

Well, as I said, you can't stay in one town a long time. I

spent better than eight years in Detroit and it was long
enough. But I'll tell you what I really miss. What I miss is the
guys. That's what I miss more than anything. I miss going to
training camp. I miss the road trips and the card games. I miss
the fellowship. The locker room, the places where it was a
pleasure to be. The practice sessions. I miss the bar where
we'd go for a beer after practice. I miss having that beer with
the guys. I miss the ballgames. I mean, when you've got a
whole team looking forward to everything, when you've got
guys showing up for practice early and staying late—well,
you've got something there. We had that perfect thing for a
while. What I miss now is my teammates.

19

GEORGE HALAS

Father of the game

Of the twenty interviews that appear in this book, none posed as difficult a problem as my interview with George Halas, the father of professional football, the Papa Bear of the Chicago Bears. The problem was simply this: Remembering that his fifty-year career as a pro player, coach, and owner has been voluminously reported, both by the press and by Halas' own published writings, what point was there in engaging him in reminiscence? Where was the gain delving into episodes that long ago had become a major part of pro-football literature? Here was a man who not only had fathered the National Football League and sat by the cradle but had provided much of the innovation that modernized the rulebook and turned the game into spectacular entertainment. What could one more interview add?

There appeared to be one approach that, so far as I knew, had not been tried. In George Halas' fiftieth year of professional football, was it not an appropriate time to explore his philosophy, if indeed he had one? Had he climbed the mountain simply because it was there, or had he chosen the role of pioneer in hope of finding a sense of grandeur that did not exist in his middle-class life? From early manhood he was a hard-nosed worker who surely would have prospered at almost any career he chose, but why such an obscure, unpromising business as football?

With three games remaining in the 1969 season, a season disastrous for the Bears, it was not the best of times to call upon Halas. The previous year he had retired from coaching, turning the job over to young Jim Dooley, one of his former players, and had gone to Scotland for difficult hip surgery. Under Dooley, the Bears scrapped for the central division title right up to the final week of the season, but in 1969 they collapsed, winning but a single game. To complicate Halas' discomfort, he had come under increasingly intense criticism in recent years, his detractors arguing that he was a cold-blooded man, or as Chicago magazine writer William Barry Furlong put it, a personality possessing "all the warmth of broken bones." Indictments of Halas contended that he was a victim of his own success, a self-made man become possessed of a feudal-baron complex; that his coaches were expected to do as George did, meaning work a ninety-five-hour week. At seventy-four he stood accused of the one charge that old men find hardest of all to take. His critics said he was antiquated.

Seated on a plain wooden chair in the sparsely furnished anteroom of the Bears' headquarters, I looked up to find Halas coming through the front door, his complexion flushed by the Chicago December. Shoulders bent, he walked with a pronounced limp, pausing to shake my hand and beckon me directly to his office. It was a spacious rectangular room, done up in all the modern executive appurtenances: paneled walls on three sides, print drapery covering the fourth, a conference table ranging down the middle of the room. Yet if the decorator had intended the room to have the crisp, clean lines that express contemporary executive efficiency, his work had been thoroughly undone. Plaques, trophies, documents, and a couple of transistor radios had been scattered about the room, not according to design but as if placed wherever space could be found. Paperwork surrounded Halas, stacked in piles on his desk and in many more piles on a table behind him.

Although his infirmity at times made it difficult for him to work out a comfortable position in his chair, he appeared on

the whole to be surprisingly energetic and still capable of the
long hours that he always had set for himself. Excusing himself, he paused during the interview to take a phone call from
Ed Healey, the great Bears tackle of the 1920s. Healey was
dismayed that the club was having the worst season in its
history and wondered if Halas still intended to hold the season's-end reunion party he had hosted annually for former
Bears players.

"Of course, we're going to have the reunion!" Halas
barked. "That's something that involves fifty years. This
thing going on now is only one year out of the entire *fifty*.
And I'll tell you something. I'll guarantee this: It will not
happen for another fifty years. No, wait a minute. I can't say
that. I'll guarantee it won't happen in another twenty-five
years."

I soon found, not surprisingly, that Halas had no ready
response to questions about his underlying philosophy. Like
a great many other doers, men dedicated to activity, he probably had seldom taken time to ask himself, "Where am I
going? What do I want from life?" Busyness, along with the
doing that went with it, was its own reward, and who is to say
it was not a worthwhile ethic? In any case, George Halas
certainly had not been the type to let himself be guided by
impulse. He was strong for planning, and for having rules by
which his plans progressed to fulfillment. In that sense he
possessed a definite philosophy, some of whose pieces came
together at intervals as he spoke to me of the past and the
present.

Assuming the reader may be only vaguely aware of Halas'
distant past, it is necessary here to relate, briefly, a few bio-
graphical facts: He grew up in Chicago, then attended the
University of Illinois, where he studied civil engineering and
played end on the football team as well as right field on the
baseball team. Following a World War I hitch in the navy,
Halas played a season of professional baseball, spending the
first half of the 1919 season with the New York Yankees
before being sent to the minors. He then returned to Chicago
and took an engineering job in the bridge department of the

Chicago, Burlington & Quincy Railroad. On Sundays he played for the Hammond (Indiana) Pros, an independent football club that played to crowds ranging upwards of five thousand against the best opponents that could be conveniently scheduled.

Apparently Halas caught the eye of a Decatur starch manufacturer named A. E. Staley, for the next year, 1920, Staley invited him to form a company football team. Casting around for a schedule, Halas suggested in a letter to Ralph Hay, the manager of the Canton (Ohio) Bulldogs, that they organize a league. Consequently, on September 17, 1920, representatives of eleven midwestern pro-football clubs met in Hay's Canton auto showroom and formed the American Professional Football Association, which later was to evolve into the National Football League. "Each of us put up a hundred dollars," says Halas, "for the privilege of losing money."

Following that first league season, a recession compelled the starch company to drop football, whereupon Halas entered into a partnership with a fellow player, Dutch Sternaman, and moved the team to Chicago. There the club has won eight championships, a total that is second only to Green Bay's eleven. Only in eight of their first fifty seasons did the Bears finish worse than third. Needless to say, George Halas became a wealthy man, thanks to a decision he had arrived at one day while at work in the offices of the Chicago, Burlington & Quincy.

As I was sitting there working away, I noted that there were three young fellows—no, two—two young fellows my age who had just come in and joined the department. And there were about six others who had been there twenty to twenty-five years. I thought, "Am *I* going to be at one of these desks twenty-five years from now?" I knew I couldn't do that. I had too much life, too much zip, too much energy to expend. And that is what made up my mind when Mr. G. E. Chamberlain of A. E. Staley Company came up to Chicago to ask me to go down to Decatur, Illinois, to become athletic director of the company—to learn the starch business and to play on the baseball team and on the basketball team and to get a professional-football team together. I jumped at the opportunity.

Now I was doing something I liked to do, and I knew that this something had a future. Certainly I never thought it would be as big as it is today, with the TV contracts and the huge crowds, but I knew it would be successful. You see, when I got out of college I realized all of a sudden that I knew a lot more football than I had known in the previous three years, and that I was capable of playing a lot better. I said, "If that's the case, the pro game has a great, great future, because that means that every player that comes out of college can improve year after year." Which was true. Later on, I found through experience that a player is at his greatest speed and body coordination at age twenty-seven. If he's a huge man, it's age twenty-nine.

Well, right at the beginning I put down a set of rules for the players. Rules about things the pro teams never thought about in those days. Rules about curfew, about meetings, about practices. No other team had ever had such rules, and I am certain of that. I asked myself, what must our players do in order to be complete football players on Sunday? One thing I insisted on was daily practice, which was something the other teams did not have. Later when they started working out every day, why, they also began putting down player rules.

One rule we had was that we never permitted smoking in

the dressing room or in a meeting or out on the field—or even leaving the park, where you had youngsters hanging around who could see you. I was trying to build an image for these players. And surprising as it may seem, all of our players in those early years received our rules very nicely—all of them except one. Fleckenstein was his name. He was a very nice fellow except on the field. There he just went wild! He would slug and poke a fellow unnecessarily. It's true that the Bears were known for bruising up people, but it was done in a legal manner, by hard-crashing blocks and tackles. Fleckenstein, on the other hand, would get us a lot of penalties and he incurred the wrath of our opponents, thereby providing them with an automatic buildup when they were about to play us.

Finally we traded him to Portsmouth. In a game between Portsmouth and ourselves, Red Grange carried the ball on a quick-opening play when, lo and behold, who should he run into but Fleckenstein. Fleckenstein hauled off and whacked Red unnecessarily, right in the face. Well, all of our players loved Red, so they took after Fleckenstein, and I think that cured him to a great degree, 'cause later in life I always enjoyed him very much.

You know, I'm a great note taker. I always take notes— always. Your mind can retain only so much, so you must put things down, and that's the reason that in my coaching days I made the players take notes during meetings. That was another of our rules. It is my contention that a player forgets 75 percent of what he has heard in about twenty minutes. I made them take notes and also made them draw up every play so they knew every man's duty. Sadly, they don't do that today, probably because there are so many plays being used and so much other work to be done that it would be just an impossibility to follow that practice. But remember, we had only eighteen players in the old days, and as a result of making our players draw up every play, why, a man could play several positions in an emergency.

You point out that I seem to have been very systematic by nature. Yes, I would say so. When I look back I think in terms of eras. I think of 1925, when we got Red Grange, as one era. Then I think of 1932, 1933, and '34, when we had Bronko Nagurski and Jack Manders and Carl Brumbaugh and fellows of that type, who typified a great team. They won championships in '32 and '33, and they won thirteen games in a row in '34, only to lose the championship game on an icy field to the Giants, who, if you'll remember, came out for the second half in sneakers. So that's the second era, and the third era was our 1940 team. That was the year Sid Luckman took over as T-formation quarterback. I had seen him play in a driving rain at Columbia University, and what impressed me was that he performed very well under extreme rainy conditions. That was one of the things that prevailed upon me to select him. In 1940 he was ready. So were fellows like Bill Osmanski and Joe Stydahar and Danny Fortmann—and such fellows as George McAfee and Bulldog Turner. And that was the year when we defeated the Redskins in the championship game, 73-0. I don't dwell on the past at any length, but when I look back I see those eras.

You ask me about the principles, or guidelines, that I have followed in business and in life. Let me answer that this way. Louis Nizer, the great attorney, wrote a book in which he said, "Nothing is work unless you'd rather be doing something else." Well, that is the principle that I've been following for years. I would prefer doing football to anything else in the world. I could have been a great golfer through the teachings of one George O'Neil, who back in the '20s and '30s was probably one of the great golf teachers of his time. He wanted me to come out for lessons. He said, "We'll go out every morning and I'll guarantee to get you in the 70s in three months." Geez, I would have loved that. And I did go out there a couple of times, but I found that it took a few hours away from football. And by golly, I couldn't stand that.

My first ten years in pro football were more fun than any time since, because I both coached and played. Later, football was still fun because I was still coaching. My greatest thrills came from being on the sideline and matching wits with the opponent and, of course, also helping out the officials. Today, that's the only part of football that I miss. I don't miss the getting-ready process, the X's and O's all week. But I do miss the Sunday afternoons on the sideline.

In the old days, when the owners got together for a league meeting, it was fun. It was really fun. Everybody knew each other, and they knew that I would start baiting George Marshall, who reacted beautifully at all times. When I knew he had a particular project in mind, I would start off ahead of time by playing it down, even though I believed in it and knew that eventually I would vote for it. I would touch on the subject and talk about the weaknesses of it and why it would not help the game. Then Marshall would get up at his end of the table and rave and rant, which I enjoyed so much. But in those days we had just one representative in attendance from each club, which made the meeting a very simple matter, whereas now you have twenty-six clubs and two or three men from each club. So you see, it becomes more of a convention than a league meeting. There's no fun in it. No, there isn't.

One of my principles was always to do anything that was to the benefit of the league, and that was the case with all of the other teams, too. They were not selfish. They did not think just in terms of "What's good for me?" They thought in terms of the league, and that's one of the reasons why the league has been so successful—why the game has grown into the greatest sport in the country. In 1936 Bert Bell, who at the time headed the Philadelphia Eagles, proposed that we have a player draft. The worst teams would pick first and the best teams, last. Of course I thought, "Well, gee, this is going to hurt us." We were one of the outstanding teams. But then I realized the draft was the best thing for the league, and I immediately went along. I did not fight it at all—not one iota.

Truthfully, I wouldn't know if today you could get the same response from owners to a proposed change that obviously would hurt their club. There are more teams involved now, and a greater variety of individuals. I question if they would give in as easily for the benefit of the league as owners did in the olden days.

You say that I am sometimes criticized for being too conservative, for being outmoded. Well, of course, that's a lot of bunk. I'm not outmoded in any sense or manner, because I've kept up with the game. If you're out for a year or so and have no connection with the game, you're dead, because things are happening so rapidly. Now here, today, the Bears have the most ultramodern of coaches, you might say, but they've made a great number of mistakes. Well, who's around to correct them? *I've* got to step in and *tell* them where the hell they're wrong. So when you can correct a modern-day coach, you're not too far behind the parade.

Mind you, I step in only in extreme cases—for example, when they're back up against the goal line and they're trying to stop the opposing team with fancy-dan defenses, and then the opposing team scores easily. Well, why the hell did you use that silly defense? At the goal line, that's when it's dog-eat-dog. So why do you have tricks by the linemen at that stage of the game? One of the linemen fails to do his trick and the opposing team's guy peels over from the nine-yard line unmolested? Why do you pull a blitz near the goal line? See, those miracle things don't *work*, not in solid instances.

Yes, I believe an owner has a right to step in, but only within the confines of the coaches' room, and then only in a limited manner—and only if the owner *knows what he's talking about*. In the two years since I quit coaching, I haven't ever tried to send a play in— never tried to interfere with their game plan or with the making up of their game plan—never tried to interfere in any way, shape, or form, unless a situation involved an outstanding mistake, my purpose being that they wouldn't make the same mistake again. And always this has been done directly to the coach, never in front of any players or other coaches or, of course, the press. I will act when there has been a stupid mistake, because the coaches are supposed to be men who are doing their job. And they are. They've learned a lot this year, and that's the reason I contend we're going to have another good team, a great team, next year. I'm that optimistic about it.

What a great game pro football is! Oh, they talk a lot about overexposure on TV, but that I don't believe in. Football is not like the theater, where the same people play the same characters day in and day out, sometimes over a period of years, and still manage to put on an acceptable play. In football you have the added advantage of players playing different roles from week to week—playing different characters, you might say. In every game they're in different scenes. And that's the reason people will never get tired of this game.

We have more teams today and more men playing the game, but this has not lowered the quality of performance one iota, and there's a very simple reason why. Your coaching in the high schools is greater than ever. The colleges now get a better player. He's well coached, well drilled. Furthermore, there's a greater number of great college coaches than there used to be. We have a lot of coaches of the same teaching

ability as the Zupkes, the Rocknes, the Staggs. So the end
result is that in professional football we get more great players than we did in the old days. Just the other day I told our
coaches that my only objection to the professional-football
coach is that because the college coaching is good, he expects
a player to step right in without further coaching. You've got
to keep developing those players. That's what I want our
coaches to do.

I recall that in 1921, when we moved our team from Decatur to Chicago, we ended the season with a profit of $71.63.
In 1922 the crowds were a little better, but again we just
about broke even. I knew pro football was a good game, but
I had no sense of destiny. We were involved in a matter of
survival. Destiny would take care of itself—the problem at
hand was how to meet the bills. If I played a historic role in
the making of pro football, I never dwell on it. I never think
about it. I never give it any thought *whatsoever*. People refer
to me as the father of pro football. So what! It sounds all right,
yes, and I hope they remember me as that. It would be nice.
But I'm not going to give it any thought, because there's too
many other things to do. Look at this damned desk! It'll take
me two years to clear up all this stuff.

EPILOGUE

Two weeks after this book was completed, I visited the offices of the Pittsburgh Steelers at 9 A.M. on a Tuesday morning. It was the day of the 1970 pro-football player draft, and because the Steelers were to make the first selection, their suite of offices already was alive with reporters and cameramen. At 10:05 head-coach Chuck Noll blinked into the television lights and announced that Pittsburgh had selected Louisiana Tech quarterback Terry Bradshaw, who scouts everywhere agreed was a marvelous prospect. "A Joe Namath with sound knees," was the way they usually put it. "The greatest arm I have ever seen," said Y. A. Tittle, the old quarterback.

One suspected that the bugle was sounding, as it inevitably does, for a change in demigods: Namath's knees were battered; he had done his network show and written his book; his floppy hair and satanic beard had come to be taken for granted. It was possible that he would remain pro-football's best quarterback for years to come, but the enthusiasm now was for a yellow-haired, trimly barbered, boyishly exuberant giant from the land of the bayous. Within weeks, Terry Bradshaw would be posing in New York studios for fashion layouts.

So it goes. The new replace the old. Last autumn, when Johnny Blood drove me north from St. Paul to Duluth to meet Ole Haugsrud, the old clubowner, Blood offered a suggestion along the way, and it drew an enthusiastic second from Dan Williams, a onetime Duluth Eskimos lineman seated in the back of the car. They proposed to take a short detour in order to show me the birthplace of Ernie Nevers, the greatest of all their erstwhile teammates. The village in Minnesota is called Willow River. It has a tavern, and as the hour was growing toward noon, we paused for a beer. Making small talk with the bartender, we were astonished to discover that he had never heard of Ernie Nevers. "Well," sighed Blood. "Fifty years from now they won't know in Beaver Falls who Joe Namath was."

In the end the demigods are mortal. Hopefully *The Game That Was* has recreated them as they once were.

MYRON COPE

INDEX

Adams, O'Neal, 156
Akron Steels, 238
Alfs, Bill, 93
All-America Football Conference, 234, 238–39, 246, 249, 262, 268
All-Stars of Ernie Nevers, 99
American Football League, 48, 72, 78
American Professional Football Association, 5, 36, 238, 278
Anderson, Hunk, 180–81, 201
Austin, Bill, 139

Bach, Joe, 260
Baltimore Colts, 268
Barefoot Boy from the Bayous, see Van Buren, Steve
Battles, Cliff, 6, 113–19, 165, 166
Baugh, Sammy, 8, 118, 148, 159–71, 190, 217–18, 224
Bausch, Pete, 204
Bednarik, Chuck, 179
Bell, Bert, 183, 283
Bingaman, Les, 263, 265–66
Blanda, George, 210
Blood, Johnny, 6, 8, 54, 59–70, 71, 73, 78, 79, 99–100, 130–31, 146, 288

Boston Braves of NFL, 113, 115
Boston Redskins, 108, 115, 117–18
Box, Cloyce, 263, 267
Bradshaw, Terry, 287
Brooklyn Dodgers of NFL, 219
Brown, Jim, 6, 245–46, 253
Brown, Paul, 7, 98, 222, 238, 239, 240–45, 246–47, 249, 250, 251, 252, 255
Brumbaugh, Boyd, 138
Brumbaugh, Carl, 281
Butler, Sol, 66

Calac, Pete, 42
Camp, Walter, 31, 238
Campbell, Hump, 197
Canadian League, 250
Canton (Ohio) Bulldogs, 127, 278
Carr, Joe, 74, 75, 127, 144
Casey, Eddie, 117
Cavenaugh, Frank, 17
Chamberlain, G. E., 279
Chandnois, Lynn, 136–37
Cherry, Blair, 268
Cherundolo, Chuck, 224, 226
Chicago Bears, 7, 8, 13, 24, 27, 43, 52, 74, 95, 104–5, 119, 146, 155, 167,

179–80, 185, 188, 201, 203, 204, 208, 211–12, 216, 231, 258, 268, 275
Chicago Cardinals, 26, 80, 104, 169, 183, 185, 261
Chicago Red Grange All-Stars, 31
Chicago Rockets, 262
Clark, Dutch (Earl), 9, 60, 83–93, 178, 257
Clark, Jim, 184, 233
Clark, Potsy, 87, 90, 91
Cleveland Browns, 7, 242, 243, 248, 250
Cleveland Rams, 93
College Hall of Fame, 267
Collier, Blanton, 247, 252
Collins, Ted, 259–60, 261, 262
Conzelman, Jimmy, 24
Coolidge, Calvin, 33, 52
Cotton Bowl game, 163
Coughlin, Frank, 23
Croft, Abe, 211
Crowley, Jimmy, 176–77
Cuff, Ward, 151, 156
Cutler, Marty, 20–21

Dawson, Len, 135
Dempsey, Jack, 53
Denny, Bill, 175
DesJardiens, Shorty, 20
Detroit Lions, 83, 90–91, 93, 104, 110, 142, 173, 178–79, 180–81, 199–203, 227, 257, 262, 264–66
Dibble, Dorne, 268
Dickey, John, 23
Dietz, Lone Star, 115–16, 117
Doll, Don, 20
Dooley, Jim, 276
Dorais, Gus, 227
Drake, Johnny, 93
Drew, Red, 147
Driscoll, Paddy, 26, 27, 30
Dudley, Bullet Bill, 6, 136, 219–27

Duluth Eskimos, 71, 75

East-West Shrine game, 97, 98, 199
Edwards, Turk, 116, 165
Ewart, Charley, 259, 260

Falcon, Gil, 20
Filchock, Frank, 167
Fincher, Bill, 35
Finks, Jimmy, 131, 136
Flaherty, Ray, 117
Flanigan, Walter, 20, 25
Fleckenstein, of Chicago Bears, 280
Fortmann, Danny, 185, 214–15, 281
Four Horsemen of Notre Dame, 64, 74–75
France, George A., 29, 33
Francis, Sam, 138
Friedman, Benny, 52
Furlong, William Barry, 276

Gallery, Tom, 46
Galloping Ghost, see Grange, Red
Gantenbein, Milt, 100
Ghee, Milt, 20
Gilbert, Walt, 79
Gilmer, Harry, 168–69, 272
Goldberg, Biggie, 177
Goldenberg, Buckets, 100, 107, 210
Gould, Alan, 86
Graham, Otto, 251–52, 253
Grange, Red (Harold), 8, 14, 27–28, 29, 41–42, 43–58, 60, 72, 74, 280, 281
Grant, Len, 154
Green Bay Packers, 8, 51, 60, 66, 68, 83, 97–98, 100–10, 118, 141, 143, 145, 151, 184, 199, 205, 210, 231
Greene, Johnny, 263
Groza, Lou, 159, 254
Guepe, Art, 163
Gutowsky, Ace, 178

Guyon, Indian Joe, 6, 35–42

Halas, George, 7, 8, 13, 24, 25, 26, 27, 29, 30, 41, 44, 52, 74, 98, 108, 132, 166, 202, 204, 205, 209, 211, 212–16, 217, 259, 261, 268, 275–85
Hall of Fame, see Pro Football Hall of Fame
Haller, Mrs. Julie, 9–10
Hammond (Indiana) Pros, 278
Harpster, Howard, 86
Hart, Leon, 262
Haugsrud, Ole, 71–81, 288
Hay, Ralph, 278
Hayes, Bob, 103
Hayman, Lew, 250, 251, 255
Heacox, Cecil, 20
Healey, Ed, 8, 13–34, 277
Healey, Luke (Mrs. Ed), 20, 21, 22, 34
Hein, Mel, 8, 156, 178, 188
Henderson, Gus, 201
Herber, Arnie, 100, 144, 146
Heywood, Ralph, 260
Hill, Harlon, 212–13
Hinkle, Clarke, 8, 9, 83, 95–111
Hoernschemeyer, Bob, 262, 263, 265, 272
Hope-Harvey team (Pittsburgh), 126–27
Hornsby, Rogers, 164
Hornung, Paul, 250–51
Hoyt, Edwin P., 238
Hubbard, Cal, 98, 100, 102
Hutson, Don, 8, 99, 100, 106, 141–50, 182

Isbell, Cece, 100, 149–50

Jankowski, Eddie, 105
Jones, Ralph, 211

Juzwick, Steve, 156

Kansas City Cowboys, 75
Kelly, Shipwreck, 143–44
Kemp, Jackie, 135
Kemp, Ray, 237
Kerbawy, Nick, 269–70
Kiely, Ed, 135
Kiesling, Walter (Kies), 136–37, 212
Kilmer, Bill, 135
Kimbrough, Frank, 195
Kinard, Bruiser, 6
Kramer, Jerry, 184
Krueger, Dr. J. T., 268
Kuechle, Ollie, 61–62

Lambeau, Curly, 54, 62, 67, 68, 69, 97–99, 99, 101–4, 105, 108, 109, 142, 143–44, 145, 146, 148
LaRue, Bobby, 177
Lary, Yale, 270
Laughead, Jimmy, 198
Lavelli, Dante, 247, 253
Layne, Bobby, 5, 257–73
Layne, Carol Krueger (Mrs. Bobby), 268
Leemans, Tuffy (Al), 6, 151–57, 219
Lenglen, Suzanne, 29, 46
Lindskog, Vic, 179
Little League football, 84
Little, Lou, 118
Lombardi, Vince, 51, 98, 100–101, 108, 139, 222
Los Angeles, George Wilson's All-Stars, 31
Los Angeles Rams, 183, 237, 239, 265
Luckman, Sid, 119, 135, 162, 208–9, 210, 259, 281
Lujack, Johnny, 259

Mandel, Fred, 179

Manders, Jack, 281
Mantle, Mickey, 272
Mara, Tim, 74, 75, 76, 78, 155
Marshall, George, 80, 115, 116–19, 129, 133, 138, 161, 162, 164, 165–66, 168, 169–70, 282
Mauldin, Stan, 185
Maxwell, Don, 53
McAfee, George, 208, 281
McCrary, Hurdis, 98
McGill, Ralph, 35
McGinley, John, 33
McGraw, "Fum," 262
McMillin, Bo, 260–61, 262, 263, 264
McNally, John Victor, *see* Blood, Johnny
Method, Russ, 79
Meyer, Dutch, 159, 163, 164
Michelosen, John, 225
Millner, Wayne, 165
Milwaukee Badgers of NFL, 65
Minnesota Vikings, 81
Modell, Art, 247, 248
Molenda, Bo, 98
Molesworth, Keith, 57
Moore, Bernie, 230
Moore, Wilbur, 167
Morrall, Earl, 135
Motley, Marion, 6, 7, 239, 240–48, 252–54, 255
Musso, George, 107

Nagurski, Bronko, 7, 95, 106–7, 281
Namath, Joe, 53–54, 103, 217, 287, 288
Nash, Bob, 26 *n.*
National Football League (NFL), 5, 65, 71, 72, 78, 81, 83, 110, 126, 127, 136, 142, 151, 188, 238, 239, 246, 249, 251, 257, 275, 278; Alumni Association, 174
Neal, Ed, 205, 211

Neale, Greasy, 179, 182, 184, 232–33, 234, 260
Nelsen, Bill, 135
Nevers, Ernie, 60, 72–75, 78–79, 80, 99, 288
New Rochelle Bulldogs, 154
New York Bulldogs, 259, 261
New York Giants, 8, 42, 52, 74, 78, 98, 117, 118, 151, 152–53, 154, 155–56, 162, 178, 188, 219
New York Yankees, 29, 43, 78
Nickel, Elbie, 131
Nixon, Mike, 226
Nizer, Louis, 281
Noll, Chuck, 139, 287
Nolting, Ray, 260

O'Hara, John, 59–60
O'Neil, George, 281
Osmanski, Bill, 105, 207, 291
Owen, Steve, 153, 155, 157

Paddock, Charley, 53
Parker, Buddy, 139, 257, 258, 261–62, 264–65, 267
Payne, Andy, 46
Pegler, Westbrook, 48–49
Philadelphia Eagles, 93, 173, 179, 182–84, 204, 227, 229, 231, 234–35, 260, 283
Pittsburgh Steelers, 68, 69, 121, 122, 127–31, 135–39, 211–12, 219–27, 258, 287
Pollard, Frederick (fritz), 238
Pool, Hamp, 215
Portsmouth (Ohio) Spartans, 83, 86–90
Pottsville Maroons, 78
Prchlik, John, 267
Pro Football Hall of Fame, 5, 8, 35, 96, 165, 173, 190, 238, 239

Pyle, C. C., 28–31, 43–49, 53, 72, 73, 74, 78

Ray, Joie, 29
Red Grange All-Stars (Chicago), 31
Reeves, Dan, 239
Rice, Grantland, 43, 76
Richards, George, 90–93, 129, 199–203
Rickey, Branch, 237, 255
Rigsby, Theo, 197
Ritter, Lawrence S., 4, 10
Robeson, Paul, 238
Robinson, Jackie, 237, 250, 255
Rock Island Independents, 13, 24, 237
Rockne, Knute, 17, 285
Ronzani, Gene, 211
Rooney, Art, 68, 121–39, 166, 219, 221, 224, 227
Rooney, Cobb, 76, 77
Rooney, Kathleen (Mrs. Art), 121
Roosevelt, Franklin D., 32
Rose Bowl game, 98, 142, 148
Roy, A. J., 195–98
Ruth, Babe, 53
Rymkus, Lou, 254

St. Louis Gunners, 77
Sande, Earl, 53
Sayers, Gale, 6
Scanlon, Dewey 78
Scarry, Mo, 251–52
Schmidt, Joe, 267, 270
Schooley, Hershell, 198, 202–3
Scott, Ralph, 30–31
Sewell, Harley, 267
Shaughnessy, Clark, 162, 206, 207
Shaw, Ed (Buck), 19
Shearer, Marshall, 220
Shipwreck Kelly, 143–44
Simpson, O. J., 50–51
Slater, Fred (Duke), 25, 237

Slivinski, Steve, 167
Slosburg, Phil, 259
Smith, Bob, 267
Snyder, Bob, 207
Speedie, Mac, 253
Stagg, Amos Alonzo, 80, 285
Staley, A. E., 278
Standlee, Norm, 109
Stautner, Ernie, 131, 258
Stein, Bill, 79
Sternaman, Dutch (Edward C.), 24, 25, 26, 30, 44, 55, 278
Strode, Woodrow (Willie), 239
Stuhldreher, Harry, 64
Stydahar, Joe, 181, 216, 281
Suffridge, Bob, 204
Sutherland, Jock, 136, 219–20, 221–22, 223–27
Svendsen, George, 107

Thayer, Harry, 231
Thomas, Frank, 148
Thompson, Tommy, 173–74, 182, 184, 233
Thorpe, Jim, 28, 35, 38, 39, 40, 41–42, 72, 127
Tilden, Bill, 53
Tittle, Y. A., 287
Todd, Dick, 167
Topping, Dan, 138
Touchdown Club in Washington, D.C., 119
Trafton, George, 55
Treat, George, 11
Turner, Bulldog (Clyde), 6, 8, 9, 95, 168, 187–218, 281
Turner, Gladys (Mrs. Bulldog), 188

Unitas, Johnny, 6, 135, 137
Ursella, Rube, 23

Vagabond Halfback, *see* Blood, Johnny
Van Buren, Steve, 173, 183, 229–36, 260

Walker, Doak, 261, 262, 263, 265, 268
Walls, Willie, 156
Walsh, Adam, 239
Walsh, Bill, 131
Warner, Pop, 39, 41, 72, 78, 80
Washington, Kenny, 237, 239
Washington Redskins, 155–56, 164, 166–70
Webster, Ralph, 249
Whelchel, Admiral John, 168–70

White Tarzan, 204–5
White, Whizzer, 129, 134, 185
Wilkin, Wee Willie, 167
Williams, Dan, 71, 72, 73, 288
Willis, Bill, 6, 7, 205–6, 238, 239, 240, 248–55
Wilson's Los Angeles All-Stars, 31
Wilson, George (Wildcat), 31–32, 45–46, 74, 207, 209
Wismer, Harry, 92–93, 201
Wojciechowicz, Wojie, 8, 173–86, 234
Wolman, Jerry, 174
Wray, Lud, 115

Zuppke, Bob, 50, 52, 57, 285